W9-DHF-814

TUDOR FAMILY PORTRAIT

CALAIS IN 1545

TUDOR
FAMILY PORTRAIT

by

BARBARA WINCHESTER

JONATHAN CAPE
THIRTY BEDFORD SQUARE
LONDON

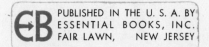

PUBLISHED IN THE U. S. A. BY
ESSENTIAL BOOKS, INC.
FAIR LAWN,   NEW JERSEY

FIRST PUBLISHED 1955

HC
254
.W5
1955

914.2
W759x

LIBRARY
FLORIDA STATE UNIVERSITY
TALLAHASSEE, FLORIDA

PRINTED IN GREAT BRITAIN IN THE CITY OF OXFORD
AT THE ALDEN PRESS
BOUND BY A. W. BAIN & CO. LTD., LONDON

CONTENTS

258010

ILLUSTRATIONS

FOREWORD

Tudor family portrait is the story of the Johnsons,
an ordinary, middle-class family, living their everyday lives
in sixteenth-century England. Few of them were remarkable people. None were poets or painters or musicians, and they
left no mark upon their generation. And yet to those who knew
and loved them, within the circle of their family and friends, they
were of as much importance as all the great and famous people
who ever lived. And for us who come after them, they are all the
more interesting because they are ordinary men and women like
ourselves. They knew, as we do, love and laughter, sickness and
sorrow, and the intimate details of their lives — the venison and
green ginger that they ate, the red wine and potent ale they drank,
the velvet gowns and ruffled shirts they wore, the carved furniture
in their rooms, the conduct of their households in town and
country, the occupation of their leisure hours, their comments on
religion and trade and the affairs of state — all this is revealed in
what is surely the most magnificent collection of Tudor letters yet
to see the light of day.

John Johnson was a merchant of the Staple, a most worthy,
sober, diligent and orderly man. He kept and filed not only all
the letters he received from his impetuous and charming wife,
from his two brothers, from his relations, friends, business acquaintances, apprentices and servants, but also a copy of every single
letter that he ever wrote, whether in English, French or Flemish,
destined for London, the country or abroad. Nearly a thousand of
these letters have survived out of a correspondence that was
originally twenty times more numerous. We may sigh for those
that are lost, but how much we have to be thankful for in the
thousand that remain! Superbly rich in life and character, these
letters chart the fortunes of a typical Tudor family, bourgeois in
the finest sense of the word, and truly representative of the age in
which they lived. They reflect as in a mirror all the fire and darkness and life of Tudor England.

The history of the Johnson Letters is a fascinating one. In the
year 1553, the firm of Johnson & Company went bankrupt, and

John's 'writings and books' were gathered together and sent to the Privy Council. The Lords of the Council forwarded the great mass of documents to the Lord Chancellor, one of the statutory judges in cases of bankruptcy, so that they could be used as evidence in the lawsuits under way against the firm in the High Court of Admiralty. When the committee of merchants had finished their examination, and the judges had given their final verdict, all the letters and letter-books, ledgers, cash-books and reckonings — the accumulation of a lifetime — were lodged for safe keeping in the Tower of London. There they lay like prisoners for almost three hundred years, the paper growing brittle and yellow with age, the black ink fading to sepia, unregarded and unregarding behind the dank and massive stone walls. At last, during the Regency, Sir Henry Ellis, Keeper of the Bodleian, began his search among the Tower records for Royal Letters. He found and published two of Otwell Johnson's which were perhaps most likely to appeal to the romantic reader of the nineteenth century — the eye-witness account of the death of Queen Catherine Howard, and that other tragic letter about the racking of Anne Askew.

It was not long afterwards that the great transfer of public records began, and the Johnson Letters were among those that reached Chancery Lane. Some of them, mostly for the year 1545, were included in the *Calendar of Letters and Papers, Foreign and Domestic, of the Reign of Henry VIII*, and several more were calendared for the *Addenda* published in 1928. But by far the greatest number remained as a unique and entirely untapped source of social and economic history among the red-bound volumes of the State Papers Supplementary.

The letters, as we have them today, run from February 1542 — March 1552. The sequence is most nearly complete for the years 1545-46 and 1551-52, owing to the chance that has preserved John's letter-books. Far fewer letters and no letter-books have survived from the early years, but only one gap occurs, from 1549-50. Earlier than the letters, and parallel with them, is a series of rather fragmentary accounts; later, in 1553, come the records of the lawsuits in the High Court of Admiralty; and seven years after that, in Elizabeth I's reign, a second series of letters and memoranda begins. Of fleeting interest compared with the great correspondence of 1542-52, they nevertheless give a clue to the fate of the remarkable man who was destined to be in turn a wealthy merchant, a penniless bankrupt and an ardent promoter of projects for the nation's trade and economic life.

My thanks are due to Dr. Alwyn Ruddock for her help and encouragement, and for the references to the Admiralty cases concerning Johnson & Company. Professor Bindoff helped me with the Flemish letters, and Dr. Ross with the French ones. Miss Mary Finch very kindly worked through the records at Lamport Hall, and I am indebted to Mr. Brudenell for permission to use the material there and also to the Marquess of Salisbury for permission to use the manuscripts at Hatfield House. Mr. Percival Boyd of the Drapers' Company gave me valuable information. I would also like to thank the officials at the Public Record Office for the help they gave me.

THE JOHNSON FAMILY

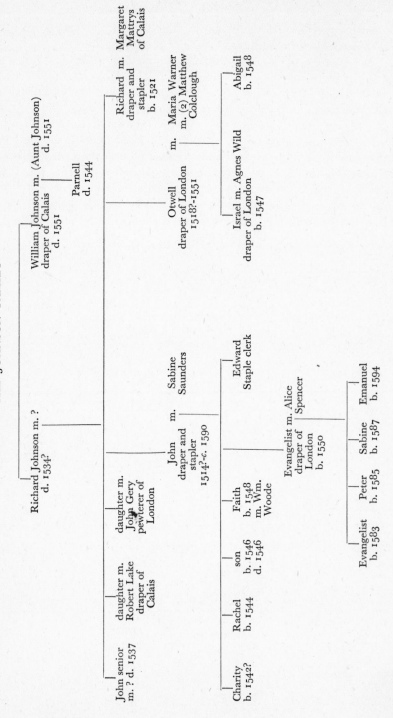

THE CAVE AND SAUNDERS KIN

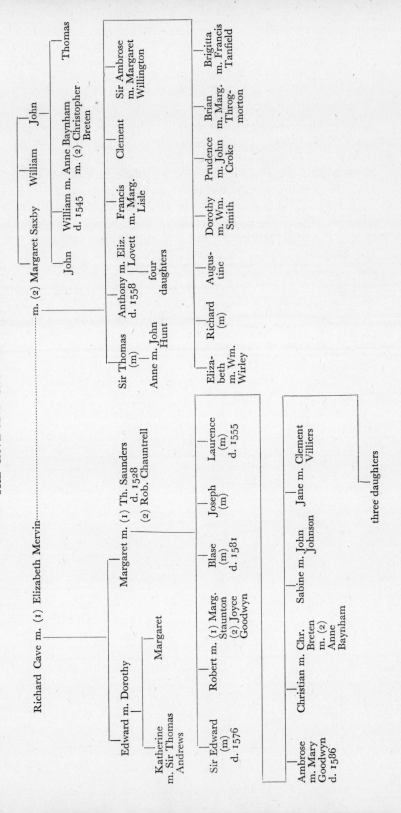

A WORTHY merchant is the heir of adventure whose hopes hang much upon wind. Upon a wooden horse he rides through the world, and in a merry gale he makes a path through the seas. He is a discoverer of countries and a finder out of commodities, resolute in his attempts and royal in his expenses. He is the life of traffic and the maintainer of trade, the sailor's master and the soldier's friend. He is the exercise of the exchange, the honour of credit, the observation of time and the understanding of thrift. His study is number, his care his accounts, his comfort his con- science, and his wealth his good name. He fears not Scylla and sails close by Charybdis, and having beaten out a storm, rides at rest in a harbour. By his sea gain he makes his land purchase, and by the knowledge of trade finds the key of treasure. Out of his travels he makes his discourses, and from his eye observations brings the models of architecture. He plants the earth with foreign fruits, and knows at home what is good abroad. He is neat in apparel, modest in demeanour, dainty in diet and civil in his carriage. In sum, he is the pillar of a city, the enricher of a country, the furnisher of a court and the worthy servant of a king.

NICHOLAS BRETON
The Good and The Bad

PART ONE

CHAPTER I

THE BROTHERS JOHNSON

IN the delicate drawings of Thomas Pettyt, the town of Calais rises sheer from the sea, encircled by its walls. The long façade of towers and battlements is broken only by the Lanterngate, with its broad archway leading into the town. Inside are wooden houses with crow-step gables and pleasant gardens, set close together in the winding streets. Here stood the ancient church of St. Nicholas, the mariners' saint, and the tall spire of Our Lady Church, where the merchants of the Staple knelt to pray. Here was the schoolhouse behind William Stevens's place; taverns like the Sign of the Ship and the Cross Keys; the leather, swordsmith and goldsmith's shops down bustling Lanterngate Street; the fish and vegetable stalls in the market place, where Flower Mary sold her cabbages and pot herbs, and delicious early fruit that came from France. Every week the clumsy market carts came rumbling in from Oye and Sandgate, villages set among the farms and orchards of the lowland countryside, with its landscape of willow-hung canals against a line of wooded hills. A stream of clear water flowed through the town, falling into the haven at a place called Paradise.

Such wares as the town lacked came in by sea, for Calais was a flourishing port, with the finest harbour on the Artois coast. All sorts and conditions of ships lay anchored in the Roads or moored at the wharves along the foreshore: great hulks bound for Antwerp with cargoes of ebony, spices and silk; pirate vessels in the guise of honest merchantmen; herring catchers, slow cogs and slender barques, their pennants streaming in the wind. The quayside was always crowded with merchants and mariners, arguing and gesticulating as the bales of goods were swung ashore, and carried into the warehouses that were only a stone's throw from the Watergate.

The story begins at Christmas 1534, in Mrs. Baynham's gabled house, looking out on the cobbled market square. At a table in the counting-house, surrounded by letters and books and boxes, his

seals and ink to hand, the chill sea air warmed by a glowing char-
coal brazier, John Johnson sat making up his accounts. He was,
according to the purser of an Italian ship, *The Salvator of Venice*, a
remarkably handsome young man: of middle height, but well
built, with a fair complexion and magnificent auburn hair and
beard. His attire on this occasion was sombre, dark fustian and
plain linen, for he was still bound apprentice, and satin doublets
and elaborately embroidered shirts were forbidden wear. He sat
now, quill pen in hand, bent over the leaves of a great ledger book,
recording his state of account in a small but exquisite handwriting.

> John Johnson ought to have that which is owing to me per
> my master, Anthony Cave, merchant of the Staple here in
> Calais, which is my father's bequest, Richard Johnson, Jesu
> rest his soul, being the sum of £54. 10s. 0d. mere sterling. . . .

> So rests nett that I am worth in money
> and good debts at Christmas anno 1534   £55   9s.   10¼d.

To Calais in the early years of the sixteenth century had come
two merchants, brothers, to make their fortunes by trade. It was
not the first uprooting that Richard and William Johnson had
undergone, for the little we know about them suggests that they
were Dutchmen, forerunners of the Protestant émigrés who were
to seek sanctuary in England during Elizabeth's reign, and whose
skill in weaving and gardening contributed so much to this country's comfort and craftsmanship. Their father was probably
Willem Jansen, a cordwainer of Geldersland, who brought his wife
and family to live in London, and eventually took out letters of
denizenship. One of his sons went to St. Albans, where he married
and settled down, trading in sheep and wool. But Richard and
William decided to try their luck in Calais, the little seaport on
the Artois coast which had been English for a hundred and fifty
years, the headquarters of the wool trade overseas, and a thriving
centre for the trade in herring and wine. Richard and William
Johnson were both drapers, and they found their opportunity in
Calais. They at once went into business together, importing
broadcloths and kerseys from England, and silks and velvets,
damasks and grosgrains from Flanders, and in fact did very well
for themselves.

As well as being a successful merchant, William Johnson was an able and public-spirited man. He rose to be Alderman of Calais, and played his part in organizing the Field of the Cloth of Gold, when Henry VIII met Francis I, and the watchers from Calais ramparts saw pavilions and tents flutter into being like so many fantastic butterflies, the gorgeous heraldic colours gleaming in the sun. William Johnson's career is the more remarkable because strict Calais regulations excluded all save Englishmen from office, and on one occasion he had to face serious opposition, when an informer ferreted out the secret of his foreign birth, and demanded his expulsion from the Council. Fortunately, William had good friends among his fellow-aldermen, and the Lord Deputy of Calais, Lord Lisle, also took his part. After many consultations had been held, they finally decided that he should remain in office.

When they were in possession of a sufficient income, the brothers married, and William Johnson was destined to live happily with his wife for many years to come. Richard Johnson, though successful enough in trade, was destined to be less fortunate in his married life. His first wife died, leaving a son whom he brought up to be a merchant like himself. The boy sowed his wild oats with a vengeance. He died young after an expensive career, and it was found that his best gown was in the hands of the Calais pawnbroker, that his wife was penniless and their little girl left to the charity of relations. In the course of time, Richard Johnson married again. His bride was probably one of the Helierd girls he knew in Calais, and they raised a family of two daughters (one married a wealthy London pewterer, the other married a Calais draper) and three sons: John, Otwell and Richard, junior, born at Calais in the year 1521. It was the eldest of these three, John Johnson, who was so busy entering up his accounts at Christmas 1534, and to whose meticulous attention to business we owe the whole magnificent sequence of the Johnson Letters.

As John wrote in his account-book, his father had died, leaving him £54 10s. in ready money, besides a little property in Calais. This of course was not riches, but by the standards of the day it was a considerable bequest, especially as Richard had other children to provide for, and as a great deal had already been spent on their education. It goes without saying that all three boys were to be merchants, like their father and brother before them, for there was no more honourable profession in Tudor

B

England, and none that was held in greater esteem. Their training had begun while they were still very young, for Richard had followed the old English custom of sending his children away from home, to be brought up in other men's houses. This was one aspect of English family life which foreigners regarded as extremely odd, to say the least of it. When, in the year 1500, the Italian diplomat wrote his masterly account of English life, *The Relation of the Island of England*, he had nothing but praise for the lavish English hospitality, the great banquets and rich silver, and the pretty widows; but the practice of putting out children of tender years he described with all the bewilderment felt by a Latin of strong family affections, faced with Anglo-Saxon coldness and reserve.

Few are born who are exempted from this fate, for everyone, however rich he may be, sends away his children into the houses of others, whilst he in return receives those of strangers into his own. And on enquiring their reason for this severity, they answered that they did it in order that their children might learn better manners. But I, for my part, believe that they do it because they like to enjoy all their comforts themselves, and that they are better served by strangers than they would be by their own children. Besides which the English, being great epicures, and very avaricious by nature, indulge in the most delicate fare themselves, and give their household the coarsest bread, and beer, and cold meat baked on Sunday for the week, which however, they allow them in great abundance. If they had their own children at home, they would be obliged to give them the same food they make use of for themselves.

The practice was of ancient origin. Born in the Middle Ages, when every aristocratic household had its nucleus of pages and esquires, it had spread with the growing snobbishness of the Renaissance, until it became a habit with the well-to-do to send their children away, rather than educate them at home and at the local schools. Where the merchant classes were concerned, the custom was to some extent founded in necessity, since for them the whole problem of education was bound up with that of apprenticeship. Company regulations forbade the apprenticing of sons to fathers, and so a merchant would entrust his son to the man who would normally be the boy's master, training him in his chosen profession, and often influencing the whole course of his career. And despite the strictures of the Italian, it was seldom that children were dispatched to perfect strangers. More often than not, relatives and friends took charge of them. When the time came for John to leave home, it was to enter the house of one of his father's acquaintances, a youngish merchant of the Staple named Anthony Cave.

Had worldly position and connection been the only consideration, Richard Johnson could hardly have done better for his son, for the Caves were a wealthy and powerful clan, foremost among the new men of the age, the *nouveaux riches*, the shrewd, rapacious, grasping gentry raised up by the Tudor dynasty. They were landowners and justices in the country, merchants and lawyers in town, sheriffs and members of Parliament. For them the sweetest plums of office were reserved, and their names appear with monotonous regularity on the commissions for the peace, subsidy and benevolence, oyer and terminer, jail delivery and sheriff rolls. Not that they lacked either brains or ability. Within the Cave family circle were several men of renown: the diplomat Sir Ambrose Cave was Anthony's younger brother; the statesman Walter Haddon and his brother James Haddon, the Protestant divine, were cousins; there was the lawyer-author Sir John Croke, one of the Six Clerks of Chancery; the big landowner Sir John Cope of Canons Ashby; there were the Hattons and Spensers, the Tanfields and Villiers, the Walsinghams, Throgmortons and Cecils — all of them drawn into that mesh of family connection and influence which was to govern England for generations to come. No doubt they were capable enough, but all the same one is tempted to echo Ralph Hythloday's remark in *Utopia*, that sixteenth-century government was nothing but 'a certain conspiracy of rich men'.

Thomas Cromwell, that hard and ambitious man, was an intimate friend and frequent visitor of the family. He, like many of the Caves, had once been in trade, but he had risen in the world since his days as a shady lawyer and sharp cloth-merchant in London. As Personal Secretary to Cardinal Wolsey, he had just begun that dizzy climb to the top of the political ladder, from which Henry VIII would hurl him to his death when the time came. For sheer mean, cold-blooded ruthlessness — he had no heart to speak of — Cromwell is almost without equal in England's history. It was he who urged on Henry the brutal suppression of the monasteries, and from those dark deeds the Caves were not slow to profit. Through Cromwell's influence, Anthony Cave's father became High Sheriff of Northamptonshire, his brothers received rich abbeys and broad lands, and he himself was presented with Tickford Priory, an erstwhile monastic property, set among the woods and streams of Buckinghamshire, which he converted into a charming country estate.

In appearance, as his portrait reveals, Anthony Cave was an undistinguished little man, short, plain and frail in health. But he possessed unusual and penetrating qualities of mind, which proved beyond the shadow of a doubt the essential rightness of Richard's choice. Respected everywhere as 'the good man' of Tickford, Anthony Cave's ideas were charitable and enlightened, far in advance of his time. He had no sons of his own and a deep affection soon sprang up between himself and John. Practically speaking, he brought John up and, when Richard died, he took the place of a father to the boy. All that John knew of his profession he learned from Anthony Cave. His master, as he always called him, handled and augmented his father's legacy, he lent him money and stood surety for him, he advised him on trading ventures in wine and herring, and at last entered into partnership with him. Years later, when there was a slight cloud on their friendship, John freely acknowledged his debt. 'I do not forget that ye have brought me up from my childhood, no more than I trust ye do remember the faithful service that I have done you, and therefore I pray you esteem me to be both faithful unto you, and such one as would be glad to do you much more pleasure and service than it is in my power to do.'

Anthony Cave took a great interest in John's education, as might be expected from the man who founded a grammar school at Lathbury in the 1530s, and eventually endowed scholarships at Oxford. More than in any other walk of life in the sixteenth century, a good education was essential to a merchant's success, for he had to read and write and handle business not only in English, but in several European languages, and also to keep accurate books of account. What Cecil called the 'wanton bringing up and ignorance of the nobility'[1] — the loutish condition of youths reared, like Orlando, among the rustic grooms and hinds

— was a problem that never troubled the merchant class, which was already famous for its interest in learning. Many individual merchants, like Cave himself, and Robert Tempest and Sir Andrew Judde among his friends, gave generously to the cause of education at a time when so many of the monastic and chantry schools were being suppressed. The great Companies were no less active. It was the Mercers who made St. Paul's School possible; later came Haberdashers', Merchant Taylors' and other schools; at Canterbury, the King's School owed much to the Company of Leatherworkers, while the Grocers were closely connected with Walwyn's School at Hereford. In this determination to acquire and promote knowledge lay the secret of middle-class success, and their gradual rise to power and influence in the nation's affairs.

John was an unusually intelligent boy, with a taste for learning that remained with him all his life, if his letters are any guide. His education was probably a fairly happy affair; at all events it is to be hoped that he was spared the brutalities that so many schoolmasters inflicted on the young at that time, and for generations after Ascham and Elyot had advocated far better and different ways. When he was past the stage of horn-book and primer, John learned to read in English and to write his letters, fumblingly at first, but later developing an exquisite Italianate hand. Latin he learned as a matter of course, shouting aloud in class from a battered grammar, parsing and construing Caesar and Ovid, even as Shakespeare was later to do. Even in Stuart times Latin was considered essential, a *lingua franca* for 'Gentlemen who go to travel, Factors for merchants and the like'.[2] As he grew older, John was taught to cipher in both roman and arabic numerals, and when he had thoroughly mastered his 'algorism' (as it was called), he learned how to cast accounts in both single and double entry fashion. Cosmography undoubtedly formed part of his curriculum, for only a few decades had passed since Columbus had sighted the islands of America, and Diaz rounded the Cape of Good Hope. Men's imaginations were stirred and quickened by the voyages of discovery, and the conquest of the sea, which held such golden promise for the future.

What pleasure is it, in one hour, to behold those realms, cities, seas, rivers and mountains . . . What incredible delight is taken in beholding the diversities of people, beasts, fowls,

27

fishes, trees, fruits and herbs: to know the sundry manners and conditions of people, and the variety of their natures, and that in a warm study or parlour, without peril of the sea, or danger of long and painful journeys: I cannot tell what more pleasure should happen to a gentle wit, than to behold in his own house everything that within all the world is contained.[3]

Sir Thomas Elyot's picture of study in a panelled room, with maps of the fabulous Indies and Cathay spread upon oak tables, the warm sun streaming through the oriel window, is a charming and attractive one. And yet for a merchant, it was only the beginning of the story, for most of what John learned came from practical experience, not from books. As soon as he was old enough, he accompanied his master in wool-buying expeditions through the Buckinghamshire countryside, watching the bargaining with broggers and growers and simple country folk, learning gradually to distinguish between good fleeces and bad. Frequently he would travel with his master to London and Calais, Bordeaux and Antwerp, so that he might know at first hand how business was transacted in the counting-houses and on Lombard Street, how wool and wine cargoes were handled and sold to the foreign buyers, how to deal with bills of exchange drawn on the Antwerp Bourse, how to clear them at the great seasonal marts — Cold, Pasche, Sinxon and Balms — and how to deal with the complex currency of half a dozen European countries.

The net result of all this was that John became a polished and travelled young man, at home anywhere in Europe, and able to deal competently with almost any situation. He could speak and write two languages, French and Flemish, fluently, and his brothers achieved an almost equal facility. Otwell, before he entered the service of Sir John Gage, the Comptroller of the Royal Household, had been apprenticed to a merchant in Calais, and had travelled far more widely in France than his elder brother. To Otwell, French came as naturally as his mother tongue; he used it in all the private and confidential passages of his letters, and indeed, in his own words, wherever 'mine English did not here so aptly offer itself to my pen'. Even Richard could be relied on to make a fair translation of a letter into French.

The youngest of the three brothers, Richard stayed at home and went to school in Calais until his father died, when John brought him over to England and apprenticed him to Anthony Cave. As the letters reveal, Richard was inclined to be a difficult youth, and Cave never gave him the trust and affection he bestowed so freely on John. It is possible that the slower Richard was made conscious that he had not his brother's natural gifts; at all events, he was given to fits of silent sulking, and sometimes would quarrel at a word, although he could be amiable enough when he wished to please. The thing that irked his master and brothers so much, however, was the fact that Richard was bone-lazy, and would do anything rather than work. His indolence was probably caused by his avoirdupois, for he was certainly overweight. The Tudors were much given to the pleasures of the table, and Richard indulged himself with the best. Once even John took him to task and told him he should get more exercise. 'For your gentle admonition to exercise bodily something, whereby the corpulency whereunto it appeareth I am subject may be avoided, I most heartily thank you', returned Richard, not a whit put out. 'At our next meeting ye shall perceive that I have prevented your brother like counsel, and now by your persuasion will further practise, so that when we come together I hope to be less than you!'

Even more than Richard's, the personality of Otwell Johnson emerges with astonishing clarity from the pages of the letters. No word-picture of Otwell has survived, but it is more than probable that he was red-headed like John, and of the three young men it is Otwell who possesses the most complete and vital character of them all. He was a gay young man, kind and generous, with a real interest in people and a rare sense of humour. Otwell must have had a singularly charming way with him, for he could always be relied on to smooth out difficulties, and even bring potential enemies round to his own way of thinking by dint of 'fair words' and expending a little time and trouble. Everyone liked Otwell, from his master, Sir John Gage, who was always 'very gentle' to him, down to the merchants of his company, his apprentices, and the workmen of the neighbourhood. Few men had more friends and fewer enemies. With it all, Otwell was shrewd and practical, managing his own and his brother's affairs with outstanding skill and success. To John, the 'beloved brother' of so many letters, Otwell was indeed devoted, and his affection was returned in full measure, for they never had a quarrel, and scarcely a day passed without one of them writing to the other.

But it is John, the eldest of the three, who most nearly approaches the time-honoured conception of the worthy merchant: handsome in appearance, dignified in his bearing, discreet, honest and self-respecting, and of sober and diligent habits. Indeed, for one so young, he was almost too seriously minded, though probably his step-brother's career of debt and extravagance had served as an awful warning throughout his childhood, and would account for his determination to avoid the primrose path at all costs. After his father's death, John became the head of the family. As such, he was consulted on every matter of importance, he took decisions that influenced the personal and business lives of his brothers, and it was his aim and object to keep them as a united and responsible family group. The key to John's character lies perhaps in his attitude towards his chosen profession. He regarded it as a most honourable estate in life, and in his eyes it assumed all the dignity of a vocation. For him, a merchant's career was his calling, to which he had been divinely summoned and appointed. Needless to say, John was a deeply religious man, even for the age in which he lived. There was another and most amiable side to John's personality: a more contented and home-loving man was never born. He adored his wife; and if there were times when that spirited young lady led him a stormy existence, he was completely devoted to her and the children, and he liked nothing better than to be at home with them in the heart of the countryside, living the peaceful life of a country gentleman, far from the turmoil of the town.

There was much justification for John's belief and confidence in his own and his brothers' future, for never before had there been such an age of merchants as the sixteenth century. Their influence would soon be everywhere, in everything, as all-pervasive as the eighteenth-century Whigs of Holland House: not only in their own sphere, but in politics as well. No Tudor statesman, however suspicious he might be of the merchant class as a whole, could entirely escape their influence, for he was himself of it, root, stock and branch. The merchant, indeed, was gradually being recognized as a most desirable member of the Commonwealth; there were more merchants than ever before, and their numbers increased with the boom in trade that lasted from the beginning of Henry VII's reign until the early 'forties. It was in these years that the merchants first rose to power, lending money to the Government, financing Henry's wars, writing treatises on economic problems, backing new industries, and promoting foreign trade and exploration. By Elizabeth's reign the position of the merchant was assured, his wealth proverbial, and his name a synonym for luxury. Contemporary writers described their magnificent banquets, their town and country residences hung with tapestry, 'gorgeous arras in rich colours wrought, with silk from Afric, or from Indy brought',[4] stored with soft Turkish carpets and delicate Venetian glass, their gardens planted with exotic flowers and fruits from overseas. With the turn of the century, English ships and English merchants were in every quarter of the globe, from Tagus to Virginia, from Java Head to Istambul. Merchants and merchandise were making England 'the wealthiest Island in Christendom'.

CHAPTER 2

THE WORLD THEY LIVED IN

THE young Johnsons grew to manhood during the springtime
of the Renaissance in England. It was a golden age, a time
when everything was new under the sun, when the very map
of the world was unfolding to show the strange uncharted seas, the
shores and islands never known before. It was an age of war and
persecution, of plague and cruelty, and yet an age of unutterable
beauty, of the rich flowering of the human spirit in so many exquisite ways that the painting and poetry, music and architecture
of that time are still the delight of those who love to contemplate
their works of genius. On the continent of Europe, the Renaissance gave birth to men of the stature of Michelangelo, Leonardo
da Vinci and Raphael, Dürer and Masaccio, Botticelli and Man-
tegna, Titian, Tintoretto and Veronese, Velasquez and El Greco,
creating a new world of vision and colour for the delight of all
mankind. Ronsard, Montaigne and Paré, Clouet and Cortez,
Calderon and Pisarro added lustre to the reputations of France and
Spain. And in the realm of religion, Luther and Calvin, Zwingli
and Melancthon wrought their mighty revolution, to be matched
on the Catholic side by St. John of the Cross, Teresa of Avila and
Ignatius de Loyola.

Beside the wealth and sophistication, the machiavellian diplomacy, the brilliant genius of Europe, England to a casual observer
appears a little provincial and *farouche*, an island kingdom
separated from the wellspring of creative activity by more than
twenty miles of sea. Yet appearances were deceptive, for within
her silver moat England was gathering forces for the consumma-
tion of her genius in Elizabeth's reign, for that immortal host of
explorers and playwrights and exquisite singers of songs. And the
early Tudor period has its own charms. The society into which
the Johnsons were born was renowned for its wit and learning, for
men of the quality of Erasmus and Sir Thomas More, for a sumptuous court that passed its time in masques and pageantry, for the
delicate lyric verse of Thomas Wyatt, and the candid portraits of

CATHERINE HOWARD

Holbein and Eworth. In these portraits we see the outward and visible semblance of the men and women of that day, the incredible richness of their dress, the barbaric extravagance of their jewellery, studded with square-cut emeralds, glowing rubies, and baroque pearls. The whole character of the man who dominated the age, Henry VIII, is revealed in a single red chalk drawing, and we can set beside it the utter repose of Thomas More, the gentleness of Fisher, the mean-mindedness of Cromwell. To read the poetry of Wyatt and Surrey is to know yet more of the spirit of the age. They sing of the times they live in, of love and spring, of hunting the deer in misty valleys, of the music of the lute and a man's voice singing, of the subtlety and poison of the Court, the shortness of man's life and the bitterness of death. From their portraits and poetry we know them well, the Englishmen of that day, in their mixture of good and evil, simplicity and cunning, good humour and sudden violence, dwelling in a land where no man walked abroad without his sword, where immense wealth lived side by side with desperate poverty and squalor, where rogues and vaga-bonds lurked on heath and highway, where pirates took their pleasure, and where disease and plague raged from one year's end to the next.

There was hardly an aspect of English life and thought that did not undergo a profound transformation in Henry's reign. It was these years which marked the transition from the careless, extro-vert, sunlit world of the Middle Ages, a world of security and stability, with the ordered hierarchy of men on earth and the saints in heaven, to the self-conscious, turbulent, creative Modern Age, where nothing was stable any more, nothing secure. The very landscape of the shires was altered, for it was in the agrarian revolution of the sixteenth century that the ancient ways of agri-culture, the open fields of the Gothic era, gave gradual place to the enclosures that we know today. When the great Divorce and the severance of the tie with Rome brought the dissolution of the monasteries in their wake, the broad abbey lands passed into private ownership, and the movement towards enclosure received all the stimulus of the urge to safeguard the rights of property. Peasant smallholders were evicted to make way for bigger and better farms, mostly for sheep, village common land was enclosed, and banks thrown up and ditches dug. Hedges were carefully planted with nut trees and hawthorn, crab apple and sloe to prevent the wandering kine; and there the wild flowers took root, the violet and rose and spindleberry, which make the hedgerow one of the fairest aspects of the English scene. A far view from Chanctonbury Ring or Churchdown Hill reveals a landscape of enclosed fields, a patchwork quilt of corn and fallow hemmed in by hedges; and a swift comparison of old maps with modern air photographs shows how little the pattern of the earth has changed in four hundred years.

Still throughout the countryside are the traces of what the Tudors built, and what they destroyed; echoes of that distant revolution that severed us from the feudal world. The noble ruins of Fountains Abbey, of Tintern in the lovely, wooded valley of the Wye, call forth romantic memories of a vanished age, and are a reminder of the destruction of Papal power. The cathedrals at Canterbury and St. Albans, the Abbey at Tewkesbury, and a host of smaller churches bear mute witness to the philistines who ransacked the ancient shrines and melted down the work of craftsmen's hands. The Tudors were great builders, and their country houses yield up the distilled essence of their world, with their linenfold panelling, long galleries and twisting chimneys, their mazes and knot gardens and bowling alleys. Sutton and Cothele and Audley End, and the merchant Kitson's great house, Hengrave Hall, are all their monuments and our inheritance. At Osterley, the exquisite work of Robert Adam decorates the Tudor shell, and as the walled kitchen garden mellows in the sun, and the ancient trees cast their shadow on the lawns, who does not wonder at the wealth that enabled the Tudor financier, Sir Thomas Gresham (whom the Johnsons knew) to buy and keep it up. Still more potent is the impression left by Hampton Court, that palace of rose-red brick and quiet green courts, with the vast panoply of the banqueting hall, and the small apartments where Wolsey walked and talked, looking out on to the river. At Cambridge, the Tudor world approaches more nearly still. In King's College chapel the carved escutcheons, rose and portcullis, gleam whitely between heraldic beasts against the columns of the nave. And among the flaring lacework of glass and stone, Henry VIII, the Tudor King, receives his Maker on terms of complete equality.

Always the figure of one man, Henry VIII, dominates the age. The force of his personality and actions can hardly be underestimated, for they influenced not only the immediate circle of

34

the Court, but every living soul in the kingdom. As a young man, and during the early years of his marriage to Catherine of Aragon, Henry had been the hopeful Prince, the darling of the ambassadors' reports. 'The King is the handsomest Prince I have ever set eyes on, above the usual height . . . his complexion very fair and bright, with auburn hair combed straight and short in the French fashion, and a round face so very beautiful that it would become a pretty woman.' He was charming, clear-skinned, red-headed and enthusiastic about everything; he was athletic, a tennis-player and horseman; he was intellectual, a linguist and amateur musician and poet, the author of the *Assertio Septem Sacramentorum* against Luther, and christened Defender of the Faith by the Pope. There was seemingly no end to his promise and accomplishments. But as the years wore on, fear and disappointment ate like acid into Henry's character, corroding most of what was good and sound, and leaving only a residue of giant will and colossal egotism. Henry might indeed have served as a model for Machiavelli. He was the crowned and anointed King of England, and he intended to remain so. Where a weaker or nobler mind might have drawn back, Henry never once faltered. Whatever steps had to be taken to ensure his impregnable position, these he took logically, dispassionately, and with apparently no more concern than if the human beings involved had been so many ivory pawns on a chessboard. The executions of Suffolk and Buckingham removed the last Pretenders to the throne; Sir Thomas More, Fisher and the Carthusians died terribly for refusing to recognize him as Supreme Head of the Church; abbots and monks were strung up like chickens when they resisted helplessly the plundering of their monasteries. The fate of Darcy, Aske and hundreds more was a sufficient warning to those who attempted to rise against him; the deaths of Exeter, the frail old Countess of Salisbury and the Earl of Surrey were examples to those who plotted about the throne. It was only a merciful illness that saved Cardinal Wolsey from the block. Cromwell was sacrificed without a qualm.

Henry in the early 1540s was still King, and yet his success had cost him dear. The man who should have been in his prime was prematurely old, a mountain of flesh, and in agony from his ulcerated leg. Such good looks as he had once possessed were gone for ever. The Holbein portraits reveal the cruel eyes, the tiny, tight-set mouth in the gross face; and not all his satin and jewels can disguise the rot that has set in, more moral than physical. Duped in foreign policy, enmeshed in two wars with France, listening all the time for the whisper of plot and rebellion, Henry was not in himself even remotely content. Perhaps in nothing is Henry's true character revealed so much as in that tragic procession of women who were at once his wives and his victims. The love affair with Anne Boleyn was understandable. Catherine had been a good wife to Henry, but she was also dull, and since she had presented him with only one sickly girl, the effect on a man of Henry's pride might have been foreseen. He would — and did — push the divorce through *maugre* the Papacy and the Empire. But that Anne should herald tragedy no one could have foreseen. It is curious that Henry, who never truly loved anyone except himself, always wanted to be loved for himself alone. After the deaths of Anne Boleyn and Jane Seymour, and the parting from Anne of Cleves, he prospected for a new sweetheart with undiminished zeal. This time he chose Catherine Howard, and although she loved another man, Thomas Culpeper, she led the King on for all she was worth. Catherine was an orphan, as poor as a church mouse, and doubtless tired of wearing turned dresses. She was dazzled by the diamonds and ermine that would be hers, bewitched by the prospect of being Queen, and her Uncle Norfolk nudged her eagerly into the marriage that promised him an accession of power. On the day that Cromwell was beheaded in the Tower, Henry married his fifth wife. After his fashion, he was in love. Catherine was his rose without a thorn, the girl who was to restore his lost youth after so many troublesome wives, who would bear him fine sons as proof of his virility. Even in public it was observed that Henry could not keep his hands off her; by day he rode and hunted as if he were twenty again, and by night he made love.

But Catherine was young, and when the pleasure of being Queen began to wear off, so did the glistening aura that had surrounded Henry. She began to think of him as any pretty girl would think of a diseased and clumsy husband, and she was still too young and inexperienced to take the measure of the man she had married. She never realized how elemental were Henry's passions, how oriental his outlook, how dangerous and subtle his mind, and how abnormally sensitive the vanity buried in that unprepossessing mound of flesh. Anne Boleyn, Catherine's own cousin, had once believed she could tame the King, and she had been wrong: it was to take all the soothing tact of a comfortable widow, Catherine Parr, to keep Henry in a good mood. There is no evidence that Catherine Howard so much as thought of Anne's fate when, bored with her unlovely marriage, she set eyes on young Thomas Culpeper again. 'I never mistrusted the Queen until at Hatfield I saw her look out of her chamber window on Master Culpeper after such sort that I thought there was love between them', said one of her women, Margaret Murray. Henry was away in the north at the time. Ironically enough he gave thanks to God immediately on his return for giving him his new Queen, 'after sundry troubles of mind which have happened to him by marriages'. The very next day, the blow fell. Catherine's enemies had been busy while Henry was away, and Cranmer confronted him with irrefutable proof of the Queen's lovers before and since her marriage. They got hold of one of her love-letters to Culpeper, signed 'yours as long as life endures', and Henry's fury knew no bounds. He called for a sword to kill her with, and wept bitter tears of self-pity and rage.

The tragedy followed its accustomed course. Catherine was sent to the convent at Syon; her lovers, Culpeper and Derham, were executed in December, and early in the New Year, 1542, an Act of Attainder was passed against the Queen. It was upon Otwell Johnson's master, Sir John Gage, that the task fell of breaking to Catherine the news that she was to go to the Tower, and with her Lady Rochford, who had acted as her go-between. Robed in black, Catherine was taken by water to the dark and miserable gate that yawned in the massive walls. Life was as sweet to her as anyone else, and she had not Anne Boleyn's steely courage. She wept so bitterly that her execution was deferred to permit her 'to reflect on the state of her conscience', while poor Lady Rochford, it is said, went out of her mind time and again. All this while, Henry stood by unrelenting, and there was never really any hope that he would forgive such a blow to his pride. Die she must, and Lady Rochford with her.

On Sunday evening, February 12th, Sir John Gage went to see the Queen, and told her that she was to die next day. As Constable of the Tower, Gage had been busy all the week past with the arrangements, some of which he delegated to his staff, among them Otwell Johnson. That same evening Otwell sat down and

37

wrote a letter to his brother, apologizing for the fact that he had been able to do no business,

> ... for I have so much been charged with Mr. Comptroller's affairs and busy commissions all this week past, that I have had no spare time to do anything else for myself nor any other; and the chief part of the same have been concerning the necessity for provision of things to the Queen's household, which I suppose will take an end very shortly, for as tomorrow in the morning she is appointed to lose her life within the Tower, as is said, where I am commanded to wait upon my master; and therefore I have made up this my rude letter overnight, most expressly to declare unto you the news aforementioned. Howbeit, for lack of leisure now, I shall gladly open a great deal more hereof at our meeting here, by God's favour.

At dawn next morning, Catherine was led to the block on Tower Green. It was cold, with the wintry chill of February, and yet the air held in it a promise of the spring that she would never see. The usual crowd of officials and servants had collected, as well as the soldiers, half in curiosity, half in sympathy, to see her exit from the world. Near the Comptroller stood Otwell Johnson, and two days later, when he had a little recovered from the shock, he wrote his letter to John. It is one of the two eye-witness accounts that have survived.

> ... And for news from hence, know ye that even according to my writing on Sunday last, I see the Queen and the Lady Rochford suffer within the Tower the day following, whose souls (I doubt not) be with God, for they made the most godly and Christian's end that ever was heard tell of (I think) since the world's creation, uttering their lively faith in the blood of Christ only, with wonderful patience and constancy to the death. And with goodly words and steadfast countenances, they desired all Christian people to take regard unto their worthy and just punishment with death, for their offences against God heinously from their youth upward in breaking of all his commandments, and also against the King's Royal Majesty very dangerously; wherefore they, being justly condemned (as they said) by the laws of the realm and Parliament

to die, required the people (I say) to take example at them for amendment of their ungodly lives, and gladly to obey the King in all things, for whose preservation they did heartily pray, and willed all people so to do, commending their souls to God, and earnestly calling for mercy upon him, whom I beseech to give us grace, with such faith, hope and charity at our departing out of this miserable world, to come to the fruition of his godhead in joy everlasting. Amen.

Your loving brother,
Otwell Johnson.

With my hearty commendations unto Mr. Cave and Mistress Cave, not forgetting my sister your wife. I pray you, let them be made partakers of these last news, for surely the thing is well worth the knowledge.

A Spaniard, nearer to the scaffold perhaps than Otwell, and certainly less hampered by the need to be discreet, wrote that Catherine cried out, 'I die a Queen, but I would rather have died the wife of Culpeper!' Otwell, too, must have heard her impassioned outburst of grief for the man she loved, but he would never have dared to put such words on paper. His letter reveals how much he sympathized, and that he felt for her as one human being might feel for another trapped 'in this miserable world', from which death provided the only escape. But had Otwell appeared too much concerned, rumour would have been busy, and the long shadow of suspicion might have fallen even on him. And to arouse Henry's suspicions was the equivalent of signing one's own death warrant.

As a member of the Comptroller's household, Otwell was in a privileged position. Sir John Gage liked and trusted the pleasant young man, and during the course of their many conversations together Otwell learned much of the doings of the Court and even State secrets. Whatever could be revealed without breaking a confidence, Otwell naturally imparted to his brother John, mostly by word of mouth, but sometimes by letter. He was at Court when Henry VIII received the submission of the 'Wild Irish' lords, while the nobles waited on the King in their most gorgeous robes of state. It was Otwell who told John of the promotions that Wriothesley and Paget received, when the first was made a baron, and the second a Secretary of State. It was Otwell again who told John what was said to the French Ambassador when the Council delivered its ultimatum of war, and what great affairs were in train when the Imperial Ambassador visited the Court.

Close to the centre of the political world, Otwell was equally well in touch with the world of merchants. The brothers were acquainted with many of the leading business men of the time, the 'great cobs' of Lombard Street, as Otwell called them, who were to do so much for English trade overseas. While Henry remained on the throne, little could be achieved, for the King demanded war and glory, not the profitable but unspectacular fruits of discovery and trade. The light that had blazed fitfully with the voyages of John Cabot and the Bristol men died down for decades. It is true that there were hopeful interludes with Rut's voyage in search of Cathay, and the voyages of Hawkins to Brazil in the early 'thirties, but not till Elizabeth's reign would the merchant's world come into its own with the voyages to Virginia and the East, and the immortal quest for Cathay. Not that the flame was ever entirely quenched; when the colossal piracy and privateering of the 'forties died down, men were found to sail English merchantmen far across the sea. Not long after the *Barbara* made her voyages to Brazil, the Barbary trade began, and soon afterwards, the voyages to Russia, Persia and the Guinea Coast. John himself must have seen the great grey elephant's head that John Lok brought back from Africa, and which Hakluyt peered at curiously as it hung on 'the worthy merchant' Sir Andrew Judde's panelled wall. Sir Andrew was an acquaintance of the Johnsons, and so were Sir William Chester, Thomas Lodge, Richard Lambert, the Offleys and the Levesons, all of them merchants who were intimately concerned in the development of trade and exploration overseas.

One of Otwell's closest friends was Armigill Wade — the godfather of his small son, the writer of affectionate postscripts on letters to John — a man who seems to typify the spirit of the early Renaissance in England, and to foreshadow the magnificent achievements of Elizabeth I's reign. To the casual observer, Wade was a typical civil servant, the Clerk of the Privy Council: but he was also known everywhere as the English Columbus, and the Johnsons must have heard the wonderful story many times from his own lips.

Six years before the Johnson Letters begin, a certain Master Hore of London, 'a man of goodly stature and of great courage, and given to the study of Cosmography', succeeded in interesting a number of young courtiers and lawyers, with the King's encouragement, in a voyage of discovery to the north-west parts of America. Among those who agreed to sail in Hore's own ship, *The Trinity*, were Thomas Buts and John Rastell (More's son-in-law); while on board the *Minion* were Armigill Wade himself, and a merchant of London named Oliver Dawbeney, with whom the Johnsons were also acquainted, and who related a great part of the story to Richard Hakluyt years later. At the end of April 1536, when all the preparations were complete, the six score voyagers and crew embarked, and the ships put out from Gravesend.

After two long months at sea, they finally reached Cape Breton Island, and then sailed north-east until they came to the 'Island of Penguin', full of wild birds, 'great fowls white and gray', which they drove into their boats and ate, and 'bears both black and white', which they captured and killed, 'and took them for no bad food'. It was here that they had their first sight of the Red Indians. One day while they were riding at anchor, Oliver Dawbeney was walking to and fro on the hatches, and he saw in the distance a boat rowing towards them across the bay. He called to the others below to come up on deck 'if they would see the natural people of the country, that they had so long and so much desired to see'. They pelted up the companion-way and manned the ship's boat, but they were not quick enough for the swift canoes. The Indians escaped upstream and fled on to an island, where the Englishmen soon lost track of them among the thick firs and pines, and the only prize they took was a decorated leather boot and 'a great warm mitten', which they found beside a dying fire.

Not long after the incident of the Indians, the ships began to grow short of food, and soon their difficulties became acute. One man killed his mate and, when the others grew suspicious, confessed to cannibalism. The captain made a courageous attempt to forestall such practices. He stood up, said Dawbeney, and made a 'notable oration', telling them that it was better to perish in body than be condemned everlastingly, both body and soul, to the unquenchable fires of hell. But the famine grew worse, and at last the men were driven to casting lots as to who should die, in order to save the others. Fortunately the arrival of a French ship that same night, well stocked with victuals, saved them. The starving Englishmen lay in wait and captured her, changed ships, and set sail for England.

The return journey carried them far to the north, so that 'they saw mighty islands of ice in the summer season, on which were hawks and other fowls to rest themselves, being weary of flying over far from the main'. They saw the faithful albatross, 'great white fowls with red bills and red legs', which they believed to be storks as they followed the ship. It was the end of October before the voyagers sighted England, and sailed into the green round harbour of St. Ives, whence they began the journey back to their own homes. Such a voyage, so long and so difficult, could not have been achieved without lasting effects on all who took part in it. Young Thomas Buts was so altered by near-starvation and misery that even his mother and father did not recognize him until, as he told Hakluyt (who had ridden two hundred miles to hear the tale), they saw a strawberry mark upon his knee. And when the King heard the story of their sufferings and privations, he was so moved with pity that he recompensed the angry Frenchmen out of his own pocket.[5]

Henry VIII was at all times capable of the grand gesture, and his regal qualities commanded admiration and loyalty from the greater part of his subjects, despite the vagaries and cruelties of his personal life. Moreover, Henry possessed several other inestimable advantages which set him above all those who plotted and hankered for his throne. With his unbreakable will, his ability to confront the Papacy, the Empire and France, Henry automatically represented the incarnation of strong and stable government, able to enforce the peace if not the prosperity for which most people longed. No one in their senses wanted a return to the aristocratic anarchy that had well-nigh ruined England in the fifteenth century. Henry was the bulwark against a return to the feudal age. And Henry, in virtue of a revolution unique in the annals of world history, was now the Supreme Head of the Church of England, representing in his person not only good secular government, but release from the control of a corrupt priesthood directed from Rome. Had Charles V permitted the Pope to grant a divorce to Henry, it is possible that England might never have broken away from the Catholic fold; at all events, the Reformation would have been long delayed. And yet it is clear that not only the intellectuals, but most people in England had advanced far in their sympathies towards reform when Luther nailed his Ninety-Five Theses to the church door at Worms in 1517. England had always been anti-clerical in feeling. As far back as the fourteenth century Piers Plowman voiced his discontent, as did Wycliffe and the Lollards, while Chaucer is as cheerfully contemptuous of the clergy as he could well be. Time had done nothing to abate that contempt in England. Fisher, Erasmus, Colet and Sir Thomas More all in turn attacked the corruption of the Church during the early part of Henry's reign. As knowledge of the reformed doctrines spread from the Continent, the forward-looking upper and middle classes embraced them with zeal and fervour. Nothing else can explain the eager co-operation that Henry received in the dissolution of the monasteries, not only from Cromwell's men, but from the Seven Years Parliament. The fact, of course, that most of the members were also among the chief beneficiaries merely made them the more fervent in Henry's cause. Mary was to find it completely beyond her power to make the rich yield up their plunder, the fair acres on which they had gorged themselves for nearly twenty years. It was one of the great permanent revolutions of English history, brought about by Henry's boredom with Catherine, his determination to have a male heir, his passion for Anne Boleyn, and his stubborn refusal to accept the dictates of a Hapsburg-controlled Papacy. Purely by accident, it happened to coincide perfectly with public opinion.

John and Otwell, typical members of the merchant middle class, leave us in no doubt as to the way they felt. They were deeply religious men, Lutheran in their conviction that only the Elect of God would be saved, Calvinist in their attitude to their calling. God was the familiar companion of their daily lives, and all their intellectual interests, apart from their work, were concentrated entirely on their religion. Otwell would end his letter 'in much haste, going to a good sermon', and once he sent his brother a copy of a morality play, with the words, 'For news I do send you the description of the great benefits and wondrous works of God, which was the Suffolk men's song, after their play of the battle betwixt the Spirit, the Soul and the Flesh that I declared once unto you.'

As one would expect, the Bible was to them the source of revelation, the directly inspired Word of God, the original authority to which they could appeal from the Church of Rome. Their very letters echo the sonorous, rounded periods of the Old Testament. The English Bible was perhaps the supreme gift of the Reformers. During the 1520s the Tyndale version had arrived in England from the Continent, only to be declared heretical by the Bishops, and solemnly burned. But in 1539, at Cranmer's instigation, the revised translation of Coverdale and Rogers was published with Henry's blessing, and a copy was ordered to be placed in every church throughout the land. Thus began the influence of the Bible in English as the source of religion, morals and literature, and on the Johnsons and their generation the effect was incalculable and dynamic. Something of this can be seen from the fact that such violent disputes and disorders arose from the mass consultation of Holy Writ that in 1543 a statute was passed, prohibiting all save 'gentlemen, gentlewomen and merchants' from reading the Scriptures. Needless to say, the Johnsons were great Bible-readers. 'Your Bible I will send you,' wrote Richard once from Calais, 'but I pray you, let me have another.' It was Richard who, in another of his letters, made special mention of the fact that the translator of the Bible, Miles Coverdale, was actually going to preach in Calais. Significantly enough, both John and Otwell were to choose their children's names from Holy Writ, without exception.

Nothing could quench their enthusiasm for the Reformation. The rebellious aristocracy, the conservative peasants might come out for the Old Religion in the Pilgrimage of Grace and the Exeter Conspiracy, but to the merchant class they were merely putting the clock back. For the Johnsons, the alternative to Henry and the Church of England was the Pope and the Catholic kings. And to them, the Pope was (as they frequently named him) the 'great Antichrist of Rome', while the Papacy was that 'great and abominable harlot of Babylon', whose tortuous manœuvrings blocked all hope of a peaceful settlement in the torn and divided empire of Charles V. It is interesting to note that when the Palsgrave of the Rhine and other German princes cast in their lot with the Protestants they had in Otwell's opinion turned 'from the Devil to God'. Both John's and Otwell's letters ring at times with a truly prophetic fervour.

Th'Emperor prevaileth against the Germans, howbeit not so much as is reported; and although God hath as it were for a season suffered the Emperor to prosper against the professors of his Word, yet I hope God will show forth his mighty arm, and send small power unto such as put on armour for the maintenance of the great Antichrist of Rome and his sinagogue, which God grant, and send us universal peace and a reformation of Popish errors.

The circle of the Johnsons was almost exclusively Protestant. One of their friends was the Staple chaplain, Parson Smith, who had once been summoned before Cardinal Wolsey for possessing Lutheran books. Another friend in Calais — it was a notorious centre of heretical doctrine in Henry's reign — was the priest John Butler, Cranmer's commissary, who was closely involved in the tragic affair of Adam Damlippe, the Lutheran friar. One of John's business acquaintances, a merchant with whom he had an account and whose family he knew well, was Henry Brinklow, better known to posterity as the reforming satirist, Roderick Mors. John's own landlord in the country, George Zouch, was excluded from Foxe's *Martyrs* only because he was fortunate enough to die a few days before the Sheriff's men arrived to take him prisoner. All these were ardent Protestants, and in John's own family there were many who were prepared to defy the law in order to satisfy their consciences. Otwell on one occasion scoured the London booksellers for a banned book, which he at last succeeded in getting — at a price.

The book of the Disputations that you write for, my brother Richard showed me that it is for Mr. Francis Tanfield, wherefore I have gotten one with very much ado, and could not have it but with secretness, and therefore it cost more than it is worth, for it cost me of truth 2s 2d sterling. My said brother doth bring it unto you; and also by him I do send you (for such news as I have at this time) th'Answer sent from Satan the Great Devil unto the Great Turk's Letter to the King of Poland, which is both notable and ingenious, with the conclusion of the Princes of Germany and other, to the withstanding of the foresaid Great Turk — very properly compiled, to my judgment.

The advanced views of the merchant middle class were in nowise shared by Henry VIII, who throughout his life remained the most Catholic of men, although gradually he moved a little to the left under Cranmer's influence. Those of his subjects who were not prepared to accept his own personal version of the True Faith had to walk delicately, for it was as dangerous for an extreme Protestant to deny the Six Articles as for a Catholic to assert the spiritual supremacy of the Pope. Henry, in fact, was a law unto himself in religion as in all other facets of the national life, and there was no room for those who disagreed out loud with his interpretation of the Scriptures. A bold and charming preacher, like his favourite Dr. Crome, who so rashly allowed the doctrine of the 'only and alonely, the throughout and eternal living God' to be proclaimed from the pulpit every Sunday, might for a while escape, but the more extreme of the Protestant clergy — Latimer and Ridley, Lever and Crowley — all had their licences to preach annulled. Sooner or later, if they would not toe the line, the choice was put plainly to the dissenters: recant or die. One of Otwell's letters reveals what happened to such as these, some of whom preferred death to the renunciation of the beliefs that meant everything to them.

Our news here of Doctor Crome's canting, recanting, de-canting or rather double-canting, be these: that on Sunday last, before my Lord Chancellor, the Duke of Norfolk, my Lord Great Master, Mr. Rich, Mr. Chancellor of the Tenths, with the Southwells, Pope, and other nobles and knights; and on th'other side the Bishops of London and Worcester, all principal doctors and deans, besides gay grayamesse, and a rabble of other marked people: the reverend father first-named openly declared his true meaning and right understanding (as he said, and according to his conscience) of the six or seven articles you heard of, as he should have done upon the second Sunday after Easter, but that he was letted from his said true intent by the persuasions of certain perverse-minded persons, and by the sight of lewd and un-godly books and writings, for the which he was very sorry, and desired the audience to beware of such books, for under the fair appearance of them was hid a dangerous accom-brance of Christian consciences, and so exhorted all men to embrace ancientness of Catholic doctrine and forsake newfangledness.

On Monday following, quondam Bishop Saxon, Mistress Askew, Christopher White — one of Mistress Fayrey's sons — and a tailor that come from Colchester or thereabout, were arraigned at the Guildhall, and received their judgement of my Lord Chancellor and the Council to be burned, and so were committed to Newgate again. But since that time, the foresaid Saxon and White have renounced their opinions, and the talk goeth that they shall chance to escape the fire for this voyage; but the gentlewoman and th'other man remain in steadfast mind, and yet she hath been racked since her condemnation (as men say), which is a strange thing in my understanding. The Lord be merciful to us all.

Anne Askew's tragic story is well known. Rich and Wriothesley racked her with their own hands, hoping to obtain some confession which they could use to incriminate others, and thus make themselves yet more secure in the King's favour. But Anne knew nothing and told nothing; she only refused steadfastly to recant her denial of transubstantiation, that first and cardinal article of the 'Whip with Six Strings'. Her death was felt everywhere as a blow to the Protestant cause, and nowhere more than in the Johnson family. John's brother-in-law and greatest friend was Laurence Saunders, a man whose known sympathies were already proving a source of danger to him. As was normal for the younger son of a large family, Laurence had been intended for a merchant's career, and was for a time apprenticed to a distant relative, Sir William Chester. So strongly did he feel a call to the ministry, however, that his master cancelled the indentures and released him to study divinity at Cambridge. One of his cousins was also there, James Haddon, the Protestant tutor of Lady Jane Grey, who was destined to die in exile at Strasbourg. It was he who introduced the young Laurence into the circle of extreme Protestant reformers, Latimer, Ridley and Lever; under their influence Saunders rapidly adopted the most advanced views. When it became legal under the Protectorate, Laurence Saunders married, although in orders; he was one of the most ardent of the Commonwealth men, and inevitably he was arrested shortly after Mary came to the throne. While in prison awaiting trial, he signed the Coverdale Confession of Faith, and then, early in 1555, he was led out to die at Coventry.

As yet, no hint of that dark shadow had fallen on the family, but it is evident from the letters to John that Laurence fully realized the difficulties of the path he had chosen, although he was not at all deterred by them. His eldest brother Edward, a brilliant lawyer who was himself attached to the Old Religion, saw even more clearly what the end would be, and shortly after Anne Askew's death he took it upon himself to warn Laurence 'to take very good heed unto myself, that I be not drowned in mine own fantasy and opinion, as other have been which after repented and acknowledged their own folly, and that he is right sorry' — runs the letter to John — 'that I should be noted to be one of the singular sort, with many mo things which were too long to write; and at the latter end, to make up all, he comforteth me, saying that he doubteth . . . my very great familiarity with Latimer . . .' His brother's advice he looked on 'as good worldly counsel, and if I had no other end to have respect unto than this present life I would follow it, but because it agreeth not to the other way, I lightly esteem it'.

It was, of course, the eternal conflict of conscience against the law, a problem that Laurence had to fight out alone. Edward's career, on the other hand, might serve as the model for any prudent, ambitious, middle-of-the-road man. Henry made him a Serjeant-at-Law, Mary knighted him a few days before his brother died, and in the fullness of time he became Justice of the Common Pleas and Chief Justice of the Queen's Bench. Notwithstanding the fact that he was a Catholic, Elizabeth made him Chief Baron of the Exchequer, and he died full of years, honour, money and estates late in her reign. Nothing reveals more clearly the difference between the two brothers than a letter which Laurence wrote to John early in Edward's reign, and which shows his lofty conception of his calling, and his passionate devotion to it.

I understand that Mr. Robinson, your churchman of Chicheley, marvelleth at my much preaching. Indeed, the miserable estate of the world is such that if there be any man found to do his duty, especially in this high ministry (as God knoweth I do it not, by a great deal), he may be as a monster among the multitude, and to be wondered at therefore. But on the other side, methinketh I may rather find some strange thing to marvel at in many of our authorised gospelling preachers nowadays, in the number of whom I conjecture I may put Mr. Robinson. There be, I say, of them that think it an high point of divinity to use seldom preaching, thereby to make it as a dainty dish — as a dish of strawberries which come but once in the year; but I take God's Word to be that necessary, quotidian, ghostly food to feed the soul withal, even as the body hath need of daily bodily food. The Lord give us eyes to see what appertaineth unto our duties, and to study to do the same, and not to lie sweating on the to-side, like sluggish, reckless stewards! Amen.

Laurence Saunders was writing when the full tide of Protestant reform was at its height. Henry had died in January 1547, leaving the kingdom to a delicate, studious boy of nine, and a Council of turbulent, ambitious men under the nominal leadership of Protector Somerset. The country was then in the throes of the plot for which the Earl of Surrey paid with his life, 'condemned to die like a traitor', wrote Otwell, while his father, the Duke of Norfolk, submitted humbly to the King. Otwell also hinted at the miraculous rumours that were in circulation about the tragic and handsome young poet. 'Du fils j'ai merveilles à vous compter de bouche at our next meeting.' Henry's death saved Norfolk in the nick of time, but when the new reign began, public opinion was still in a whirl of apprehension. One can sense John's anxiety when he reported to Anthony Cave: 'Yesterday the King was carried by land from Westminster to Syon, and this day by land also to Windsor, and there is buried as this day. Other news here is none that I have yet learned, but that all thing is well, Our Lord continue it.' What was to come was still unsure, and few could have forgotten the ancient proverb: 'Woe to the land when the King is a child.'

Their fears were to be justified, for seldom had England to suffer such a government. The new Council was comprised of power-ridden megalomaniacs, as greedy as they were inept, and riddled with corruption. Their first actions showed the mettle of which they were made. Somerset, in possession of the King's person, got himself created Lord Protector, and dukedoms, earldoms and marquisates rained on the rest. Yet this same reign was to mark the triumph of the Protestant cause, and make it still more certain that Mary could not succeed. The conservative element was practically excluded from the Council. Somerset, Seymour, Warwick, Southampton and Northampton all favoured the new learning and the reformed religion, and they at once began to remove the barriers which Henry had imposed. Somerset himself was a genuinely tolerant man, and he brought about the repeal of the Proclamations Act and other legislation against heresy. Notable reformers — Bucer, Peter Martyr, John à Lasco — flocked in from abroad, and in London the great preachers drew crowds daily to St. Paul's Cross and the city churches. The Edwardian Prayer Book was published, and the Litany; the clergy were allowed to marry; the meaning of the Sacraments was redefined. It was now the turn of the Papists to recant. Bonner, the hated Bishop of London, was 'stalled in the Fleet', and Stephen Gardiner, the Catholic Bishop of Winchester, was sent to the Tower, and eventually deprived of his office. 'That the old Winchester is become a new quondam,' Laurence Saunders wrote to John, 'I know you be a good clerk to say, Amen, and if it be so, I must needs say Deo Gratias.' London was in a ferment, as can be seen from a letter which Otwell wrote to his brother in May 1547, when the excitement was at its height.

After I was entered (brother) into my news within th'enclosed, I could not stay my pen but to write all; and therefore here for more of our Londonish religion news, know that Mr. Dokker (I say) Doctor Smith of Witless or Witterton College made of late a book of unwritten verities, which I hear say he is now agreed with veritably to unwrite them again; and the confession of his fault and ignorance in his first doing shall be put forth in fair print, into a thousand copies perchance, because few or none shall see them, and he himself shall be at his liberty to prove an honest man hereafter, if he can, without any open recanting as these whoreson herewigges were wont to do, that were wont to say that sola fides doth justify: howbeit (I thank God) there hath nothing else been preached at the Spital these last sermons, but that almost, and Down with Ceremonies, Down with Ceremonies of the Bishop's of Rome, etc., too long here to recite particularly. And thus again farewell.

Dr. Smith had to recant, but he suffered nothing worse than that humiliation, for Protector Somerset governed with a mildness that was all too rare in the Tudor age. He desired to make no martyrs and, while he lived, he held legal violence in check. Religious persecution was one of the greatest evils of the sixteenth century, and yet, bad as it was at times in England, it was inconceivably more dreadful on the Continent, where the Reformation and Charles V's struggle to maintain his vast empire, began a bloodbath that lasted for decades in Spain and France and the Low Countries. Beside the foreign kings, Henry appears as an angel of enlightenment in matters religious. In England, by not drawing conspicuous attention to one's beliefs, it was at least possible to follow one's own religion in comparative peace. On the Continent, this was never the case. As early as the 1540s, when the Placards were up in the Netherlands, Anthony Cave was sending accounts of the Emperor's 'extremities in burnings and punishing all against the Papish sect', and the English were shocked at the tales of the 'poor Christians' escaping from the pogroms in Antwerp. Indeed, when the Molenmeester of Haarlem came over to England and made his way down into Northamptonshire to see John, probably with the aim of founding an early colony of weavers there, Otwell sent him off with the words: 'I would have sent him unto you a-horseback, but his own choice was "rather to be a confessor afoot, than a martyr a-horseback", as you know their common proverb goeth.' Religious persecution had become part of the normal life of the Low Countries.

The Johnson family themselves were to be very closely involved in an incident that must have left its mark on them all, and hardened, if possible, their resistance to everything that savoured of Rome and the Emperor. Richard was married in the autumn of 1547, and shortly afterwards he went to Antwerp with his wife's brothers. He was trying to clear up some business transactions there, when news reached him of what had happened to his wife's Aunt Mattrys.

... an evil chance happened to my aunt Mattrys at Saint Omers, where she is retained prisoner for certain foolish

258010

LIBRARY
FLORIDA STATE UNIVERSITY
TALLAHASSEE, FLORIDA

words spoken against an image of Saint Adrian, and what will come of it I know not yet. The matter is put up to the Regent's Court, so that it hath cost him a great deal of money and me some, and I fear more will or it be ended. . . .

Death was the penalty for such an offence, and there was every likelihood that Aunt Mattrys would in fact die. An age which executed queens was not likely to extend more chivalrous treatment to a merchant's wife. The only hope lay in taking the case up with the highest authority in the land, and it seems that all the Cave and Saunders relations went into action without delay. As sincere Protestants, they approached Protector Somerset himself, and the great man intervened personally on her behalf. He summoned the Imperial Ambassador to his presence, and in the course of the interview he brought the matter up, trying to make light of the whole affair, excusing the indiscreet words by saying that the woman 'had taken more drink than she should have done' — a slander on Aunt Mattrys's good name which was more than justified by the circumstances.

Unfortunately, the international situation, and England's relation to it, were such that the Emperor had the whip hand. Charles V could not have disapproved more strongly of the Somerset Government and all it stood for; he deeply resented the fashion in which his cousin Princess Mary was being treated, and the Netherlands Government were in no mood to make concessions where none were necessary. Van der Delft did indeed report the whole conversation in great detail to the Imperial Council of State, but the most that they would allow was a relaxation of the full penalty: the death sentence was commuted to one of imprisonment. 'It seemed', the Ambassador wrote after he had broken the news to Somerset, 'that the Protector was not over-pleased at this, for he had ready minutes of the charges, and evidence that your lordships had sent me. But I did not fail to point out to him that the correction was very favourable, and requested him to use his endeavours to prevent their subjects from committing in future any similar scandal, to which he replied, "That is quite right".'

It is to be hoped that Aunt Mattrys did not languish long in the Flemish prison, but that her friends were able at last to secure her release. Alas, the rest is silence, and there is no further word of her fate in the letters. But that the Imperial Government should have treated an English national in such a way must have had its effect on the circle of her family and friends, and their grief and indignation are not difficult to imagine. Such incidents could only worsen the already strained relations between England and the Empire, and by Elizabeth I's reign the word Catholicism had become synonymous with that of the Inquisition. Late in life, and despite all his misfortunes, John's one great consolation was that in Elizabeth's England they had freedom to follow 'God's glorious gospel' in the face of all their enemies.

Religious persecution and continual wars by land and sea were the natural accompaniments of the Johnsons' lives, and indeed of sixteenth-century life as a whole. This alone would be sufficient to account for that deep strain of melancholy which haunts the greatest verse and music of the Tudors, echoing as it does the swiftness of man's days on earth, and all too frequent pain and death. But there was a third and even greater shadow over their lives, that of sickness and the plague. Disease and pain, for which there were no merciful drugs and anaesthetics, was something that everyone had to endure as a matter of course. The only remedy, when John once cut his finger in Calais, was a germ-ridden plaster of diaculum (lead) and herb o'grace; Lady Cromwell for days suffered such agonies of toothache that she could not move out of the house; Otwell endured shuddering attacks of ague, for which nothing could be prescribed. Anthony Cave was seldom well, and the sad dilemma of the doctors is illustrated in Otwell's letters to John in November and December of 1544. 'Doctor Augustine saith that he hath none ague nor other disease but weakness, and himself confesseth that if he might return to his stomach or appetite, and sleep, he should soon after recover strength enough to get away from this City.' But a few weeks later it was still the same story. The doctors simply did not know what was wrong. 'Mr. Anthony Cave commendeth him heartily unto you,' wrote Otwell, 'continuing still in much weakness and great pains of his limbs, now one then another, without any express sickness else within his body, as his physical counsellors say, but yet his weakness is such that he can in nowise presume to ride neither in chariot nor on horseback, to get home to Tickford any time before Christmas . . . without a much more present recovery than doth yet appear in him.' Always a prey to insomnia and other ills, Anthony Cave's health went from bad to worse, and yet there was nothing that the doctors could do, either to cure him or relieve his sufferings.

The Tudors to us seem hard, and yet their stoicism and apparent indifference to pain was perhaps the only way they had of demonstrating that they could be superior to mortal ills. And of all that they had perforce to bear, surely nothing was more terrible than the plague. Brought from the East centuries before, the virulent bubonic plague had decimated the country during the Black Death, and was still the Tudor scourge, taking its toll year in and year out, until the Great Fire burned the City to the ground in 1666. The Tudors were not, most of them, clean. Except for the naturally fastidious (and this did not by any means include the rich and aristocratic), they commonly spent their lives in conditions that would not have disgraced a slum. Rats and vermin debouched off the ships and bred and multiplied in the sweating wood and plaster houses, crammed together in narrow, dirty alleys, where bugs and lice were accepted as part of the normal course of things. The floors of many houses, as Erasmus remarked, were covered in layers of rushes and filth; more often than not, the household slops and excrement ran in the foul gutters of the streets, where pigs rooted and hens pecked among the dunghills. The overcrowded houses, with no facilities for cleanliness, and no provision for sanitation, were the breeding-ground of all contagious diseases, and especially of the plague. The dread sickness took little account of seasons of the year, although it always seems to have been at its worst during the warm summer and muggy autumn weather.

Letters to John mention the outbreak of the autumn of 1543, when the artist Holbein was among those who died, and when the lawyers transferred themselves *en masse* to the sweeter air of St. Albans. John's cousin, Sir John Cope, refused point-blank to come to London, even though his financial credit was at stake; he recounted the fears he had at being even in the country, for one of his cousins had dropped dead of the plague not long after leaving his house. The disease spared neither old nor young, and there was no telling where it would strike next. In the summer of 1544, John lost a promising young apprentice, Thomas Holland; his brother-in-law, John Gery, lost his little daughter, and the coming of autumn 1545 brought tragedy into Otwell's house.

Young Henry Johnson, his prentice lad, fell ill and soon afterwards died.

> It hath pleased God this day to take Henry Johnson, my
> boy, from me by death, and doubting whether it be the
> plague or not, I am resorted to my brother Gery's house, and
> there will continue this fourteen days at least. I pray you,
> let Thomas Barwell my friend be secretly certefied thereof, to
> th'end he make not his wife privy of the same too rashly.
> You may show him it was of the plague, because else he or his
> wife (perchance) would think that he was cast away for
> lacking of looking unto, which I take God to judge was not
> so, for he died in mine arms, Our Lord have his soul and all
> Christian, and keep you in health. . . .

Unable to make up his mind whether it really was the plague or
not, Otwell decided to go and stay, as a precautionary measure,
with his brother-in-law; but it seems that he may have carried the
germs with him, for not long afterwards one of the boys in the
house fell sick.

> God Almighty hath still his scourge for me in his hands,
> for on Wednesday last he struck William, my brother Gery's
> lad, with the plague as we suppose, for he complaineth much
> under his arm, and is become very sick, so that therefore I am
> whipped home again to mine own house into Lime Street
> (for other place to go to I have none), and trust there to take
> no hurt, for the Lord is mightful to deliver or preserve his
> elect in the midst of all tribulations, to him be all honour and
> glory for ever; beseeching you not to take any sudden conceit
> for my sudden return again to my foresaid house, for surely I
> think my boy died of no plague, albeit he went away so sud-
> denly. His time was come, and so shall all ours at the Lord's
> pleasure, who be our guide thereunto. . . .

Otwell stayed at home and worked in his counting-house,
hoping and praying for the boys' safety and his own; but alas,
only four days after he fell ill, William died of plague:

> My said brother's boy, that I writ you was visited with the
> plague at my being in his house, died on Sunday at night last,
> and so I am altogether at home in Lime Street again. Let God
> do his pleasure with me — and yet I pray you do not think

D

that I despise your writing, wherewith you persuade me to have some honest circumspection to myself. No, not so, but as the case is I have none other refuge but home to mine own, where I trust is no danger for me.

Otwell remained in good health, untouched by the contagion all around him. For some reason or other, probably because of the large numbers of children there, it seems that John Gery's house suffered more than most; for again in 1548 Otwell was writing that one child had died there, and 'two more sick, whereof one of them at the writing hereof was full of God's marks'. It was, all things considered, remarkably courageous of Otwell to stay in the City at all, for hundreds left London as a matter of course at such times, staying with relations in the country if they could do so, and camping in the fields when they could not. But in 1548 the epidemic was so terrible that even Otwell yielded at last to his brother's persuasions, and agreed to stay at Glapthorn Manor for a while, until the worst was over. Otwell, however, loved London, plague or no plague, and it seems that a fortnight of country life was as much as he could bear. At the end of two weeks he was back in his beloved City.

Always, it was the cities and towns that suffered most severely during the outbreaks of plague, and Calais endured almost as much as London, for during these years it was overflowing with foreign soldiery, and became a veritable death-trap. Every year saw dreadful outbreaks to which there seemed no end; the Johnsons' young cousins were among the victims, and their friends among the staplers suffered heavily. Nothing could be more difficult than to be brave under such horrifying circumstances. Even John's stomach would not serve him to tarry longer at Calais than need be, and there are reports of the Lieutenant of the Staple flying back to England as fast as the ship would carry him, and of husbands leaving wives to die alone. Surely one of the most tragic letters ever written is that in which Margaret Baynham described what had happened in her comfortable home in Calais. Her letter reveals the anguished Tudor belief that they had no right to be happy in this world, and that they were on earth only by the sufferance of a cruel and jealous God, who indeed bore far more resemblance to Jehovah than to the loving spirit of the New Testament.

Anno domini 1545, the first day of April, at Calais.

Master Johnson, I do right heartily thank you for the good beer you sent me, albeit that a great part of the same hath been drunk with much, much lamentation and mourning. For upon Palm Sunday in the morning perceived we manifestly that John Crant (which had complained seven days before) was sick of the plague, whereupon I and all my household were glad to void my house. The same self day after Evensong, Margery, one of my sister Plankney's daughters, waxed suddenly sick also of the same disease, whereupon my said sister forsook her own house also, with such wares as she had in her shop, and went to my garden in Maisondieu Street, where she and I with a great number of young fruit do continue in great sorrow and heaviness of heart, God be merciful unto us, help and comfort us. And what shall become of these two sick persons we are uncertain yet, but they are very weak and feeble. They be in God's hands — Almighty God be merciful unto them, and restore them their health again if it be his pleasure.

Thus doth God chastise and scourge me from time to time (first by the death of my husbands, then by the death of my two brethren-in-law, my sister's husbands, and now with John Crant, on whom of late I bestowed so great cost) to keep me in awe and under correction still. I beseech his almighty goodness, even as he daily reneweth my sorrow and heaviness, so mercifully to send me patience in all my trouble and adversity, and to obtain the same the better, I desire you and good Master Cave to pray for me. From Calais, as is above rehearsed.

By yours to her power,

Margaret Baynham,

widow.

This being written in the morning, John Crant and Margery my sister's daughter departed this world about eleven of the clock before dinner. Now is our lamentation and mourning greater than ever it was before, Almighty God be our comfort.

PART TWO

CHAPTER 3

LOVE AND MARRIAGE

THE shrewd Italian author of *A Relation of the Island of England* once remarked that he had never seen an Englishman really in love, 'whence one must conclude, either that the English are the most discreet lovers in the world, or that they are incapable of love'. Allowing for his Latin lack of sympathy for the English temperament, his strictures were probably true enough. Tudor Englishmen were not of a noticeably romantic disposition. They were practical and prosaic, toughened by a harsh upbringing and the struggle to survive. Until Elizabeth came to the throne, they lived in a world almost untouched by feminine ideals and illusion: masculine standards everywhere prevailed, and both men and women had to conform to them. In that world, romantic love played little part; the results, as in poetry, were usually tragic, and so not generally followed. Love and marriage were poles apart. The aim of the Tudor merchant was to live as comfortably and die as rich as he could, and marriage accordingly assumed its proper place in the natural scheme of things. First and foremost, it was a sound business proposition: many a credit balance was saved, many a ledger put in the black by a good-sized dowry. And moreover, with its useful and ever-widening circle of friends and relations, a prudent marriage would inevitably improve a man's prospects in life. It was unthinkable not to marry, not to found a family: love and happiness were anyway a matter of chance, and most sensible men and women were content to leave all the arrangements in the hands of parents and go-betweens.

And yet, although the profitable and practical were the avowed Tudor aim, in spite — or perhaps because — of it, the ideal of romantic love was beginning to undermine the cast-iron code of earlier years. Margery Paston, beaten black and blue by her mother, nagged and bullied by her family, did at last succeed in marrying the man she loved, bailiff though he was, and though her family and the Church were against her. *Romeo and Juliet* breathes the spirit of English romanticism, even though Verona is the setting of their love story. In the middle years of the sixteenth century, life was more comfortable, ideas more civilized than even fifty years before. Where no great possessions were involved, and no family pride and alliances had to be considered, many middle-class marriages must have been as much a matter of affection as coldblooded bargaining over dirty lands. Most people were well aware of the nagging misery that ensued where no love existed, and with thoughtful parents the happiness of their children must always have had at least an equal claim with worldly considerations. 'How often have forced contracts been made to add land to land, not love to love?' wrote the dramatist Heywood. 'And to unite houses to houses, not hearts to hearts? Which hath been the occasion that men have turned monsters and women devils.'⁶ John's master, Anthony Cave, made it a condition of his will that his daughters were on no account to marry for lucre or money, but 'as God disposes, and on the advice of their kin'.

In this respect, at any rate, John Johnson was more fortunate than many young men of his time, for he could marry where he pleased with complete freedom of choice. There was no anxious or calculating father to force his inclination, no maternal prejudice to overcome. But being a sensible young man, he did not altogether disregard the opinion of his elders when he married Sabine Saunders. This girl with the lovely, unusual name, of purest Renaissance feeling, was his master's niece, and one of the younger daughters of Thomas and Margaret Saunders. Of Sabine's birth and early years little is known. The house at Sibbertoft where she grew up could never have been dull, that much is certain. It must have been alive with the shrieks and laughter of children, tearing through the garden on fine days, and round the house when it was wet, and with the servants arguing and hallooing at the top of their voices. It would seem that even their father was worn out with the strain of trying to remember who was which among his twelve children, for when he made his will he mentioned none of them by name, but simply left everything to the care of his eldest son. Sabine could scarcely have known the conservative and Catholic Edward, so much older than she was herself, and absorbed in his legal career. Even in later years, when she was grown up and married to John, Sabine would refer to him as 'my brother Serjeant', and never by his Christian name. Another of her brothers, Robert, also took to the law, and was admitted to the Middle Temple some years before she was born. Blase the wealthy merchant, Joseph the farmer, Laurence the Protestant divine and Ambrose, the youngest of the family (like Richard Johnson, he was apprenticed to Anthony Cave), together made up the sum of Sabine's six brothers, and she had five sisters as well. Of two of them, Jane and Christian, Sabine was always very fond, but her favourite companion was perhaps her brother Laurence, for they were much together in later years. In many ways each was the complement of the other: the brother unworldly and intellectual, the sister lively, practical and gay.

Sabine was probably no exception to the common Tudor practice of sending children away from home to be brought up, particularly since there were so many at Sibbertoft, and her mother married again soon after Thomas Saunders died. Much of her young life was probably spent with her aunt and uncle Cave at Tickford House, where she and a handful of other girls, aided by horn-book and primer, would have managed to 'scramble themselves into a little education' — much after the fashion of Mrs. Goddard's boarders in *Emma* — make marchpane, and sew a fine seam. If their parents were both well-to-do and interested in the new learning, English girls often received an excellent education at this time; the daughters of Sir Thomas More, the Princess Elizabeth and Lady Jane Grey are a few of the notable Englishwomen that the early Renaissance produced, with their knowledge of classical and modern languages, their rhetoric, philosophy and divinity. But as yet most feminine education was strictly practical, with no pretensions to being intellectual, or even ornamental. Woman was made to be wife and mother; her sphere was bounded by the walls of her home and garden, by the people within those walls, and by everything that pertained to the useful domestic arts. Even in Elizabeth's reign, the heroine of Lyly's *Euphues* could write: 'I have wished oftentimes rather in the country to spin, than in the court to dance, and truly a distaff doth better become a maiden than a lute, and fitter it is with the needle to practise how to live, than with the pen to learn how to love.'

It is not to be supposed, however, that Sabine pined for Greek and Latin, nor that she revolted, like the heroines of Victorian novels, against the eternal 'pricking in clouts' — Sir John Haring-

ton's name for embroidery.[7] Sabine was a normal little girl;
there was no need for her (like Lady Jane Grey) to escape into a
kinder, gentler world; and nature had not endowed her with the
unique and dazzling brilliance of an Elizabeth. When there were
more agreeable and amusing things to do, it was not in Sabine's
nature to sit for hours mewed up with a book. At all times Tickford House was full of people, young and old, for Anthony Cave
was a hospitable man and loved to entertain. In summer when the
days were light and warm, there was walking and riding (which
she loved); there were plays to see when the travelling companies
came their way, and the morris dancing and racing and wrestling
at the village fairs. And when the winter evenings began to draw
in, there was singing to the lute, and dancing and story-telling,
and the hectic parlour games that the Tudors adored; there were
endless hours to spend chatting about nothing at all, when the
wind howled in the woods outside, and the firelight glowed in the
tapestried rooms, and threw strange shadows on the panelling.

It was here, at Tickford House, beyond a shadow of doubt, that
Sabine first met John Johnson, the handsome apprentice with hair
as red as King Hal himself, who used to come over from Calais
several times a year and spend hours shut up with her uncle,
poring over heavy volumes of accounts, and arranging the details
of their trade. John had most likely known Sabine from the time
she was a child; he had watched her grow up; he knew that he
loved her, and was going to marry her if he could. As for Sabine,
what she was like to look at, no one will ever know. No Holbein
painted her coiffed demurely in white linen like Mrs. Pemberton,
or in a whelk-shell head-dress like Queen Jane, with the soft black
velvet caught becomingly to one side. Whether Sabine was beautiful or plain, or whether like Wyatt's mistress she was 'not fair, but
lovely to behold',[8] whether she had bright chestnut hair and fine
sparkling eyes, a smile that showed white even teeth, and a pretty
voice, no one will ever know, although it is pleasant to imagine
that she was as pretty as she herself would love to have been. But
it matters very little, because the one certain thing is that John
loved her with all the love and tenderness of which he was capable.
The cautious, sober, intelligent young merchant was drawn in-
tuitively and irresistibly to the impulsive, lively and wilful Sabine.
She was, as he so often wrote, his 'entirely beloved'. The course of
their love affair, however, was even stormier than is usual, for,

gay and quick-witted as her talents were, she was not possessed of a sweet and gazelle-like disposition. The courtship of Sabine must have cost John more concentrated thought, time, trouble and money than anything else in his life. All her relations approved of the 'towards young man', as Cave fondly called him, but it is difficult to believe that their approval or otherwise would have weighed with Sabine. She was a wayward young lady with a determined will of her own, seldom in the same mind about anything twice, and about him least of all.

During the year 1538, when John was abroad, it seems that Sabine was seldom out of his thoughts. The account he kept of his personal expenditure reveals that she was remembered at frequent intervals, with 'a little maund full' of ripe, sweet French cherries, picked in May; with gay silken ribbons; with 'a neck-kerchief for my mistress' and delicate bone-lace from Antwerp as a token of his love. It is also worth noting the effect that the pursuit of Sabine had upon John's personal appearance. He who had once been content with his 'work-day gown', and honest but supremely unexciting fustian, now apparently burgeoned forth into silken dalliance. The accounts show him buying fine lawn shirts (three at a time) of Antwerp making; new shoes, new slops, new nether hose; doublets of striped satin and russet satin and bombasine; Spanish cloaks and surcoats enriched with parsemano work, or gold and silver lace. His best gown was sent for furring; he bought new gloves, and 'a hat dressed with laces' off one of his friends; even perfume to make him smell like the lily. When next he dismounted at Tickford House he must have been the very glass of fashion and the mould of form.

If she had held out before, it is evident that she could not resist him now. Not long afterwards, they were formally betrothed. Sabine was probably about nineteen or twenty at the time, for although it was by no means unusual for girls to be married, like Juliet, at fourteen and even younger, the better sort of people frowned on child marriages and were well aware of the dangers involved. 'The effects that for the most part ensue thereafter', wrote one Elizabethan author, 'are dangerous births, diminution of stature, brevity of life, and such-like'...'[9] The Spanish philosopher Vives held that eighteen was the ideal age for marriage, and Sir Thomas Elyot's Zenobia elected for twenty. Sabine is unlikely to have been married much earlier than twenty, for her uncle Anthony Cave, whose word counted for much in the family circle, felt strongly on the subject, and specifically forbade his own daughters to marry before they reached that age.

After the formal betrothal had taken place, preparations began for the wedding, which seems to have been held in the autumn of 1541. Sabine's dowry, indispensable for a Tudor bride, had been left to her by her father and grandfather, so that her eventual marriage was considered as a matter of course. It was worth more than a hundred marks in money, and would have been handed over to John some time before the actual ceremony took place. As well as her dowry, of course, Sabine had the well-filled hope chest that every girl carried with her to her new home: piles of snowy linen, sheets and blankets and furnishings, and all the new wardrobe of clothes that made up her trousseau. The Tudors adored any excuse for enjoying themselves, and family and friends doubtless took full advantage of the opportunity a wedding gave, riding in from miles around to be present at the feast, each wearing the colours of bride and groom, and receiving their wedding gloves and scarves as token gifts. Sabine, arrayed in her white wedding gown, wearing beautiful embroidered gloves and with a coronal of flowers on her long hair, was led in procession to the door of Tickford church, where the marriage service was read and the gold betrothal ring placed on her wedding finger. After the ceremony, it was usual for the bridal group to enter the church itself for prayers and benediction by the priest, and the bride and groom drank from the loving-cup with the sops in wine. Once the ceremony was over, the fun began. Everyone rode back to Tickford House for the wedding feast and ate their fill of the rich spiced dishes and delicate fruits and drank deeply of the potent ale and wine. The singing and dancing and merry-making went on for hours, with all the old customs of bedding the bride, flinging the stocking and drinking sack posset, which everyone heartily enjoyed.

Thus Sabine entered the married state. There is no record of her feelings as a bride of a few months, but marriage seems to have agreed with John. Rather surprisingly, Tudor men, as well as women, seem excessively eager to enter the yoke of matrimony. There are few jokes about reluctant bachelors and surrendering freedom, and it seems that the comfort and privileges of the married state were regarded as more than offseting the drawbacks.

So we find one Flemish friend sending John his compliments the summer after the wedding. Adrian van Weede's remarks, said Otwell, were 'after his accustomed merry fashion', and they give us an insight into the sturdy, common-sense attitude to marriage that was characteristic of the sixteenth century.

Très cher Sieur Otuel Janson, à vous me recommande tant que je puis, et au Sieur Jan Janson. Je vois bien qu'un poil de con tire plus que dix chevaux qui sont à craindre. Les Hollandais m'ont dit que votre frère devait venir en brief en Anvers, mais il faut que sa femme soit contentée premier, comme de raison. Nies, j'ai espoir avec le temps on pourra bien parler à lui à loisir, et qu'il se contentera de sucre, car il est douce comme nous autres.

Not long after Adrian had made his bawdy jokes, John did indeed go abroad, leaving Sabine for the first time since their marriage. His feelings were surely not less sensitive than those of his admired contemporary, the Earl of Surrey.

> What day I quit the Foreland of Fair Kent,
> And that my ship her course for Flanders bent,
> Yet think I with how many a heavy look,
> My leave of England and of thee I took,
> And did entreat the tide, if it might be,
> But to convey me one sigh back to thee. . . .[10]

John's friends knew how he and Sabine were feeling, and they did their best to comfort and reassure her that all was well. After he had been in Calais for a few days, cousin Thomas Saxby wrote and told her that her 'bed-fellow at the making hereof was in good health and merry, with all our loving friends here', trusting that the dull business of selling wool and fells to the Hollanders would soon be finished, 'and then ye shall have him the sooner with you, for I assure you he thinketh only to be at home with you, as ye would have him with you'. It is evident that John grudged every moment spent away from her, a state of affairs that must have been delightful and highly gratifying to Sabine.

Several years of marriage did not change the lover into the husband. There is no doubt that John and Sabine loved each other passionately. They were blissfully happy in each other's company, and utterly miserable when apart. During his enforced sojourns abroad at the Staple, they wrote each other long and loving letters, not once in a while, but many times a week. The local carrier, that 'ordinary ambassador between friend and friend',[11] would call for Sabine's letters at the manor house, and take them with the loads of wool and fells to Otwell's house in Lime Street. There Otwell (who was occasionally not above reading other people's love-letters) would give them into the care of a friend or sea captain making ready for Calais, or into the hands of the Dover post, and they would eventually reach the impatient John. Sabine's letters are delightful to behold. She has a candid, open hand, but she can never quite manage to keep the lines straight on the paper, and so she always ends up higher on the right side than on the left. Her spelling is all her own and, being a woman, she naturally disregarded the logic and order so dear to the masculine mind. Love and cheeses are wonderfully mixed in her letters. John's tuition, however, and a few years of constant practice improved her writing out of all measure, although she never achieved Olivia's 'sweet Roman hand'.[12] Sometimes for fun she seems to have taken the pen away from him, when he was busy in the counting-house, and copied whole paragraphs or stray sentences into his precious letter-books.

As for John, his affection and contentment increased with time. Sabine was the one person in the world with whom he could truly be himself, take off the mask of dignity and aloofness that the merchant must wear in public. Only with Sabine could he relax and find release. That small, exquisite handwriting of his becomes larger and more generous when he writes to her. Once, when there was a delay in the post, she taxed him with not writing often enough. 'With all my heart, entirely beloved,' came the reply, '. . . I think by this time I owe you not a letter, but I think I have by this time paid you letter for letter, and yet suppose I you to be two or three letters in my debt since my coming from you. Yea, if my diligence in writing continue towards you, I do not see how ye will be out of my debt before Easter!' (It was then November.) When at last his letters came, Sabine was almost complacent as she contemplated the stout packet that lay before her. 'I do perceive your diligence in writing to me, for the which I right heartily thank you,' she replied prettily, 'and also desire you to continue the same.' She indignantly rejected John's charge that it was she who had not written to him. '. . . You do find fault with me that you had no letters from me in fourteen days. The fault is not in me, and so I trust you will say yourself if all my letters come to you, for I am sure I never sent you so many letters in so short space.'

Their letters to each other are full of domestic news, the everyday stuff of life which has meant so much to so many from the beginning of time — news of the children, and of their friends and relations, of the gathering-in of the rents and tithes, of the sheep-shearing and the wool-winding, and the little luxuries that are to be bought abroad. Sometimes they tease each other, write nonsense, long passionately for the other to be with them. 'Your letter of the 5th of this present month I have received, for the which I thank you,' wrote John to his 'loving heart', 'being glad ye perceive so well what a good husband I am, and I trust you will let it be an example to you to be the better wife unto me.' And Sabine would reply 'in most loving wise' to her 'well beloved husband (Master I should say, because it doth become me better to call you Master than you to call me Mistress). . . .'

England in the sixteenth century was renowned far and wide as the 'Paradise of married women'. It was a country where the women were 'beautiful, fair and well-dressed', and where not only did they have 'more liberty than perhaps in any other place', but where they knew well how to make use of it.[13] The ideal held up to the Tudor wife by one of John's contemporaries, Gervase Markham, was that of 'sanctity and holiness of life'. She was to be a woman of 'great modesty and temperance, as well inwardly as outwardly', and in sentences that would need the voice of Miles Malleson to do them justice, he continues: 'Inwardly, as in her behaviour and carriage towards her husband, wherein she shall shun all violence of rage, passion and humour, coveting less to direct than be directed, appear ever unto him pleasant, amiable and delightful; and though occasion, mishaps or the misgovernment of his will may induce her to contrary thoughts, yet virtuously to suppress them, and with a mild sufferance rather to call him home from his error than with the least strength of anger to abate the least spark of his evil.'[14]

Sabine, needless to say, does not in the least resemble this paragon of all the virtues. She was not at all submissive, either inwardly or outwardly, and virtuous suppression was utterly impossible to one of her impetuous and flame-like disposition.

When contrary thoughts welled up in Sabine's heart, she uttered them regardless. 'With all my heart, good wife (but sometime a shrew)' begins one letter from her 'loving husband', and yet another ends: 'Farewell, and goodnight, wife. I had almost said good wife, but that it were sin to lie, as ye know; nevertheless my hope is that old fashions will be left, and then if I will not say good wife I shall be worthy to be called liar!' John was not made for the role of Petruchio. A mild-mannered, peace-loving man, he and Sabine got on as husbands and wives have always done, in the pleasant companionship and occasional bickering of married life, compromising in a way that was to their mutual satisfaction. As Sabine wrote to John: 'If you will do as you did promise me, you shall perceive I will do as you will have with as good will as you desire it of me.'

During the late summer of 1545, John had made arrangements to go to Calais for the wool sales, but found himself unexpectedly delayed over the land purchases that he was making for Anthony Cave at the Court of Augmentations. Sabine was filled with dismay when she heard the news. 'If this your tarrying now do make you to lie at Calais in winter,' she wrote, 'I beshrew them that it is long of. You do write that you be weary of London, but my trust is you be not weary of your own house, nor of nobody in it . . .', signing her letter, 'Your loving and obedient wife that will be!' Fearing that he might go hungry in Otwell's bachelor household, she sent him presents of cheeses and chickens and pigeon pies in the carriers' carts, and begged him, when he reached Calais, not to walk abroad in the plague-ridden streets. 'Desiring you most heartily to keep yourself well till you come home to me, and then I will keep you so well as God will give me grace.' He was her 'well-beloved', and she ended her letter with a kiss, 'by your loving wife, that lives in hope'.

In Calais, John sat down to write his reply by the light of a flickering taper. The little room he lodged in at Mrs. Baynham's was chilly, and outside lay the impenetrable darkness of a winter's night.

Jesus anno 1545, the 8 in November,
at Calais.

In most loving wise I have me commended unto you, trusting of your health. Your letter of the 2nd of this present month I received this day, and perceive that ye received my letter by Dunkerley but the day before. If he rode about the country with the gelding I bought of him fourteen days or he came at you, he played a knavish part with me, and show him, and that I am not content to be so used at his hands.

My coming into England shall be, if God send me life and health, eight or ten days before Christmas, and therefore within this fourteen days I will write to you against what time ye shall send up my horse to London. The death is here not very sore; howbeit, we be all in God's hands: as it pleaseth him, so be it. I will keep myself for your sake as well as I can, and at my coming home I am content ye have the keeping of me. Howbeit, I may not be no more shrewdly spoken to, nor yet curstly looked on!

As for the sale of Mr. Griffin's wool I force not of, but that my father hath disappointed me of his wools it grieveth me. I perceive now his friendship is but feigned — howbeit, I trust I shall live. If ye either speak or send to him, let no less be declared than that I conceive it unkindly, as I have no other cause.

I perceive ye have sent Richard to London for £40. I pray you, desire Harrison to get as long time of Mr. Bickill's as he can for his wools, for I can now appoint him no more money before Christmas. Desire Harrison to show you how much wool I shall have of him above 2,000 stone, for I esteem to have above by the money he hath had of me.

I pray you, send for no more money to London before Christmas, for I have none to spare. As the Lord knoweth, to whom I commit you in haste, going to my bed at ten of the clock at night — and would ye were in my bed to tarry me! I bid you Goodnight, good wife sometimes!

By your loving husband,
John Johnson.

To my loving friend Sabine Johnson
be this delivered at Glapthorn.

The letter, wedged into some captain's wallet, travelled across the Channel, and at last reached Glapthorn Manor. Sabine pulled the sealing thread, broke the scarlet wax and read the letter through. Then she sat down at the table in the parlour, pen in hand. 'I am glad to hear that I did please you so well at your last being at home,' she wrote saucily, 'praying to the Lord to give me grace that I may do always so; and whereas you do wish yourself at home (I would no less), and desiring you most heartily to come home so soon as you can, and keep yourself well, good husband. . . .'

John's next letter was in a half-solemn, half-provoking strain.

For lack of other matter, ye desire me to remember you, my wife, and children, and will me to keep myself well, etc. I am in the hands of God, whom it may please to dispose me according to his godly will, and he it is that knoweth what is best for us. If it will please the same God to send me life (as your prayer is), then I shall help the bringing up of my children the best I can, and so provide for them and you as nigh as God will give me grace. But if God will otherwise dispose me, you must be content to receive it thankfully at the Lord's hands.

And where ye hope if but one man in the whole world should be kept from death, it might be I, if it pleased God, it is true that all is in his hands; howbeit, if it came so to pass (as there is no such likelihood!), ye were like to lose me, your husband. For if there were in this town no more men left but I, the women of this town would keep me perforce from you, and then ye were never the better! By Saint Mary! I should have much ado to please so many women! God save me from being troubled with many women, for I have much ado to please you alone, as ye know! I pray you, keep yourself well that I may find you merry at my coming home, for here be many fair widows would have me, if ye would not be angry therewith. As the Lord God knoweth, who keep you, in haste.

By your loving husband that would
fain be at home,
John Johnson.

If by any chance he had hoped to provoke Sabine and make her a little jealous, he did not succeed. Sabine knew, and John knew that she knew, that there was only one designing widow in Calais who could possibly be offering him consolation: Margaret Baynham, a charming, tactful, soothing and obviously pretty woman, who seems to have had an annihilating effect on all the men in

Calais. Sabine, however, neatly disposed of Mistress Baynham in two short sentences. 'Husband, you do write there be many fair widows in Calais that would be glad of you, if I would not be angry. The truth is I had rather they had every one of them two husbands than you should be troubled with them!' The sting lay in the fact that Margaret Baynham had loved, and lost, exactly that number of husbands. But after all, Sabine was in a sweet and contrite mood. 'Your promise made to me I will not say but you kept, and so have I, and will do to the uttermost, without any bond or allegation; and when it shall please God to send you home, I put no doubts but that we shall agree very well these cold nights. . . .'

John and Sabine loved each other dearly, in spite and because of the occasional storms that made their lives more vivid and interesting, and themselves more sharply aware of each other. Their mutual affection and dependence increased rather than waned with the passing of the years, and John's frequent, enforced absence abroad could hardly make Sabine's heart more loving than it was already. One autumn in Calais, John fell ill of the ague, that unpleasant disease, akin to malaria, which was one of the minor scourges of Calais. The little seaport had what Sir Thomas More described as a 'barren soil and wretched climate'. It was surrounded by acres of damp marshland, and beyond that were the slow-moving, stagnant channels that drained the low-lying farmland, while through the town itself there flowed a conduit of water, used doubtless as a dumping-ground for anything and everything that the citizens chose to throw out of their windows. When the news reached Sabine that John was ill in bed, being nursed by Mrs. Baynham, she grew into a fever of impatience to be with him. Despite the cold November weather, she waited only until her bags were packed, and her little black mare saddled, before setting out for London with Thomas, the groom. In a day or two she reached Lime Street, and nothing that Otwell could say, no argument that John was getting better, had the slightest effect. She was determined to take the first ship for Calais, and off she went.

At London, the 5th in November,
1546.
Brother, trusting that your amendment increaseth rather than otherwise, I commend me unto you. And according to

my doubt in my last letter since my coming from you, my sister your wife's unbelieving of your amendment is grown into such desperation, in a manner, that no manner of persuasion could stay her from coming over unto you at this instant — which, if it be as discreetly done as rashly or woman-like, I refer to your judgment. I can think no more in it than other men may do. Well, I trust she shall arrive safely, and without long sojourn at that side the sea, I hope ye will both repair over together, God maintain both your health.

Other things I have not as now more largely to write you of, than I have heretofore done by Marcus the post, with letters from Mr. Anthony Cave. My wife should have kept my sister company over to Calais, if she had been in case convenient thereunto, but she can show you (if she will) that it was not meet so to be.

Your business with Mr. Kirkham she hath left me word of. I shall do therein what I can, but I doubt he will not so well regard me as he would do you, or her (at least) for his promise' sake, and therefore if it take not effect according to your mind, blame not me, and so I said to my said sister your wife. Thus, in much haste, fare you as well as myself. In haste (I say),

Your loving brother,
Otwell Johnson.

In case my business here, both for you and myself, had not been urgent, I could have been content to have played the fool over myself with my sister. Howbeit, th'adventure had been somewhat dangerous to have trusted ourselves both in one ship, and therefore I thought it best to forbear the same at this time of the year, and so suffered her to play the fool alone for this voyage. I trust you will take no displeasure therewith, nor with this my writing, for I do it for no disdain, but to make you merry, if you will take it well.

To my loving brother John Johnson, merchant of the Staple, at Calais.

As soon as she landed at Calais, Sabine went straight to John's side. She nursed him back to health, gave kind-hearted Mrs. Baynham 'immortal thanks' for her help, and got John safely home

to Glapthorn Manor as soon as he was fit to sail. They spent
Christmas there together, enjoying themselves quietly with the
children, and refusing all invitations to spend the holidays with
their friends and relations. Sabine took good care of John, but
despite all she could do, the ague attacked him again in the spring,
and the doctors declared that he was not well enough to go to
Calais for the wool sales. His master, Anthony Cave, much dis-
turbed by this second attack, sent him much good advice to
'beware of surfeiting and cold. For any worldly business forget not
your own health', and Otwell held special consultations with the
physicians in London. Their prescriptions can be seen; and if they
did not cure the ague, they could at least have done John no harm.

To my sister I send a certain gum, by th'advice of Mr.
Alban Hill, to put into her wet perfume that she useth to
occupy in your house: the same, beaten very small with
rosewater and cloves a few, is very comfortable for you. All
dry perfumes are nought for you, but a close perfuming
chafer were better to be used than th'open dish. If she have
none, let word be sent, and I will provide her one here. Also
Mr. Hill doth not think it ill for you to use now and then one
of the pills that I brought you myself, for they will amend
your stomach very perfectly. And so Our Lord continue
your health. . . .

Occasional references in the letters to 'woman service' and
'women's fantasies' reveal that Otwell was more than a little
inclined to feel superior to the feminine half of creation, even while
he was bewildered by the quicksilver and intuitive workings of the
feminine mind. But that John and Sabine's marriage was happy
he could not deny. It was a family joke that Sabine was utterly
miserable away from John, and could only be 'restored to perfect
health' by his 'presence with her'. So contented did John look
that Otwell's thoughts in the spring of 1545 began to turn towards
marriage. Otwell was much given to complaining of the lack of
good food, and indeed everything that goes to make a pleasant
home, in his lonely bachelor quarters, and it seems at last to have
dawned on him that the simplest way to be comfortable was to
take a wife. There was also another reason. While he himself was
not attached to anyone, a girl he knew had fallen deeply in love
with him. Maria Warner was the pretty daughter of a well-to-do

merchant, and so much did she want to marry Otwell — and him alone — that her family were making the first overtures on her behalf. One spring morning, when the trees were green with the first delicate young leaves, and the sun shone warm after the winter's cold, a merchant named Robert Sonning came to call on Otwell, as he sat working in his counting-house. Sonning revealed himself as the appointed go-between, declared something more of Maria's passion than the young man knew already, and sounded him gently about his own feelings. After Sonning had left, Otwell sat down to write the news to his brother, begging him at the same time to keep it secret. To make it doubly safe from Sabine's naturally curious eyes and merry wit, he wrote in French, a language that she did not understand.

Touchant la matière de quoi eûmes dernier pourpos ensemble à votre département d'ici, à ce matin j'ai été ému de par Robert Sonning, lequel m'a déclaré que les amis de la fille ont cent livres sterling, argent comptant, prêtes à me bailler avec elle, et ils soushaitent fort que je ne la veuille refuser, car elle ne porte faveur à autre personne du monde que moi, eut-elle dix fois davantage. Response je n'ai fait aucune, sinon comme je vous déclarai d'avoir donné à son frère. Je pense que la chose se trouvera forte honnête, et par ainsi je suis délibéré d'en deviser plus avant, comme je verrai bonne être. At our meeting, with the Lord's help, you shall hear more, et cependant, ayez la bouche cousue, je vous prie.

There can be no doubt that Maria had lost her heart to the charming young merchant; 'she would not favour anyone in the world but me, even if she had ten times more money'. It was not long before Otwell made up his mind, and indeed he had already decided within himself that he would marry Maria. In May he was writing to his brother: 'La matière que touche à la fille que savez, je la vous recommande, ainsi et quand bonne opportunité se donnera.' As the head of the family, John was very much concerned in the match-making, for all the negotiations — the settlements, the handing-over of the hundred pounds' dowry, the trading partnership to be arranged between Otwell and Maria's brother, Bartholomew Warner — were in his hands. Fortunately there was goodwill on both sides. Everyone wanted to forward the match, and everything went well for the betrothed couple. During the autumn of 1545, everything was settled to their satisfaction, and Otwell wrote to tell John how grateful he was for the 'painstaking and conclusion made with Bartholomew Warner, for the which I most heartily thank you, and am very well contented with that you have done, trusting to find him no less my friend than he hath promised you that he will be, the living Lord prospering his affairs'.

Already, it seems, Maria's dowry had been handed over and used in Otwell's business transactions, although the date of the wedding had still to be fixed. They planned to have a country wedding at Christmas, among their friends at Glapthorn Manor, when an unexpected delay took place, as Otwell wrote, 'concerning my coming down unto you with Maria, my woman shall be'. Her brother Bartholomew was in Calais with his master, Sir John Wallop, and the Richardsons, with whom Maria was staying in London, refused even to entertain the idea of her travelling into Northamptonshire alone with her fiancé, unless they received written authority to say that she might go. Ideas of propriety were strict in the sixteenth century and, much as Maria desired to go with Otwell, she bowed to the rules of decorum. From what we know of Maria's gentle, affectionate disposition, it is unlikely that she would anyway have rebelled, although it is impossible to imagine Sabine in a similar situation not doing exactly as she wished and going with John willynilly. When Bartholomew did eventually arrive in London, he received a letter summoning him back almost at once and he was, said Otwell, 'so very earnestly desirous to see the solemnisation of our matrimony celebrated while he may be at this side the sea', that he begged them to hold the wedding in London. He generously offered to bear all the expense of Maria's trousseau and the wedding breakfast, though this, said Otwell, was to be 'as moderate as may become our honesties, by God's grace'.

May it therefore please you, gentle brother (as very heartily I beseech you) to take pains to repair hither yourself, and my sister your wife (if she can quietly attempt to travail so far) about th'end of the next week, and then we would proceed to our doings on Monday before Candlemas Day, which shall be the 25 of this present, for longer than that day it cannot be deferred, to perform Bartholomew's mind at least. I trust you have made no great preparation for my coming unto you about this business; howbeit I am thoroughly persuaded of your gentle affection towards me, and the like thing I do experiment in our friend above-named, wherefore I can be content (as alway I have been, and God willing so will continue) to subject myself to both your wills, viz. to marry here first for his pleasure, and then to come down to you and marry there again (if you think it good) for your pleasure.

Disappointed though they might feel that the delightful pre-parations were not to be made in their own home, John and Sabine consented willingly to the new arrangements, and doubtless travelled to London to attend the wedding. Otwell and Maria were married by special licence from the Faculty Office at the end of January and, however optimistic the bridegroom was about the cost of the festivities, they must have made a largish hole in Bartholomew's purse. All their friends had to be invited and entertained. There were casks of French, Rhenish and Spanish wines to be bought, pastries and confectionery, spices and con-serves of fruit, and, as always, great baked venison pasties. Otwell himself sent down a warrant to Higham Ferrers for a doe to be killed in the Forest, and wrote of the yards of fine Flanders materials that were needed for Maria's trousseau, with 'many other toys and necessaries . . . pour ma fête'. On such great family occasions as this, merchants were not used to stint themselves.

In contrast with Otwell's happy marriage, the course of Richard's love affair was anything but smooth. He loved Mar-garet Mattrys of Calais and she returned his love, but from the veiled hints and curiously oblique references in the letters it is clear that her people put every obstacle in Richard's path that they possibly could. Money was probably the trouble. The Mattrys family were wealthy, while Richard was comparatively poor, and there was another, richer suitor for her hand. Early in the summer of 1545, soon after his own engagement, Otwell was reminding John to 'stir the coals earnestly in the matter' while he was in Calais, and months later John wrote to Parson Philip Smith, the Staple chaplain, to enlist his help and that of Margaret's aunt Spicer. He promised to make 'such reasonable offers in his behalf that I trust they shall have no power to say nay', but the months came and went, and still (according to Margaret's sympathetic brother) there was 'no good news'. It took more than two years of tears, entreaty and negotiation before the family's consent was won.

At last, however, they gave in, and the wedding was arranged for the autumn of 1547. It was held at Calais, where Richard and Margaret afterwards made their home, and the ceremony probably took place in the Church of Our Lady, where the Staple chapel was, and where Thomas Betson's jewel hung. All the Johnsons were invited to the wedding and they eagerly made ready to cross the Channel. Only Sabine was slightly aggrieved, for although John had, as he said, been 'much entreated' to desire her presence, he pretended for weeks that he had given a flat refusal on her behalf, saying that he knew it would be far too much trouble for his wife to come. Sabine complained that she could not tell from his letter whether he wanted her to come or not, but as the harvest was nearly finished she made up her own mind. 'Husband,' she wrote, 'if I chance to come without any more bedding, I do not doubt but I shall be welcome to you. My brother parson will come with me, if I come.' She and Laurence Saunders rode up to London to join Otwell, Maria and Richard, and all five set sail for Calais.

Many of the arrangements had been left in Otwell's capable hands. There would, he knew, be plenty of wine in the cellars at Calais, and the Mattrys family would take care of the fish and fowls and luxuries of all kinds. But there was one thing that England alone could provide for the wedding feast: venison. In the capacious depths of a huge green trunk he sent over six large venison pasties, and with them the 'excellent good flesh' of nearly a whole raw buck, giving John detailed instructions for seeing to it as soon as possible after the sea voyage, and baking it in pastry with 'new pepper . . . if cooks there think it good'. Otwell was also responsible for buying at least part of the bride's trousseau, including her wedding gown — Maria probably helped to choose the material for this — and it was shipped over to Calais in time for the ceremony.

In the packet of cloth are 3½ yards of fine cloth that cost 17s the yard (et ultra, say ye!) for the bride's wedding garment, and an upper-body to spare; in a greater piece, 6½ yards for her second gown, and like upper-bodice to spare; and 3 yards for her aunt Spicer . . . Cloth for Margaret's petticoats was bought with th'other abovesaid, but my wise man forgot the same out of the truss, I beshrew his heart; but Laurence Spender shall bring the same very shortly, and all other things necessary. And thus I pray you that my brother Richard and I may be heartily commended to his spouse, and all her friends and ours. He doth write me from Tickford yesterday that it will be Friday at night ere he can be here, and then with speed he come towards Calais; and my sister your wife when she cometh, and my Mary and I will follow as fast as we can, God willing.

No one in the letters stays single if they can help it, for Tudor men and women clung firmly to the belief of the immortal Doctor that, while marriage might have its pains, celibacy could not possibly have any pleasures. The Tudors, indeed, married as often as they could lawfully do so. Death was the decree absolute of the sixteenth century and, once released, the surviving partner rushed joyfully to the altar again and again. Henry VIII was by no means the only much-married king in Europe (Philip of Spain had four wives), or citizen in his kingdom: the only difference being that he assisted the course of Nature. Sabine's grandfather married twice, so did her mother and her stepfather. Her cousin Andrews at Charlton married twice, and her niece Frances Breten married three times in all, as did aunt Cave, Anthony Cave's wife, who survived three husbands before she decided to erect the handsome marble monument in Chicheley church to the man who had loved her in her youth.

Widows of course were fair game, for their jointure and lands were usually far richer than the dowry of a young girl, and besides, widows *liked* to marry again. 'It is not considered any discredit to a woman to marry again every time that she is left a widow,' wrote the Italian observer of the English scene, 'however unsuitable the match may be as to age, rank and fortune.'[15] And the playwright Greene, in Elizabeth's reign, said practically the same thing. 'The call of a quail', he wrote rather nastily, 'continueth but one quarter, and a widow's sorrow only two months: in the one sad for her old mate, and in the other careful for a new match.'[16] Both writers seem to have uttered the plain, unvarnished truth. The disagreeable, discontented Duchess of Suffolk was painted by Holbein beside her handsome young Master of Horse; Mrs. Fayrey, the energetic business woman of the Johnson Letters, married twice, and so did 'gentle Mistress Baynham'. John once offered to sell Mrs. Baynham's fells for a good price for her in London, 'unless', he added with a smile, 'ye would have them shipped to Calais, and to be called a rich widow!' Such a rumour, once begun, could be relied on to bring an endless train of suitors in its wake. There was apparently no prospect more delightful to contemplate than that of a rich and willing widow. Sabine herself liked to play matchmaker on occasion, and when one of their friends, John Jennyns, a none-too-well-off merchant, lame in one leg, was in search of a wife, she invited him to come and inspect the 'rich widow, which was Peter Edwards' wife of Peterborough', with a view to matrimony. Indeed, everyone did their level best for 'my limping master'. 'John Jennyns most heartily thanketh you for your goodwill', wrote John to Anthony Cave, 'and desireth you if ye think the widow meet for him, and that she will be content to hear such a suitor (which he would know gladly or he travelled far), he desireth you to send him word, and he will come to you.' The reply from Anthony Cave was not altogether encouraging, for John's master was wholly on the side of genuine attachment, and not worldly considerations. 'I would be glad he were well matched', he returned, but regretted that he was not sufficiently well acquainted with the lady to be able to offer an opinion on 'how the party stands'. He promised, however, to write again if he perceived 'any towardness, or that she is meet for him'. Eventually the lady was rejected, not on account of her lack of beauty, but because she was not wealthy enough for the fortune-hunter. 'Except it be to amend his living I will not advise him to travail,' was John's conclusion, 'nor I think he will not.'

The time that elapsed between exchanging one gold wedding-ring for another was sometimes scarcely long enough to allow a polite interval for mourning and weeds, certainly not the conventional year of Victorian times. Occasionally, indeed, the situation resembled nothing so much as *opéra bouffe*. Sabine's much-loved sister Christian died in the late spring of 1545, leaving behind her a houseful of children, and an apparently inconsolable widower, whom John tried to comfort in the following letter.

Jesus anno domini 1545, the third day of April,
at Glapthorn.

Your letter (beloved brother) I have received by William
Albury even now, at my coming home from London. And
whereas it hath pleased God to call to his mercy my sister
your wife, for whose departure ye make great moan and
have a troubled heart, surely, brother, though ye have no less
cause than so to do, forasmuch as such departing of friends
is a great grief unto all fleshly hearts, yet my trust is that the
Spirit of God shall so work in you that ye may receive all
thing at his hand spiritually, and to esteem all worldly and
fleshly things transitory even as they be, and not to take them
for a punishment in this world.

For God doth work his Will according to his unsearchable
knowledge, which Will when it is fulfilled on us may neither
be taken as a punishment, nor yet by suffering thereof we to
make any satisfaction unto him, for when we have all done
that we can, yet be we unprofitable and deserve nothing: but
Christ's death and Passion hath made a whole satisfaction
unto the Father for us. I beseech you therefore in the name of
God to quiet yourself in time, and to say as we be taught,
Thy Will, Lord, be fulfilled, and not ours.

Our old amity I trust shall nothing be minished (though
God have wrought his Will), but for my part I hope shall
rather be increased, and to my power I will be as ready to do
you pleasure as ever I was, hoping of no less friendship at
your hands than I have had. I shall right heartily desire you
that we may meet as we have done, trusting that these holidays ye will be here, whereof both my wife and I would be
glad. I promise you, if much business did not let me, I
would be with you or it were long . . . As the Lord God
knoweth, to whom (after commendations unto you, with the
same from my wife) I commit you, and him I beseech to send
us merry meeting, that we may with one esprit glorify God
the Father of Our Lord Jesus Christ, to whom be praise for
ever and ever, world without end.

Your loving brother-in-law,

John Johnson.

This 'gentle and fruitful' letter was thankfully received and duly taken to heart by the unhappy Christopher Breten, although, as he said, his 'naughty flesh' would scarcely submit to his irreparable loss.

That summer, Sabine's cousin William Saxby died, leaving his wife with four young children to provide for, and a new baby on the way. The appropriateness of a match between Anne Saxby and the sorrowing widower was immediately apparent to Sabine, and early in September she set off on a visit, armed with a proposal of marriage from Christopher, and a letter of virtuous exhortation from John. The young widow's reply, as given by Sabine in her letter to John, is a revelation of all their thoughts and feelings.

Jesus anno 1545, the 10 of September,
at Glapthorn.

In most loving wise, well-beloved husband, with all my heart I commend me unto you, with desire of your health, and praying to the Lord to continue the same.

And to certify you that I have delivered your letter to Mistress Saxby, she and I being alone; and without moving anything to her, she gave you thanks for your letter and also for your goodwill, and said that she had a husband that did love her so well as a man could love his wife, and if she should have one that would not love her and her children, it would be a grief to her. Then did I declare to her my brother's honest behaviour to his wife, with many words, the which were too long to write. Her answer was that she would not set her mind to no man till she was delivered and churched, and then as God shall provide for her; saying it is but a while since her husband died, and that she thought no man would be so hasty to move any such thing to her, her husband dying so lately: in nowise she would make me any grant that my brother should come to her, thanking him and you both for your goodwills. This week I look for Parson Saxby, to whom I will break the matter, and desire him to move it to her again; to whom I think she will make a plainer answer than to me.

You shall receive herewith a letter from William Laurence, wherein you shall perceive what he writes. I sent him answer by his boy that you had nothing to do with the gentleman, but with Laurence, and the bargain that he made you look that he shall perform it. Other answer had I not to send him, for I know nothing of your mind concerning that matter. You shall understand that you have seven wool-winders of work (and they shall lack none).

I do write this week to my brother Otwell for money for Harrison, who hath all the money that you left me. And thus Jesus be with you, in haste.

> By your loving wife,
> Sabine Johnson.

To my loving friend John Johnson, merchant of the Staple of Calais, be this delivered at Calais.

Within a few months Anne had agreed to marry Christopher. He was not by any means rich, or even young, and he had ten children; but still he was a lawyer, and he farmed his own land in Northamptonshire. Doubtless Anne could not afford to be too delicate in the matter of a husband. Christopher could at least offer her a home and affection, and she was relieved of the dreadful necessity of living alone and trying to provide for her children with no one to help her. Marriage was then, as it is still, the best possible career for a woman, although it was not the only alternative for Anne, had she been so disposed. Many intelligent women in the sixteenth century were extremely career-minded. Not only were a number of trades open to women as of right, like the London silk-women's guild, but also a widow automatically became a member of her husband's company, and could trade like an ordinary merchant. The Johnson Letters contain frequent references to these capable and money-making women. One of the most remarkable is Jane Rawe, always referred to by Otwell as 'the Hazebrouck woman'. She ran a private exchange business with great success, travelling from her Flemish centre at Hazebrouck to London, Antwerp and Calais as the needs of her firm required. Thomas Rose's wealthy widow continued in business as a fellmonger (of all things) until she decided that she liked the single life no more, and married her late husband's friend, a butcher and fellmonger named Purvey. The redoubtable Mrs. Fayrey, an old friend of the Johnsons, was the widow of a prominent stapler, and no mean business woman herself. Otwell had the healthiest respect for that determined matron, for she fired searching questions at him on all matters connected with her business transactions, and had no mind to be cheated of even a farthing. Gentle Mrs. Baynham, on the other hand, succeeded in being efficient without losing any of her feminine charm, and both John and Anthony Cave used to vie for the pleasure of entertaining her when she arrived in England. The delicacy and sweetness of her letters give no hint of the very capable business woman she really was, farming hundreds of acres of land in Calais, running a comfortable boarding-house for her stapler friends and trading in wool and wine and herring with the Johnsons and other merchants of her acquaintance. Anne Saxby was her daughter, but it seems that she had not inherited her mother's business acumen; she made no effort to take over William's business, but most willingly married Breten. Late in January 1546, the 'knot' was 'knit up between' them that was to make them both happy. 'I pray God send them comfort of each other', were John's words to a mutual friend, and indeed the match he did so much to promote seems to have been an unqualified success.

But if it was possible to marry as often as one was legally free in the sixteenth century, divorce was almost non-existent, and those who offended the rigid moral code of the time became the outcasts of society. Christopher Breten, who, from whatever motive, took another woman to wife a bare six months after Christian died, was himself to cast out his own daughter. The story is a tragic one, and the more so because it was enacted under John's own roof at Glapthorn Manor. Sabine had taken this young niece into her house before Christian died, and she grew so fond of her that she begged Breten to let her come and live with them indefinitely. 'And so God judge me,' he was later to write, 'it was never in my mind, nor yet in my wife's for anything I yet know to take her away so long as you would have her, but as it is now chanced, I had rather than a great piece of that little I am worth, we had all been otherwise minded.' For several years, all was well, but during the winter and spring of 1546-47 John's illness seems to have disorganized the household at Glapthorn Manor. Devoted to her husband, Sabine gave him all the time that she could spare, even neglecting the children to be with him. Certainly she could have had little time for the niece who lived with them, and who indeed must have been left to her own devices and the company of the servants for days on end. There was little to do, and plenty of time to dream in, when the girl's eyes lit on a handsome young workman, a journeying wool-winder by the name of Rede. It was Rede who seduced her.

In a small household like Glapthorn Manor, hemmed in by people at every turn, it was impossible to keep the affair secret, and when Sabine's niece began to suffer from morning sickness, one of the servants began to gossip in the village. The news spread like wildfire while Sabine was abroad, happily attending Richard's wedding. 'Whoever hath now accused her', wrote the distracted father, unable to believe that such a thing could have happened, 'might as well have given my sister knowledge thereof, before her coming from home towards Calais, as to blow it abroad in both your absence, to the slander of your house and your poor friend; and deserved as small thanks at your hands, in my poor conceit, in uttering of it, as it hath been uttered, as the wench should have done if she should have committed the same lewd act within your house.'

When John and Sabine were informed of what had been going on, they did what everyone seems to have done when they found themselves in difficulties; they consulted Otwell, and begged him to help them. It was Otwell who had the unenviable task of riding through Northamptonshire in the dark and bitter winter weather to seek out and interview Rede and ascertain whether he had in fact committed 'the devilish feat'. When Otwell told the wool-winder that 'the wench had confessed it', Rede swore blind that it was none of his doing, and Otwell, though he 'laid it very earnestly to his charge', could get nothing more out of him. Not that that was the end of matters, for justice in the sixteenth century was always rough, often summary, and frequently carried out in private without benefit of judge or jury. The men of the family now stepped in. 'Brother,' wrote Breten, 'use your discretion in trying out this matter, and for the poor wench, handle her as ye will. I will be shortly with you, although, I thank you, I never came before with an ill will. I trust I shall then perceive somewhat of the truth. If she may be cleared of this feat (as my trust is in the living God, *veritas liberabit*), it shall be at your pleasure and my sister's whether ye will be any more troubled with her . . . I have no mistrust that ye will use indifferency herein, and so I shall require you to do, and more I will not. . . .'

But as for the unhappy girl, rumour on this occasion proved only too true, and Christopher Breten took steps to cast her from his bosom. He had once, he said, hoped to marry her well. 'At the death of my wife, I take God to judge nothing so much did comfort me as the trust of her good bestowing.' But that was impossible now and, while the family could doubtless have forced Rede to marry her, it was unthinkable that they should have to acknowledge a low, common wool-winder among their connections. Christopher Breten's letter, however, reveals that he was not quite so cruel and inhuman as to leave her utterly destitute in her plight. He is writing about Christmas-time, in the year 1547:

> After all hearty commendations unto you and my sister your bed-fellow, and also my brother Laurence, with the same from my wife, I am very sorry my daughter — whom I would God had pleased to have taken before she had been fully one day old — hath given so much occasion towards the evil bruit that hath been bruited and spoken of her, as I do now think by your writing (the more sorry therefore) to be true. And yet I am forced to say, as I said before, for the bruit being as bold as may be, and as true as I now perceive by you is like to be, there be some very near you or in your house that be nothing to be praised for the bruiting and setting it abroad as it hath been done, although (as truth is) it be a common thing pertaining to lewdness to have their evil conditions (as they be many here, I am afraid) manifested abroad.
>
> Brother, as against Rede ye have so compelled me by your writing to suppose him to be an offender, that I shall desire you with other my friends to help to punish him as he shall be found worthy, being nothing glad I have or should have occasion so to do. And for my daughter, God amend her (if this be true) shall have for my part the broad world to walk in. I pray God give her grace and me also to repent and amend (as much as in us may be) all things that be amiss, and if any have misreported her, to give them like grace.
>
> Brother, if ye perceive the thing to be so great that she be not worthy to resort again into your service, I shall desire you till we may meet, that ye will see them where she hath been recompensed for their charges and pains she hath put them

F   87

unto; and I shall, God willing, see you recompensed with most hearty thanks; and after, let God (if so may please him) and herself provide for her. Thus, fearing to trouble you again with a long letter, and also requiring you to ascertain me in writing what ye think to do, or would have me to do in this matter, I commit you unto the tuition of the living God. Scribbled at Teken, with a heart nothing merry (God in whom all comfort and remedy is, amend it at his pleasure).

By your loving brother and
assured poor friend,
Christopher Breten.

The time hath been so troublous that I could not conveniently come unto you, requiring you in the meantime as indifferently as ye may to learn out the whole truth, and to let me have your friendly advice and help to convey her somewhere out of the way, if it be true that she hath declared unto you, etc.

To his well-beloved brother and friend, Mr. John Johnson, this be delivered at Glapthorn.

What the poor girl's fate was remains a mystery. If her father relented, he would probably have supported her and the child in some remote country farmhouse, to eke out her days among the spinsters and the butterwomen; if not, she would indeed have been abandoned to wander through the highways and byways as best she could. It was about this time that the unpleasant side of Puritanism began to show itself in England. One of Otwell's apprentices was to relate how 'the goodwife of the Cock & Star is in the Counter, and hath been this sennight; and one day this week some of her neighbours doth think she shall ride in a cart for playing an harlot's part. The Lord be merciful unto us all, and God change all their devilish hearts and minds, and strengthen them and us with his holy word'. The good and the kind among her neighbours wished her no harm, but then, as so often, the conscience-ridden fanatics had it all their own way. Even Henry VIII was touched by this aspect of the Reformation, which was certainly alien to the good-humoured, rollicking days of Chaucer's England. During the spring of 1546, the King's celebrated conscience prompted him to order the dissolution of the Stews, the notorious brothels on the Southwark side of the river, where all the light ladies of London plied their trade. It is pleasant to end with Otwell's letter, which reveals how much the prospect delighted and amused him, and that he at all events preferred to laugh about such things, than sit down solemnly in the ashes and moan about the wickedness of the world.

For news, understand that the morning of your hence departing, Doctor Cox preached at Paul's Cross of the King's pleasure and the Council's determination to have the Stews dissolved, and to set all the gentlewomen at large. Forsooth! In my fantasy it would have done prettily to have assigned every one of them to a chantry for occupying, and to none other, and therewith to have suffered them to have been the great Bishop's tenants still, and every one of them to learn to row in wherries upon the Thames, for furnishing of their rooms that are taken up to serve the King at the sea in his ships; and by this means, within a year or two, we should have better store of mariners for the common service of the King and merchants also than we have now! Well, God save the King, and send us all of his grace competent to his glory and honour for ever, Amen.

CHAPTER 4

THE FAMILY AT GLAPTHORN

A N estate in the country was the dream and ambition of every Tudor merchant. Visiting foreigners stood amazed at this fondness of the English for country life. 'Every gentle-man flieth into the country', they observed with surprise. 'Few inhabit cities and towns, few have any regard of them.'[17] The streets of London held no such fascination for its wealthy merchants as did the faubourgs of Paris for Frenchmen, or fair Florence for her citizens. Englishmen desired only to escape from the crowded city streets, from the stream of letters and bills of exchange that flowed into the counting-houses, from the bales of goods mounting ever higher in their warehouses, from the racket of carts and coaches and porters, all the 'vast confusion' of Paul's Walk,[18] and the ceaseless babel of foreign voices that chattered and dinned in Lombard Street. Only in the sweeter, quieter air of the country could they relax from the cares of business, and find peace. There they could take their ease, walk in the garden with their favourite spaniel at their heels, and enjoy the company of their neighbours. They could play the squire among the villagers, quarrel with the parson, and marry off their daughters to the local gentry. And loving the countryside as they did, they could watch the eternal progress of the seasons: the warm spring that released them from the winter's cold, the perfection of summer, and the rich harvest of the autumn.

> This maketh me at home to hunt and to hawk,
> And in foul weather at my book to sit,
> In frost and snow then with my bow to stalk,
> No man doth mark where so I ride or go,
> In lusty leas at liberty I walk . . .
> Here I am in Kent and Christendom,
> Among the Muses where I read and rhyme.[19]

It was in the country that John Johnson chose to make his home when the time came. For some little while after their marriage, he and Sabine had lived with Anthony Cave, and many of their friends must have thought they would eventually settle down in the neighbourhood of Tickford House. But however kind the Caves were, and comfortable though the great house was, they wanted, naturally enough, to be by themselves, and to have their own home. Sabine's family came from Northamptonshire; her mother and brothers, her sisters and all her friends were there, and when one of her cousins offered them a house at Polebrook, there seemed every reason for them to accept. Polebrook is a little village lying a few miles south-east of Oundle, near the water-meadows of the river Nene. From the cousin, Parson Thomas Saxby, John agreed to rent the parsonage house, with other small houses nearby, the glebe farm, and also all the tithes of wheat, hay, milk, chickens and calves that belonged to the living. The rent was £3 6s. a year, as John's journal entry for December 31st, 1542, reveals:

> My wife, Sabine Johnson, oweth for chest of
> ready money: and is for the sum of 33s mere
> sterling the same day paid to Sir Thomas Saxby,
> Parson of Polebrook, for the full payment of his
> half year's rent for the farm of the parsonage
> of Polebrook, due at Michaelmas last past. Sum   £1 13s. od.

When John wrote that journal entry, they had been at Polebrook only a few months, since just before the harvest was got in, and they did not remain there for very long, hardly more than a year. Possibly John never intended the parsonage to be his permanent home. It was too small for a growing family; moreover, he was making money fast at this time and he wanted to live in a fashion more in keeping with his income. When it came to selecting a permanent residence, the Tudors had exacting views, which Polebrook probably did not meet. Dr. Andrew Boorde, the celebrated writer of the day, laid it down that the house must face east and west, but not south, for while the 'East wind is temperate, frisk and fragrant', the south wind was extremely unhealthy. The situation of the house had to be airy, and yet sufficiently near wood and water for all the varying household needs. Above all, the prospect must delight the eye with the harmony of nature. 'I had rather not to build a mansion or a house than to build one without a good prospect in it, to it and from it. For if the eye be not satisfied the mind cannot be contented, the heart cannot be pleased; if the heart and mind be not pleased, nature doth abhor.'[20]

At all events, when an acquaintance, Sir Thomas Brudenell of Deene, one of the wealthiest landowners of the neighbourhood, spoke to him about a manor house and farm which he held of Lord Cromwell, and which he was thinking of letting, John immediately went over to view the place, and eventually decided to take it. Glapthorn Manor, as it was called, lay within easy riding distance of Polebrook, a few miles to the other side of Oundle, in a belt of rich farmland. A shallow stream wound its way through the home meadows, and all around was a prospect of wooded hills — Shire Hill and Hostage Wood, Wymond Hill and Southwick Wood. The rent was £8 a year, and at such a price John decided he could afford to live at the manor house, and retain Polebrook as well. The only person to be disappointed by the change was Anthony Cave, who in his heart had always hoped that John and Sabine would settle near him in Buckinghamshire. However, he made the best of it, and offered to help them all he could.

I perceive that a farm of Mr. Brudenell's is offered you, and that ye think to conclude for it. If it be a thing that ye like and hope to have profit by, I am glad of it, but I am sorry that ye will settle so far from this country. Herewith I do send a letter to Mr. Brudenell in your favour, which if it may do you any pleasure I shall be glad of. I am but smally acquainted with him, but I know him, and I think he knoweth me.

John leased the Old Manor House (known locally as Browns' Manor), a fine stone and timber building set in a great garden. It was one of those small manor houses which had been built all over England at the end of the fifteenth and beginning of the sixteenth centuries, country houses like Cothele in Somerset, or Middle Littleton in the Cotswolds. It was doubtless a rambling, comfortable place, with few pretensions to style, and owing little or nothing to the classical symmetry of the Renaissance. Built often around a small courtyard, or in a rectangular block with two short projecting wings, the Tudor manor house still kept the lofty mediaeval hall, with the long light oriel window, and the parlour leading off the upper end, where the family could be by themselves when they chose. At the lower end of the hall was the buttery, leading into the kitchen, with its pantry, stillroom and dairy, and the wine-cellars down below. A simple flight of stairs led up to the first floor, where lay the bedrooms of the family, while above were the nurseries and attics to which the children and servants were consigned.

At Glapthorn Manor there were fine gardens. Beyond the flower garden with its curious knot-beds lay the kitchen gardens, a pool stocked with freshwater fish — pike, perch and bream — and a stream of clear water flowing through the meadows beyond. To one side of the house there was a magnificent apple orchard, covering an acre of ground, exquisite in the springtime when the trees were clouded with pink blossom, and again in the autumn, with their hanging russet fruit. Not far away was a grove of ancient walnut trees, and all around were the gentle wooded hills. Glapthorn Manor was a pleasant place to live, and so John and Sabine must have felt it, for while they enjoyed all the advantages of country life, yet they were near enough to the village and the highway not to feel cut off from their neighbours and the outside world. Before the summer of 1544 began, the documents were signed and sealed, and John and Sabine, with the baby Charity, and a bevy of maidservants and menservants, were all established at the manor house.

Young as she was (and she could not have been more than twenty-two at the time) Sabine was the mistress of a large household and responsible for the welfare and conduct of everyone beneath her roof. Not only were there the children and John to be cared for, and the apprentices and servants, but there was a constant stream of guests as well. Otwell and Maria were frequent visitors at Glapthorn Manor, so were Robert and Laurence Saunders, her cousin James Haddon, and most of their friends. It was nothing for Sabine to have seven people staying with her all at once. 'In most loving wise, well-beloved husband,' she wrote to John one spring, 'I commend me unto you, and so doth my brother Villiers, my brother Breten, Mr. Baynham, and all their wives, with my sister Smith, the which good company hath been with me all this Whitsuntide; and we all would have been glad of your company, the which if wishing could have done we should have had (but patience!) ... I have had a lack this three days that you say a woman doth never lack, for with cold I have been so ill that I could not speak. But I will not beshrew them it is long of.' Sabine was a strong and healthy young woman, but it seems that she was prone to suffer from laryngitis, for in another spring we find her writing to John: 'I have had an impediment this four days that many would have their wives to have it all the year; for four days I could not speak — it came with a cold.' But even when she was well, or when the guests were as considerate as Anthony Cave, who begged them to 'make me no stranger: I mean, to use any other provision but ordinary, which shall best content me', guests naturally took some looking after. The one thing that a wealthy merchant expected of his wife was that the house should be run smoothly and graciously, and that he should not be troubled by petty domestic problems. It was on Sabine that everyone's comfort and well-being depended, and the creation of that comfort was both an art and a vocation. As mistress of the house, she had in Markham's words to be '... of chaste thought, stout courage, patient, untired, watchful, diligent, witty, pleasant, constant in friendship, full of good neighbourhood, wise in discourse ... secret in her affairs, comfortable in her counsels, and generally skilful in all the worthy knowledges which do belong to her vocation'.[21]

Sabine's duties were by no means confined to the purely ornamental. Country households in the sixteenth century were almost completely self-supporting as far as the necessaries of life were concerned, relying on their own resources for food and drink, clothes and fuel. Sabine had to look after all the household, doctor their ailments as well as she could with herbal remedies, and sometimes scold them into common sense. She had to supervise the work of the house, the inevitable dusting and polishing and cleaning, the washing and ironing, the sewing and spinning; she had to arrange the menu for the week's meals, the breakfasts and dinners and suppers that the entire household sat down to, and all the baking and brewing that went on; there was the cultivation of the flower and vegetable gardens to attend to, and the dairy as well, the milking and cheesemaking, the butter-churning and cream-skimming, the feeding of the pigs and poultry, the egg-collecting, and the marketing of all the surplus produce at Oundle market. Besides this she ran the big farm in John's absence from home, directing the wool-buying and winding and sheep-shearing, buying cattle and horses, collecting the tithes and rents, seeing to the repairs of the barns and houses, paying the bills and keeping the accounts, and looking after village affairs generally. If Sabine was occasionally out of temper, it is hardly to be wondered at. 'May Fortune sometimes', was Anthony Fitzherbert's airy remark, 'that thou shalt have so many things to do that thou shalt not well know where it is best to begin.'[22] The contemporary *Mulierum Paean* has a few lines in the same vein.

> Estates commonly where I go
> Trust their wives to overlook
> Baker, brewer, butler and cook
> With other all, men meddleth no whit
> Because the woman hath quicker wit.
>
> My lady must receive and pay,
> And every man in his office control,
> And to each cause give yea and nay,
> Bargain and buy and set all sole
> By indenture other by court roll,
> My lady must order thus all thing,
> Or small shall be the man's winning.[23]

Sabine ran the house, but John provided the money. And while the best advice urged Tudor husbands to be generous to their wives, John Lyly was careful to say: 'Let all the keys hang at her girdle, but the purse at thine; so shalt thou know what thou dost spend, and how she can spare.'[24] Arguments over money were as frequent a source of open or concealed difference then as now. Fitzherbert had it that most wives and husbands deceived each other now and again over income and egg-money,[25] but it is rather difficult to see how Sabine could have done this. John was the kind of man who liked to see everything down neatly in black and white, and Sabine had to give him an account of every farthing that she spent. Every time John gave Sabine any housekeeping money, he made an entry in his journal:

The 13th day of July, anno 1543.

Accounts of household at Polebrook oweth for chest of ready money: and is for the sum of £3 mere sterling the same day delivered unto my wife for the necessaries of the house.   Sum   £3 os. od.

One month later, another £5 was sent down to her from London while he was abroad and, during January 1544, payments for 'th'accounts and reckonings of Polebrook' totalled £4 8s. By the end of March, Sabine was evidently running short, for John had to lend her money. 'My wife Sabine Johnson oweth for chest of ready money: and is for the sum of 30s mere sterling the same day (March 26th) to her lent — £1 10s 0d.' Everything was meticulously noted down, whether it was 'two basins of latten' that her mother bought for her at Harborough Fair, or a heavy turning mill that was used to grind the corn. At first, Sabine kept her own account book, but in later years, after they had moved to Glapthorn Manor, the household accounts were handed over to young Thomas Egillsfield, and at the beginning of the account book for 1550 is a long list of the sums of money handed to him by his mistress, with the dates when it was given.

It is clear from the letters that Sabine was no Dora Copperfield, but a very practical and thrifty young woman. She kept good account of the money that was in her hands, and in time John came to rely on her completely for the conduct of all his business affairs while he was abroad. Otwell in London would be given a note of how much money she would be likely to need, and it would be forwarded to her from time to time. Sometimes she needed more money than usual, and on one occasion, in the autumn of 1545, her demands were the cause of a first-class family quarrel. In all innocence she wrote up to Otwell to send her more gold, not knowing that her letter had crossed with one of John's. 'I pray you, send for no more money to London before Christmas,' he had written to his beloved, 'for I have none to spare.' Otwell himself was unusually short of cash. Sales were down, they had been making heavy purchases, and Maria's dowry money (besides the money from the wine sales) had all been used up. 'Your wife's warning most commonly for money is very sudden,' Otwell complained, 'and divers times not agreeing with your remembrances that you leave with me. I pray you, warn her thereof by your next letter.' When Sabine's next letter came, demanding £40 immediately, so that she could pay the wool-buyer Richard Harrison, and with it a barrel of new red wine, the effect on Otwell was explosive.

Of this bearer, your servant, I have received your letter of the 2nd of this month, requiring by the same to have £40

63

sterling sent you by him for Richard Harrison (as you write),
which I do perform with very great difficulty at this instant,
all in fair gold. But I beseech you right heartily not to take
upon you from henceforth to send your man so suddenly to
me for any more money, at Harrison's appointment or otherwise, without some honest declaration unto me before by writing of his or your necessity, in such wise as I may have reasonable leisure to provide for the same to the least loss that
may be.

It is neither your husband nor I that keep any such store of
money laying by us, that Harrison can have of us what he will
appoint, with sending of your man for the same. And truly,
at this instant I am out of doubt that your husband doth not
once think of one penny that ye would have sent for now, for
he neither spake, left remembrance, nor writ unto me of one
groat to be sent him, since the sending of the last £25 to Tickford — and yet have I paid here for Harrison to Mr. Laxton,
since my brother's going over, £20 that he left not me one
penny for; I did the like long since to Mr. Barnes, Alderman,
also for him, with £28 and odd money. Let Harrison therefore content himself, I pray you, and do you consider that your
husband is extremely charged with wares, and can as yet make
no sales; and the things so being, forsooth it is no small deal of
money that hath been furnished to Harrison since Midsummer
last.

Well, say unto Harrison of these things that I have written
you above what you think good, but by my troth, I will return
your man empty the next time that he cometh in such haste
as he doth now, without some knowledge aforehand, and
especially when I am sure that my brother doth make no
reckoning of such sending. . . .

Let everything therefore be used from henceforth as it ought
to be . . . Red wine I would you had as much as you would
drink, if I knew how to send it you. In case I should take upon
me the sending down of a rondlet, I know not how it should be
accepted of all parties. Howbeit, you shall have it if you will
send me word so. . . .

Otwell was to find out that his sister-in-law had a temper that
was at least the equal of his own. Sabine would not permit anyone

except John to dictate to her what she should or should not do, and Otwell soon realized that he had loosed the whirlwind. When the next batch of letters came up from the country, he guessed quite accurately that they contained 'much matter of displeasure against me, for therewith I had one from her myself, not so gently written as she was wont to do!' Sabine had in fact written as follows to John:

Jesus anno 1545, the 8 in November,
at Glapthorn.

In most loving wise, entirely beloved husband, with all my heart I commend me unto you, being right glad to hear of your good health by two of your letters received this day. In your letter of the 26 in October you writ of your safe arrival at Calais, of the which I am glad to hear of; and whereas you would that you were at Dover coming home, even so would I (and yet do beshrew them that keep you there this cold weather). I am sorry that they die so fast at Calais, Our Lord cease it when his most merciful will is, in whose hands is both sickness and health, praying you with all my heart to keep yourself well, and then God will spare you to provide for me and your two maidens, with a many more.

Your wool winders will have done within these thirteen days. You shall understand that Harrison had need of money, for the which I did send for to my brother, as I have written you in my letter sent when I sent for the same money; wherefore my brother was very angry, and had thought to have sent home my man without, saying that you left no such commission with him. But when he had fumed well, then he bethought himself, and sent me £40, of the which Harrison shall have no more than he must needs.

Also I have had a great fond mind this three weeks to drink red wine, for the which I did send to my brother, who saith 'he would send me some, but he cannot tell how it would be taken of all parties'. I will take pains rather than I will write to him again, although I have a great mind to it, as the Lord knoweth, who send you health. In haste.

By your loving wife, that was never
thus weary with writing,
Sabine Johnson.

If I can hear of a gelding for your saddle, I will do that I can to make away Don. Dunkerley's horse shall be well kept, and one of his eyes, for the other eye is out. Goodnight, good husband, with all my heart.

To my loving and beloved friend, John Johnson, merchant of the Staple of Calais, be this delivered at Calais.

Sabine also poured out the whole story to the sympathetic Richard Harrison, who took it 'in the nose' and rounded on Otwell, writing to him 'rashly' that he need 'take no care of any money that is sent or delivered unto him, for he knoweth me for no owner thereof'. Otwell by this time was disgusted. 'I pray you answer them both for me,' he wrote to his brother, 'for I will not.'

John indeed was forced to play the part of peacemaker between all three of them. He told Sabine that she might not have such 'light occasions' to be offended with Otwell, that she should have all the money she wanted, and as for the wine:

> I am sorry ye had not red wine when ye would have had it, but ye may not be too lightly displeased for the lack thereof. Perchance he could send you none good, or there was some other let. I hope he will send you some shortly, and then all displeasures will be blown over. I pray you, when it cometh, prove if it do make frogs creep, and send me word. Here is good store of new wines of divers sorts: if it might be conveniently, I would ye had part thereof. I wish you some thereof even with all my heart, and could be content to pay for it on that condition, as the Lord knoweth, who send you health, as us a merry meeting.

Sabine was not entirely convinced, especially when no red wine materialized. 'You be desirous to know if frogs will creep', she rejoined. 'My trust is they will creep, but when, God knoweth.' With his brother, John took the line that it was all a great fuss about nothing, and that he must look on the whole affair 'as proceeding from a woman'. Otwell, however, was still rather cross. 'Her excuse to you of her displeasure, for my refusing to send her red wine, is also like a woman's tale, for I had no way to do it than but to have sent some in a bottle by Richard Preston when he was here. Well, she shall not be long without some, if that be all the cause of her grief! Better a bad excuse than none!'

It was doubtless the gentle Maria who helped to coax Otwell into a good humour with his tempestuous sister-in-law, and in his next letter he proffered the olive branch, reproaching her for being so 'strange' towards him, and sending her the bottle of new red wine that she longed for. 'If you be content to let anything pass that is done . . . or spoken of, I will do the like: or whether you will do so or not, truly I will not once think of . . . the matter, for I must of force from henceforward practise to forbear a woman speaking in her angry mood, as I would look to have any pleasantness proceed from her . . .' The allusion to his forthcoming marriage, and the delicious red wine he sent, softened Sabine's heart. Indeed, before she received the wine, she had already forgiven him, as she wrote to John.

> . . . Doubt you not but the grief that was between my brother and me will be done or you come home, although he hath written ungently to me; and when I have good wine I will thank you for it. And I thank you that you wish me part of your good wine: but if I had venison I would not *wish* you it, but would *send* you it. . . .

The explanation of Sabine's taut nerves and shifting moods that autumn was very simple: she was going to have a baby, and if Otwell had known this, he would have walked half way round London to gratify her sudden whim for new red wine. In an age of enormously large families, and women worn out by continual child-bearing, Sabine was unusually fortunate. Ten children had been the lot of her sister Christian, who was evidently quite young when she died; but if the letters are anything to go by, Sabine's babies came at respectable two-year intervals, almost with the regularity of a planned family. Charity, the eldest little girl, was born some months after the move to Polebrook in 1542; and Rachel, the second daughter, was born at Glapthorn Manor in November 1544. Otwell hailed the news of her birth in his usual cheerful fashion.

> Brother, I commend me very heartily unto you, and to my sister your wife, being very glad that she hath sped so well, albeit it is much besides my conjecture: but the Lord's gifts

are to be received with much joy, as I doubt not but that you take this. This bearer was told the child's name for to have showed me, but it fell besides his horse or out of his panniers by the way. Only he doth remember (as he saith) that Jacob's wife was so named in th'Old Testament, which I know not but if it were Rachel. There is no great force in the matter, considering that all thing is to God's glory and my sister's comfort and yours, with all your friends here.

In the autumn of 1545, when John left her to go to Calais, Sabine was with child again, and Maria went down into the country the following spring to be with her at the confinement. John had been summoned to Calais yet again and, since she naturally wanted him to be with her when her time came, Sabine wrote begging him to come home.

Jesus anno 1546, the 17 in May,
at Glapthorn.

Well-beloved husband, as heartily as heart can think I commend me unto you, trusting in the living Lord that you be in health, daily praying to the same Lord to continue the same and to send you well home, trusting that you will be at home shortly to bid gossips. To appoint the time, it lies not in me, and whether it shall be before Whitsuntide or after, Our Lord knoweth, for I stand in doubt; wherefore I most heartily desire you to make all the speed home that you can. And do you think, good husband, what a great comfort it shall be to me to have you here at that time, trusting in the Lord that he will send you a son; but whatsoever it be, pray we to the same Lord that it may be born to his honour and godly will.

Husband, you shall understand that I with your little ones and your house be in health, with all other your friends in these parts, the Lord be praised.

This day I sent you a letter, answer to yours of the 8th of this present, wherefore I have at this time but little to write you of, as the Lord knoweth, who send you health and your gentle heart's desire. In much haste.

By your loving wife,
Sabine Johnson.

Richard is still buying of fells, and hath not yet made up a load. Harrison will provide you of as much wool as he can, and even so will I. I have sent this day to my brother Breten with your letter, and at Richard's coming home I bade him come by my father's, to know whether you should have his wool or no, and to my cousin John Lane to know if his wool and my Lady Lane's were sold: if not, to get some promise of it for you; and also to know if my Lord Montagu's wool were sold, and Mr. Warne's of Broughton (but that, I think, my brother Breten will stay).

To her well-beloved friend John Johnson, be this delivered at Calais.

With two daughters already, John and Sabine longed for a boy, and this time their hopes were not disappointed. But alas, the baby lived only a few weeks, and they grieved bitterly over him. 'Brother, I am sorry (if God had been otherwise pleased) that ye have lost your little, little fair summer flower,' Christopher Breten wrote to them. 'I trust both you and my sister will take it no otherwise but even as the loss of a flower, and he that hath taken that shall refer you another (I trust shortly)'. But it was to be some years before the longed-for son and heir arrived. In 1548, Sabine was with child again, and the whole family sent her their prayers and good wishes for her safe delivery, hoping that she would this time have a 'goodly boy', but all to no avail. A few weeks before Christmas, another small girl came into the world and was christened Faith. Otwell could not resist teasing John a little, for the opportunity was too good to be missed.

Going about to close up this letter, an honest man of Walgrave brought me yours of the 9th of this present, which I have no time now to answer in never a point of it. Only I praise God with you for my sister your wife's good deliverance, and beseech him within these twelve months to send you Hope to your Faith and Charity, seeing you are better practised in getting of wenches than boys! But all be to God's glory. By my brother Richard at full, I will enlarge more matter unto you. . . .

Always the children were welcome, and always the husbands' main concern was for their wives' safety. The sixteenth century was not an age of antiseptics or even cleanliness, and the risks of childbed were such as almost every woman had to take. One can imagine what Bartholomew Hosse's wife had gone through when he wrote to John, 'Sir, it is so that I was full purposed to have been with your mastership the Sunday last past, but it has pleased God of infinite goodness to have sent my bed-fellow delivered of child, of the which she is very weak of, and I am sorry to leave her lying in that case.' The woman who had a clean and skilful midwife — and most of them were addicted to the brandy bottle — could count herself fortunate indeed. Sabine at least could call on her married sisters to help her, as this letter from Clement Villiers shows.

Brother, with like hearty recommendation unto you and my sister as you have written to me, I give unto you and my sister for your gentleness showed unto us at all times. And, Sir, I heartily greet old Jane my wife well, and I shall be well content that my wife be with my sister to do you pleasure, and for her comfort, and I pray God make my sister a glad mother when time shall be, and I shall pray for her. No more to you, but I pray Jesu send my sister good speed in her business, and you with all yours good health unto the pleasure of Almighty God. From Hothorpe.

> By your assured brother-in-law
> to his power,
> Clement Villiers.

Brother, I give to you and my sister hearty thanks for your fish.

To my loving brother John Johnson, give this.

It was the spring of 1550, and soon afterwards Sabine was indeed a glad mother, for the long-awaited boy was born. They christened him Evangelist in token of their joy and thanksgiving, and almost at once he becomes the 'young master' of the letters, the adored only son for whom nothing was too good. When he was two years old, we find Sabine writing to London and asking John to buy a doll for him. 'A pair of shoes for Evangelist bring with you', she begged. 'And I pray you, cast away a little money of some baby for him: my sister Gery can do these things well.'

With her sisters and servants to care for her, Sabine was never expected to be on her feet before she was well enough. Faith was born early in December, but it was not until the following January that Anthony Cave suggested that Sabine would have 'waxen strong' enough to pay them a visit at Tickford House. She stayed at home, in her warm and comfortable bed, between the finest sheets that the linen-press possessed, while friends and relations and god-parents flocked around. Everyone in the neighbourhood came to see the new baby in her rocking cradle, bringing beautifully embroidered baby clothes, corals and rattles, and presents for Sabine as well. Christenings, which were always held soon after the baby was born, were a fine excuse for good company in an age which adored entertainment of any kind.

John and Otwell were both good husbands, and they tried to make their wives as comfortable as they could. For months beforehand, they ordered and shipped home luxuries from abroad. John had hardly learned that he was going to become a father one year (it was March, and Rachel was not born till December) when he paid out 6s. 6d. 'for a sugar loaf', as he wrote in his journal, 'against she lay in'. A stream of nice things travelled down from London, 'two loaves of sugar and a bag of spices', 'comfits for my sister your wife', a 'pot with succat', dates, prunes, raisins, oranges, sugar-coated caraway and coriander seeds, and, of course, new gowns for their wardrobes. John once presented the Calais goldsmith with several ounces of silver 'to make a casting-bottle for rosewater', and wrote urgently to have it finished some months later, 'for my aunt Cave is upon her laying down of child, and then it should be occupied, as Our Lord knoweth'. No doubt Sabine and Maria both possessed such silver perfume bottles, fashioned with round bowls and long, slender necks. The bedrooms where the children were born were as comfortable as money could make them. The Queen's room was, of course, equipped with arras hangings, with crimson satin curtains to the bed, fine lawn sheets, and a coverlet of ermine embroidered in blue velvet on cloth of gold, with silver bowls and ewers. Clearly no merchant could afford to provide on such a scale, but they did their best. Otwell once completely refurnished Maria's bedroom when a new baby was on the way, asking John to make the purchases in Antwerp.

My Mary's next child-bed chamber shall lack a large Brussels tick of the best making, of 11 or 12 quarters broad, which would be ready garnished there, and also two or three pieces of arras blue say, not too light of colour. If you can, I pray you refuse not the buying of these things for her, as for a groaning-chair of that colour my sister your wife hath charge of for her, and for spices such as she buyeth for herself, namely pepper, and child-bed junkets also; moreover, small cushions, ½ dozen of green and as many of blue. And so again fare you well.

Otwell was no less anxious than his brother to raise a family. In the spring after his marriage to Maria, he took her down to the country and left her with Sabine; it was just before the baby boy was born. At intervals, Otwell wrote teasing messages to his bride: 'Brother, with my hearty commendations to you, my sister your wife (mother to fair young boy, I trust, long before this time), and to my poor Mary, not being able (as I doubt) to bear neither boy nor wench . . .' When the first good news came, he sent his delighted congratulations, 'being no less glad of my sister your wife's prosperous bringing-forth of her fair son and yours, than I am heartily sorry for my poor Mary's sorrowfull languissement', and asking John to 'comfort my poor wife (as I am sure you do!) and provoke her to mirth as much as you may!'

But Otwell's wish was to be granted, and soon. Early in May the following year, 1547, he could hardly disguise his impatience for the child to be born — 'My Mary, with her great belly yet' he wrote to John. On May 26th the baby finally came. It was a boy, and was baptized that same day at St. Dionis Backchurch, near where they lived. The new father displayed the most enormous pride, telling John the news with a nonchalance that deceived no one.

News I have none to write you of, but that I am sure you heard yesternight by George Grant at Tickford, touching the good deliverance (the Lord be praised) of my Mary with a jolt-headed boy on Thursday last, in the morning, betwixt four and five of the clock. And Sir Ambrose Cave, Mr. Armigill, and Mistress Richardson gave him his name, Israel, whose seed was multiplied like the sand of the sea; and so I beseech God bless him and his posterity to his glory, that he and all we may be the right Israelites in spirit before his sight, both here and in the world to come, Amen. In haste scribbled, being yet fasting, at two of the clock in the afternoon.

Israel (and how easy it is to divine the family's religious beliefs from the names they gave their children) was born in the Lime Street house, but in the spring of the following year Otwell and Maria moved to their new home in Lombard Street, the very centre of mercantile life and thought. The news that Maria, like Sabine, was once more with child was given in Otwell's usual style, 'with hearty commendations to my sister your wife's belly from Mary my boss the belly'. Early in the summer, Maria's second child was born, and this time it was a girl.

Brother, almost forgetting to make you partaker of my Mary's joy and mine, understand that on Wednesday last, somewhat before nine of the clock in the night, she was well delivered (God be praised) of a fair daughter, who was named the morrow after at her christening Abigail, th'interpretation whereof in English is (as my brother Francis Warner sheweth me) 'my father hath rejoiced', and so I beseech God my sister and you may do of that she now beareth, praying you also to make my father and mother Warner, with other our friends at Lynn, privy hereunto at your next going or sending thither, with commendations from both their sons Bartholomew and Francis, who be both here at this present.

Although Maria, as Otwell put it, was 'mother and nurse to Israel', Sabine was rather wealthier than her sister-in-law, and her children were put out to a wet-nurse, some bouncing country-woman in the village. They remained at the breast for what seems an inordinately long time today. Charity (like Juliet) must have been almost three years old when her mother wrote: 'Your two little maidens be in health; Charity is weaned and is come home.' Rachel was still with the wet-nurse in the autumn of 1545, and would continue to live with her foster-mother for another two years. She was near enough to the manor house for Sabine to visit her frequently, and once the child picked up some illness, probably from the cottager's children. 'My daughters shall have God's blessing and mine,' wrote John, 'and am glad of Rachel's amendment. I pray you, come not much at her your-

self, lest ye get the disease yourself.' It is very probable that the
child had smallpox, the curse of the sixteenth century, and the
ruin of many a woman's beauty. Both of Otwell's children had
it, as one of his apprentices told John. 'Israel and Abigail hath
had the smallpox, but they are meetly well again now, thanks be
given to God for all his gifts.'

John was extremely fond of his two children. Like the celebrated Roman matron, he was given to calling them his 'two
jewels', an affectionate and charming description that Sabine
duly echoed in her next letter, although a year or so later, when
they were round her skirts, it was 'Our brats be well, thanks be
to God'. Young and impatient, eager to enjoy life while she
could, and with far too much to do, Sabine was perhaps not a very
tender or loving person where young children were concerned.
The Tudors, living in a world where extreme pain was a commonplace of existence, were indeed not really very understanding in
the way they used their children, and 'spare the rod, spoil the
child' was a general rule. The treatment that gentle, intelligent
Lady Jane Grey received at her parents' hands is well known, and
it is on record that the Duke of Norfolk once informed Princess
Mary that, were she his daughter, he would knock her head against
the wall until it was as soft as a baked apple. Nor is there any
reason to suppose, from the accounts of the time, that other children as a whole led happier lives at school or at home. It is not
to be imagined that Sabine was as unamiable as some parents
but, all the same, it is evident that the old saws were ingrained
in her. The summer after Charity came home from her foster-
mother, plague broke out at Glapthorn, and someone died in the
village. The little girl was hastily packed off to her uncle and
aunt at Teken, and John wrote the following letter to his brother-
in-law:

Since my coming from Polebrook on Sunday was a sennight
(beloved brother), I perceive Charity, my little maiden, was
carried to Teken by reason of one being dead out of Armeston
of the plague. It was a very bold deed to trouble you and my
sister with her; howbeit, because of your gentle offer made
unto my wife and me at your being at Polebrook, we were the
bolder, and shall desire you to be no less bold of us if we may
do you any pleasure, in anything that lieth in us.

My wife saith she doubteth much that my sister and you will make Charity a wanton in suffering her to have her will, and then she shall do her a shrewd turn, and cause her to have strokes hereafter. I pray you, therefore, let her be kept in awe, and not suffered to eat much flesh meats for warts' breeding, and thereunto she is much inclined by complexion.

To Christopher Breten and his wife, surrounded by their large brood, the presence of Charity could have made very little difference one way or another; one child more could easily share someone's bed, and be squeezed in at the table. They promised, however, not to spoil her, and Teken House must have agreed with the little girl for, when next Christopher wrote, she was 'merry and in health, I pray God long to continue it unto his pleasure; and where in your letter ye give my wife and me thanks for the pains Charity should put us unto, I trust ye will not so think, for the having of her is no pain, but rather pleasure, and so we esteem it, and I pray you do the same'.

Always in the country there was this constant danger of plague, brought in by carriers and travellers and people fleeing from crowded London. In the autumn of 1545, it raged as severely in Northamptonshire as it did in the City and in Calais. 'Ripon hath buried one of plague', wrote Sabine to John, 'and at Oundle they die still, wherefore I fear this town.' Mr. Ripon was one of their friends at Cotterstock, only a mile or two away, and in his next letter, John told Sabine what to do.

I have now received your letter (well-beloved wife) of the 23 of the last month, which hath been at Antwerp, and is come again. I perceive thereby that Ripon hath buried one of the plague, and that ye fear it will come to Glapthorn. As long as it cometh no higher than Cotterstock there is no fear, by the grace of God, but if God should visit Glapthorn, I pray you remove to Polebrook with all your youth, and leave no more at home but two of your maids and Jasper, the shepherd, and John. I cannot perceive but ye shall be in great danger if the plague come in Glapthorn (as God defend), for that ye shall not keep . . . out of the town.

All through November it ravaged the countryside, although

fortunately Glapthorn was spared. At Cotterstock, poor Ripon suffered terribly, as Sabine told her husband.

I did write you that Ripon had buried one of the plague. You shall understand that for the space of a month he had none sick, trusting that all had been well, and now, within these eight or ten days, he hath buried out of his house either eight or ten persons of his children and servants. At Oundle they die sore, Our Lord comfort them.

The following year saw no relief and, when the warm weather came, John decided that Polebrook was the safest place, and transferred the whole household to the parsonage, except for those who were left behind to look after the animals. He wrote to Anthony Cave:

It hath pleased God to visit us at Glapthorn with the plague. One house is infected about the church, and a child hath a great sore which is like to break, within two houses of my house, which hath caused me to remove my youth and household hither. And although it hath been troublous to me, chiefly because of the winding of my wool, yet I am in more quietness and in less fear than I should have been there.

In the autumn, Sabine went to stay for a while with Otwell and Maria in London and, while she was there, she received the most alarming news. The plague had come to Polebrook, and not only there, but to Newton and Sibbertoft and Teken, where Charity was still staying, and to most of the little towns and villages of the neighbourhood. Glapthorn itself was fairly clear, and Christopher Desborough's sickness was thought to be only some new ague; nevertheless John Ferne and Margery and other servants had fled in terror from the manor house. Sabine had no idea how things were left at home, and she wrote to John to ask him to let her return into the plague-stricken district, if only for a few days, so that she could collect Charity from Teken, where there were 'at least twelve or thirteen children in the house besides my cousin Hatton's and mine' and see to the ordering of the farm.

John Ferne and Margery is gone, but he doth not write me in what order my house is left, wherefore, if it please you, I could be content to go home and see some order set in my said

houses, and then to go or come whither it shall please you.
For wheresoever I be, I shall not be in quiet to think how
rawery I left everything, not thinking to tarry so long from
home.

If you do go into France, I pray you, give me leave to go
home, and I will promise you I will not tarry at Glapthorn nor
Polebrook not two nights, for I am as 'fraid to be sick as any-
body. It is better for me to go now than to tarry any longer —
the sooner the better. If they should die sore at Polebrook and
Glapthorn, we were in ill case for looking to our cattle, being
at this time unprovided, both men and maidens.

Those children who survived the dire diseases that menaced
their lives, and who had sufficient spirit not to be cowed by their
harsh upbringing, must have been amazingly independent and
self-reliant, for from the earliest days they were accustomed to
being jounced around the countryside from one house and one
aunt to the next. 'Charity is at Peterborough', wrote Richard
Preston to his master, 'and so I have not heard of Evangelist since
he went, God send him health; I will see him shortly.' Sometimes,
the children all trooped over to Church Langton, and they probably enjoyed themselves there, for the utter simplicity and
sweetness of Laurence Saunders's disposition would have endeared
him to his nieces and nephews. At other times they went on long
visits to their cousins Judith, Anna and Martha at Tickford
House. 'I thank you for my wanton wench Faith', wrote John to
Anthony Cave. 'Ye shall receive a gown for her, and three more
for my cousins.'

Thanks to the letters and journals that have survived, we know
a little of what the interior of the manor house was like. The
principal room was, of course, the great hall. This was probably
furnished much like that of their cousin Cope's at Canons Ashby,
with its high roof and dais and oriel window, the great table for
the family and guests, long trestle tables with benches for the
servants, court cupboards to hold the plate and cutlery and latten
candlesticks, and chests to hold the linen. An open fire burned in
the middle of the hall, with the smoke ascending through the
louvre in the roof timbers. Most of their furniture was of oak,
simple and solid. The great trees were felled in the forest nearby,
and carved and joined by country carpenters like Kett and Jan-

kinson at Glapthorn. Elm, beech and pine were often used as well, but few of the elegant Stuart woods were theirs — the rosewood, tulip-wood and ebony from the East, the soft lime that Grinling Gibbons loved to work with, and laburnum and walnut for veneers. It is sometimes stated that all the walnut wood used in cabinet making at this period came from abroad, and that walnut trees were not planted in England until late in the sixteenth century.[26] But there was, as we know, a grove of fine old walnut trees at Glapthorn Manor as early as 1510, and when John was living at the manor house in 1548, Otwell wrote down to him: 'I pray you, remember my walnut tree timber, that I may also have it here before my said going over, for to put it forth to working, and to have it ready shortly after my coming again, by God's grace.' If Otwell thought it was well worth the trouble and expense of having the timber carted to London, it is certain that much of the furniture that John and Sabine owned was also made of walnut wood.

At Canons Ashby, where John and Sabine often stayed, one of the walls was hung with 'a painted cloth of Pavia and another of Mars'.[27] Tapestry proper, loom-woven, and as lovely as *La Dame à la Licorne*, was the prerogative of the rich, and seldom found in small country houses. John's Flemish partner, Michel Mulier, shipped two pieces from Antwerp to Lynn, which were doubtless destined for some aristocratic household; similarly, the great tapestry hangings shipped in the *Salvator of Venice* in 1553, illustrating the Story of Poetry, Absalom and Tamar, and the Story of Saul (the size of the *atelier* where they were made can be seen from the number of identical pieces), were clearly for the *sala* of some Spanish nobleman. Far less expensive to buy were the 'piece of white say, and another piece of honest sad blue say . . . both of the best making that is made for hangings' that Otwell ordered from Antwerp, and which cost about 20s. Fl. apiece. Painted linens were cheaper still, and a French visitor to England in 1558, Monsieur Perrin, commented on the widespread use that was made of them.[28] Sabine was fond of painted linens; they covered the bare plaster walls with brightness and colour, they shut out the draught, and they were cheap. The price was no small consideration when there were active children in the house. We find Otwell writing one December to tell his brother that 'the painted cloths are not yet amended where the colours were hurt, but against the next week I am promised to have them ready'.

Their floors were boarded with solid oak, or let in with flag-stones. Only the very richest could afford such wonderful work — the true product of the Renaissance — which John ordered from Antwerp, not for himself, but for Otwell's master, Sir John Gage. The order was sent through his own agent at Antwerp, Robert Tempest.

> I send you herein the pattern of a chapel of Mr. Comp-troller's of the King's House, which he would have paved, but before the paving-stones be provided, his desire is to know the charges thereof. By the pattern ye shall perceive that the place where the altar standeth is 8 foot broad and 20 foot long: that would he have paved with stones drawn with antiques of the best fashion. The middle place is 10 foot broad and 17 foot long: that would he have also with antiques-work, but not of so costly as the other, nor not both of one work. The nether place is 7 foot broad and 20 foot long: that he would have paved with plain stone, unwrought, of colour green and yellow. I pray you, the soonest ye can let my brother be certified what all will cost, and he shall again write you whether ye shall go through with it.

More than any other room in the house, the parlour was the centre of family life. Smaller than the great hall, it was easy to keep warm, and mostly faced south, with leaded panes that let in the sun and the light. It was the one room in the house where the family could be by themselves, and dine alone if they wished. Harrison relates that where tapestry, arras work, or painted cloths were not in use, the walls were 'ceiled with oak of our own, or wainscot brought hither out of the east countries, whereby the rooms are not a little commended, made warm, and much more close than otherwise they would be'.[29] John himself bought such wainscot panelling for Anthony Cave at King's Lynn, and he was so taken with them that the following year he shipped over a hundred panels for his own use in the *Neder Yere of Antwerp*. These were packed carefully into keels when they arrived at Lynn, sent down by water to Yaxley, and then by carrier to Glapthorn, where they were used to panel the parlour. The local carpenter was kept busy during the winter of 1550. 'To Kett for boarding of the parlour — 5s 4d' runs an entry in Thomas Egillsfield's account book. By spring the work was finished, and Sabine was delighted with the result. 'My parlour is well-nigh trimmed', she wrote to John. 'I trust it will be ready against your coming home.'

The complete refurnishing of the parlour was delayed during her visit to the Continent, but shortly after her return home '6 dozen of curtain rings, which cost 18d' were sent down to the manor house. At Canons Ashby the windows were hung with curtains of yellow say, but the colour that Sabine chose at Glapthorn was probably green, for on her waxed and polished oak floor was an oblong green carpet, four ells long and two ells broad. Floor carpets were becoming increasingly popular as ideas of comfort progressed, although sweet herbs and rushes were still strewn. The carpets came, of course, from Antwerp, and John several times received commissions to buy them for Anthony Cave and Christopher Breten. Chairs were prized possessions in the sixteenth century, and the parlour at Canons Ashby, although it was furnished with nine stools, could boast only one chair. John, however, was somewhat more addicted to comfort than his spartan cousin, for it was 'chairs' in the plural that were often sent to Sabine. These were probably box-type or cacqueteuse oak chairs, and must have been extremely uncomfortable to sit on, since upholstery did not come into general use until the seventeenth century, when matching sets of chairs first began to be made. The Stuart chairs, fashioned of walnut, with velvet backs and padded seats, appear positively luxurious beside the surviving monuments to Tudor endurance. Indeed, Sir John Harington, Queen Elizabeth's godson, said that the old-fashioned wainscot stools were 'so hard, that since great breeches were laid aside, men can scant endure to sit upon them'.[30] Cushions were used, of course, some of velvet, and others beautifully embroidered. It is pleasant to read that cushions were among the most frequent purchases for the manor house. A whole 'dozen of cushions' was once sent to Glapthorn from Flanders, and yet others were bought in London. Many of those at Glapthorn were made and embroidered by Sabine herself, for she was a most accomplished needlewoman.

Sabine's parlour was able to display an expensive clock, certainly a shelf of John's books, including Froissart and the Bible, and works of devotion — 'three stories of Scripture' were bought for John in 1547. At Canons Ashby there was a 'pair of tables of brazil with a lock, and men of box and brazil', probably a chessboard and chessmen to help while away the time; and also, for the entertainment of his guests, an 'old great Venice lute', one of those seductive, melon-shaped lutes like that of the Giorgione painting, and which lies athwart the step in Jan Steen's *Morning Toilet*. In the sixteenth century, no evening was complete without music and singing. John himself could play the lute, and he wrote the words 'lute-strings' on the back of one of his letters, as a reminder to buy some more. A painting also hung on the parlour wall at Glapthorn — the 'painted story of the Scripture' which Robert Andrew bought for John in Flanders at a price of 7s. Fl. One unusual feature of his cousin Cope's house was the large number of paintings there, including a portrait of Henry VIII, one of Mary Magdalen writing, another of Poverty, and of Lucretia Romana (the last two being valued at 3s. 4d. each). A sea picture hung on one of the walls in the parlour, and opposite it was 'Cabota his map', evidence of the owner's interest in exploration and the new-found world.

The parlour at Glapthorn was warmed by the traditional open fire, where the great logs burned for a week at a time, the ashes being raked out early in the morning and fresh kindling put in. Most of their fire-irons came from the workshops of the Low Countries and were made of wrought iron or shining brass, like the 'andirons, fire shovels and tongs' ordered by Anthony Cave. Wood fires and candlelight went together and, when the autumn evenings began to draw in, the housewife took her latten candlesticks from the cupboard.

> Provide for thy tallow ere frost cometh in,
> And make thine own candle ere winter begin.[31]

Candles were to be the sole source of light for reading and sewing for centuries to come, but candle-making was an odorous, time-wasting business. Despite Tusser's advice, Anthony Cave (and probably Sabine as well) preferred to buy supplies readymade from the Mortons of Oundle, rather than have the maids spend hours dipping tallow at home. The candles were of various weights and sizes: tall, fat ones that would burn almost an hour at a time, and slender tapers and rushlights to light the way to bed. The Oundle merchants would be called on to supply dozens at a time.

For my candle, I pray you speak to John Morton to make me 24 dozen. I would have of 4 in the lb, 6 in the lb, and 8 in the lb: of each 4 dozen, and the rest of smaller sorts; and that he will send them hither as shortly as he can, for I cannot tell how to send for them.

The warmest and most comfortable place to be in Tudor England was undoubtedly in bed, those huge four-posters with swelling bed-posts, vast testers and voluminous curtains that amaze all who gaze on them today. John went to a great amount of trouble over the great bed that he and Sabine were to sleep in at Glapthorn Manor, visiting the houses of his friends to see if he could decide which style he liked best, and trying to get it copied. His favourite was Armigill Wade's, but Otwell liked Sir John Gage's, then reposing at a merchant's house in Mark Lane.

Sir, this day in the morning I received your letter of the 12th of this month, wherein your only desire is that I should remember your bedstead of the fashion of Mr. Armigill's, which, forsooth, I have looked upon, and do not like it so well as that of my master's, which is here at Mr. Tate's house in Mark Lane. And therefore I have made no great haste to have caused one to be made at Calais, but suppose to have you better sped here in London, and better cheap, for Mistress Wade showed me that hers cost above 20s sterling the only bedstead, besides the hanging. And besides that, Nicholas, the joiner that should have been the workman for yours, is every day sick of a drunken axe during this hot weather, so that I have done nothing for the same at Calais, but I will cause some honest workman here to take the matter in hand, and perform it honestly to your mind, I doubt not.

When it was at last made and finished, the great bed was sent down to the country by cart, to be followed in 1544 by another that Robert Joiner had carved, and yet a third soon after that, to accommodate their guests.

Sprung mattresses did not exist in the sixteenth century, but a wool mattress was placed on top of the bed-boards, and would, if properly stuffed, have been warm and comfortable. On top of the mattress went the expensive feather beds, regarded as a luxury in the middle years of the century, and imported almost always from abroad. Otwell once reminded John 'not to forget a Brussels tick to furnish the roomth of your own bed', and John paid £2 6s. 8d. for 'two ticks and for making' which he ordered for Anthony Cave. They could be had cheaper than that, for he once imported six feather bed ticks for Sir John Gage, costing £2 10s. 7½d. There is no mention of sheets in the letters, but doubtless Sabine used them, as did most well-to-do people at this time. There were also long bolsters and down pillows, and woollen and fustian blankets, over which went the quilts and coverlets. 'My little house needeth two or three quilts to lay on beds this winter, if it please you to buy them', Otwell wrote to his brother abroad. One kind of quilt that was in vogue was the Spanish coverlet, such a 'coverlet white of Spanish felt' as John sent to his mother-in-law at Sibbertoft one winter, when she was ill, and also bought for Lady Brudenell at Deene. In the best bedrooms there were tapestry coverlets, 'in cypress chests my arras counterpoints',[32] such as Sir John Cope used at Canons Ashby.

Tudor bedhangings were often in the last degree magnificent. Shakespeare's 'valance of Venice gold in needlework'[33] might fitly describe the coral satin, embroidered in gold and silver, that adorns the King James's room at Knole (the original cost was £8000); and the Venetian Ambassador's room is sumptuous — sea-green Genoa velvet against gilded wood. Merchants, restrained by the depth of their purses, made do with 'blue velvet and tawny satin', like cousin Cope, or yellow satin with scarlet fringe. Otwell and Maria preferred arras blue say, with a matching colour-scheme of green and blue cushions. To every Tudor room has to be added the intimate personal belongings that express the personality of the woman who uses it. Sabine no doubt had her ivory combs and brushes, her looking-glass, cosmetic jars and trinket-box, 'basins and ewers to lave her dainty hands'.[34] There were presses in which she hung her silken, satin, and worsted gowns, shelves on which she laid her caps and gloves; there were the chests and coffers and chairs, Turkey carpets, velvet cushions, and bright flowers, roses and carnations, in slender glass vases.

We know that Sabine, like most women, loved flowers and gardening. She planned her garden at Glapthorn Manor long before the move took place and asked her brother-in-law to help her. Otwell duly visited the London seedsmen, buying quantities of 'seeds for my sister's new gardens', which were sent to the manor house in time for the spring sowing. Every spring after that, fresh consignments were sent to her from the City.

> In March and in April, from morning to night,
>   In sowing and setting, good housewives delight,
> To have in a garden, or other like plot,
>   To turn up their house and to furnish their pot.[35]

Gardening was already one of the chief English delights and vocations. Tudor gardens, with their curious knot-beds, their formal walks, shady pleached alleys, lawns and herb-plots are justly famous, and it was during this period that many decorative and useful plants were introduced from abroad. The gardening books of the time include elaborate instructions for growing window plants and herbs; and outdoors Sabine doubtless grew as many different flowers as she could obtain: primroses, violets, wallflowers and narcissus, columbines, paeonies, damask roses, larkspur, lilies and marigolds, sweet williams, carnations, pinks and snapdragons, and innumerable herbs, such as lavender, rosemary, and many more, which were used for medicinal as well as decorative purposes. Flowers were everywhere in England, and it was about this time that a visiting Dutchman wrote that 'their chambers and parlours strawed over with sweet herbs refreshed me; their nosegays finely intermingled with sundry sort of fragrant flowers in their bedchambers and privy rooms, with comfortable smell cheered me up, and entirely delighted all my senses'.

It was this same Dutchman who commented so favourably on the good order of English homes, 'the neat cleanliness, the exquisite fineness, the pleasant and delight furniture in every point for household, wonderfully rejoiced me',[36] and there is no reason to think that Glapthorn Manor fell short of this standard, for one has the impression throughout the letters that impatient, energetic Sabine was the last woman in the world to put up with dirt and dust in her home; the more credit to her. Whatever else might be lacking in her household, one feels sure that the floors were regularly washed and swept, clean rushes put down, the furniture polished, spotless bed- and table-linen used, and the whole house turned inside out at every spring-cleaning. It is, however, only fair to admit that in many places still, and certainly earlier in the century, England was not the cleanest of nations. Erasmus had many astringent remarks to make about the filthy state of English houses, and it is well known that Cardinal Wolsey was forced to hold a pomander to his nostrils when he passed through the palace courtyards, in order to avoid retching at the offensive stench, though the large size of royal and noble households was probably the root cause of this, since it made good housekeeping and proper supervision well-nigh impossible. Even in John's time, Anthony Cave was furious to find that his London house had, through a misunderstanding, been let, 'knowing the demeanour of men's servants, that in their near friends' houses will do many displeasures, so that I fear many inconveniences shall ensue . . .' The Tudors suffered much from vermin because of their lack of cleanliness and disinfectants, and fleas, bugs and lice abounded in the wooden walls and floors, in the wardrobes and presses. Tusser gave what was clearly commonplace advice on how to deal with them.

> While wormwood hath seed, get a handful or twain,
> To save against March to make flea to refrain,
> Where chamber is sweeped and wormwood is strown,
> No flea for his life dare abide to be known.[37]

The lack of sanitation and good drainage systems inevitably complicated matters, and in many places a state of nature prevailed. In the towns, despite the regulations of the municipal authorities, all the household refuse was dumped in the streets, and mounds of filth bestrewed the roads. Otwell's vivid remark is redolent of the age he lived in: 'The more that dirt is moved, the worse it stinketh.' Privy and cesspool were the rule, and every house contained its quota of pewter chamber-pots; Otwell sent two down to the manor house on one occasion. The water-closet, invented at the end of Elizabeth's reign by her brilliant godson, Sir John Harington, was destined to remain in utter oblivion for centuries, until the discerning pioneers of the Victorian age brought it into universal use among civilized people. But even with all the handicaps, those who had a mind to be clean and fastidious, would be. It is interesting to see that when John asked Henry Southwick to commission a military tent for Sir Thomas Brudenell, he stipulated that there must be room for the jaques.

Mr. Brudenell, my friend, hath desired me to provide a round tent, such one as I bought two years past for my uncle

Sir Ambrose Cave. Whether ye have the same in remembrance or not, I cannot tell, but I shall heartily desire you to be a mean to help him to one, sent to London the soonest may be. As I remember, it should be 24 foot wide, made with a place for a jaques joining to the tent . . . My uncle Ambrose's cost me 12 angels, but Mr. Brudenell is content to give an angel more to have it well done . . . Mr. Brudenell's colours be blue and red, which I pray you let be the colours of the fringes; and that ye disburse I will repay you with thanks where it shall please you to appoint me.

Laundry was one of the greatest problems in a house as full of people as Glapthorn Manor. In London there were professional laundresses, descendants of the fifteenth-century Beatrice le Wimplewasher and Massiota la Lavendere,[38] but country households had to rely on themselves alone. Fortunately at Glapthorn Manor a stream ran through the meadows near the house, and the linen could be washed in the running water, beaten clean with big wooden bats by the maids, their sleeves rolled up to their elbows. There was also a well in the courtyard from which the water was drawn in buckets, to be heated in great copper cauldrons like the one John supplied to his friend, Parson Mowyer of North Kilworth. Weighing nearly 25 lb., it must have been no small work to fill and heat. While in fine weather large quantities of washing could be pegged out in the sun and wind to dry, it would have taken days in the cold, damp winter months, and for this reason it was the practice in most households to put the dirty linen on one side, and have one or two big washes a year. A letter written by a certain George Pierpoint (no connection of the Johnsons) seems to confirm this custom. His wife, he told his brother, was sending various things for a new baby, including

. . . her christening laces, her best bearing-sheet, such as they be, and a pair of her best sheets, one of the which my wife occupied at her last lying-in, the which is clean, and hitherto forgotten to be washen. But she hath sent them both because ye shall perceive she doth mean well. She would desire, when the said two sheets hath been occupied as ye think good, she might have them home unwashen, because this is an evil time of the year to dry and make linen white in.

To help her with all the work of the house, Sabine had plenty of maids. The sixteenth century was an age when cheap domestic servants abounded; John and Sabine had seldom to visit the hiring fairs, for girls were only too anxious to go into service with a good master and mistress. Months before they arrived at Polebrook parsonage, they received a letter from William Howham, who wanted them to employ his daughter.

Jesus.

Sir, in my best manner I recommend me unto you, and to my mistress, heartily desiring God of your good welfare. Sir, I understand that you intend, by the grace of God, to be resident and dwelling in this country. Sir, I have a daughter which hath been at service three or four year in the country, and broken with all works for a woman to do, and now of late she is comen home after her term. If you be unprovided, I would be glad it might be you to have her; and by my faith, if I did know any vice or conditions by her, she should not come. And I pray you of answer hereof, for unto such time as I hear from you, she shall not be fast with no man. I would that it would please you to have her. No more, but Our Lord send you of his grace, Amen. At Peterborough, on Fast Tuesday, anno 1542.

By your that I can,
William Howham.

To John Johnson, merchant of the Staple at Calais, be this delivered at London.

There is no telling whether William Howham's daughter was engaged or not: probably she was, for a new household could always use a willing servant. All those who were employed at Glapthorn Manor a few years later, in 1550, are mentioned by name in Thomas Egillsfield's account-book. The most important in a manor house like Glapthorn was, of course, the cook, the 'best woman servant' capable of taking charge of the 'whole housekeeping',[39] who could 'bake, brew, make white bread and malt, and able to oversee her servants'.[40] In the rich and aristocratic households, the cook was often a man, sometimes even the 'musical-headed' French chef beloved by the Elizabethans.[41] Good cooks were as difficult to come by then as now, and Anthony

Cave's wife had the utmost trouble in finding one (or rather, Otwell did) for Tickford House.

> Your letter of the first of this month (loving brother) I received yesterday of my brother Richard. And for the young man cook you write of, that Mistress Cave spake unto me for, you shall understand that he can in nowise be had of his master because he hath not above three years to serve of his prenticehood, and there is none other in the house but he and another unthrifty roper of any bigness, to do him any good service: which thing I pray you declare unto Mr. Cave, with my hearty commendations unto him and to his wife, according to my duty, being very sorry that I can do them no pleasure in this behalf.

In Sabine's household, Joan Cook had charge of the kitchen. Her wages to us seem appallingly low, as indeed they were: twenty-one shillings a year, and all found. As she apparently received no money allowance for the livery she wore, her petticoats and kirtles, and aprons and hose and shoes were doubtless given to her by Sabine. Mistress Joan was often hard up, for in June 1550 she received an advance of two shillings on her wages, and another two shillings in July, and not until October was she paid the two-and-fourpence due to her 'for full payment of her quarter wages due at Michaelmas last'. A decade or so later, the Northamptonshire Justices were to allow a maximum wage of twenty shillings a year to a servant of Joan's standing, with an allowance of six-and-eightpence for livery.[42] They permitted the second woman servant of a household, less skilled in matters of housekeeping, a wage of eighteen shillings a year, with five shillings for her livery; and in Sabine's house it was Richard Preston's wife who came nearest to this sum, with the fourteen shillings paid her 'for her wages due the first in September'. There seems little doubt that this was her yearly wage; had it been only six months' money, she would have been earning more than her husband. There were two other maidservants at the manor house, but their wages were far below the top rates allowed to the 'mean drudge' of the Justices' report, for they at least could earn ten shillings a year and their livery. At Glapthorn, Bess Bainton received 'for her wages, 6s., for her livery 6s.', while Bess Horseley was paid six-and-eightpence a year, her clothes being given to her by

Sabine. There were also two young girls in the house, probably under eighteen, whose names were 'Marie' and 'Doretie'. They were too young to be paid wages, but naturally their clothes and food were found, and perhaps a little pocket-money given them occasionally. Entries by Thomas Egillsfield record two pairs of shoes being bought for them from the local shoemaker, at a shilling the pair. To help in emergencies, such as spring-cleaning, sheep-shearing, harvest and Christmas, women would come up from the village and give a hand. Samson's wife came up one December, and did ten days' work at a penny a day.

The maidservants worked hard, getting up at dawn in summer, and almost as early in winter, and they were kept busy all day at housework and kitchenwork and dairywork, in sewing and mending and spinning, and the hundred-and-one tasks that have to be done in a big house. Because of their status in life, and the little money they earned, only the simplest enjoyments of life could come within their reach. In some houses, like Sir John Harington's, where the master and mistress were strict, they were fined when they were late, or when the beds were not made to time, or when they were heard to swear. But most houses were not so organized and gloomy, and in some the maidservants managed to have fun, in spite of their poverty. When Jane Villiers was staying with Sabine, after Evangelist had been born, she received a note from her husband that must have made her return home with all speed, as fast as her mare could carry her. It is not, of course, improbable that Clement, feeling slightly neglected, should have intended just that.

> Wife ... I have much ado to rule my slumber, for my maids doth rise in the morning by the bull belling, and I by nine of the clock; and our cheese is put together by two of the clock; and our hens fly up to the rooster by four of the clock; and your maids' lattice pellets fly at midnight! And thus fare you well until your return.

Perhaps the best picture of the Tudor maidservant, her life and her work, comes in a poem written by a man who was only a few years younger than John himself. It is a charming poem,[43] and it rings with remembered truth, a portrait of some willing country girl he knew when he was young, some Marie or Doretie of years gone by.

With merry lark this maiden rose,
And straight about the house she goes,
With swapping besom in her hand;
And at her girdle in a band
A jolly bunch of keys she wore;
Her petticoat fine laced before,
Her tail tucked up in trimmest guise,
A napkin hanging o'er her eyes,
To keep off dust and dross of walls,
That often from the windows falls.
Though she was smug, she took small ease,
For thrifty girls are glad to please;
She won the love of all the house,
And pranked it like a pretty mouse,
And sure at every word she spake,
A goodly curtsy could she make;
A stirring housewife everywhere,
That bent both back and bones to bear.
She never sleeped much by night,
But rose sometimes by candle-light
To card and spin, or sew her smock;
There could no sooner crow a cock,
But she was up, to sleek her clothes,
And would be sweet as any rose.
Full cleanly still the girl would go,
And handsome in a house also,
As ever saw I country wench.
She sweeped under every bench,
And shaked the cushions in their kind;
When out of order she did find
A rush, a straw or little stick,
She could it mend, she was so quick
About her business every hour.
This maid was called her mistress' flower.
She bare the keys of ale and beer,
And had the rule of better cheer.
She was not nice, nor yet too kind,
Too proud, nor of too humble mind,
Too fine, nor yet too brave, I trow.
She had, as far as I do know,

Two fair new kirtles to her back;
The one was blue, the other black.
For holy days she had a gown,
And every yard did cost a crown,
And more by eighteen pence, I guess;
She had three smocks, she had no less,
Four rails and eke five kerchers fair.
Of hose and shoes she had a pair;
She needed not no more to have;
She would go barefoot for to save
Her shoes and hose, for they were dear.
She went to town but once a year,
At Easter or some other day,
When she had licence for to play.
I had forgotten for to tell,
She had a purse she loved well,
That hanged at a ribbon green,
With tassels fair, and well beseen;
And as for gloves and knives full bright
She lacked not, nor trifles light,
As pins and laces of small cost.
I have to you rehearsed most
Of all her goods. Now to the form
And making of this creeping worm.
Her port was low, her face was fair;
It came no sooner in the air,
But it would peel, her cheeks were thin.
God knows she had a tender skin.
The worse mis-shape this minion had,
Her legs were swollen very bad;
Some heavy humour down did fall.
Her foot was narrow, short and small,
Her body slender as a snig;
But sure her buttocks were full big;
That came, I think, from sitting mich;
And in her side she had a stitch,
That made her oft short-winded, sure.
But her complexion was full pure.
She was well made from top to tail;
Yea, all her limbs, withouten fail,

Were fine and feat. She had a hand
There was no fairer in the land,
Save that with toil it changed hue.
Her fingers small, her veins full blue;
Her nails a little largely grown;
Her hair much like the sun it shone;
Her eyes as black as jet did seem;
She did herself full well esteem.
Her lips were red, but somewhat chapped.
Her tongue was still and seldom clapped.
She spake as she were in a cloud,
Neither too soft nor yet too loud,
And tripped upon the floor as trim,
Ye would have thought that she did swim
As she did go, such was her pace.
She minced fine, like Mistress Grace,
That at the Dagger dwelled once,
Who made good pies of marrow-bones.
I dare depose upon a book,
She was as good a maiden cook,
As ever dressed a piece of meat;
And for a banquet, small or great,
And raising paste, she passed still.
As soon as flour came from the mill,
She made the goodliest cakes thereof,
And baked as fair a household loaf,
As e'er was seen or set on board.
What needs more talk? At one bare word,
The greatest lady in a shire
She might have served seven year.

CHAPTER 5

THE PLEASURES OF THE TABLE

F OOD is a magic word, for it is the means whereby life is sustained. We can, if we must, do without many things on earth, but if we are denied food, we die. To eat is therefore a necessity, but to eat well is both a delight and a blessing, and indeed has always been esteemed so from generation to generation. Foremost among those who enjoyed good food and wine were the Tudors, and it may be doubted if even our Victorian grandparents brought such a fresh and lively interest to the pleasures of the table. They ate, of course, far too much; the amount of food they consumed at one sitting would be fabulous by any standards and, in comparison with the austere menus of to-day, almost beyond the reach of the imagination. Philip Stubbes, writing at the end of the sixteenth century, remarked that 'Nowadays, if the table be not covered from one end to the other as thick as one dish can stand by another, and to every dish a several sauce appropriate to his kind, it is thought unworthy the name of a dinner',[44] and the menus of contemporary banquets, the recipes of Tudor cook books, and the everyday provision of the Bouche de Court, provide ample proof of his statements. No noble household would have thought itself worthy of the name unless it sat down, not only to 'beef, mutton, veal, lamb, kid, pork, cony, capon, pig or so many of these as the season yieldeth, but also red or fallow deer, beside great delicates wherein the sweet hand of the sea-faring Portugal is not wanting',[45] not forgetting innumerable dishes of sea and freshwater fish, salads and fruit. During the 1540s, however, when the cost of living was rising by leaps and bounds every year, it is doubtful if ordinary middle-class families could possibly have provided on such a lavish scale every day. 'Gentlemen and merchants keep about one rate,' wrote Harrison, 'and each of them contenteth himself with four, five or six dishes, when they have but small resort, or peradventure with one or two, or three at the most, when they have no strangers to accompany them at their tables.' Most merchants dined at noon, after an early breakfast of bread, ale and meat, and they sat down to supper at six o'clock in the evening, especially those who had acquired the sophisticated London manners. By Harrison's time they were wont to begin their meals always with a fresh salad, and end with a dessert of 'fruit and conceits'.

To the Johnsons, no less than to their friends and relations, it is clear that food was one of the main interests of life, and one of the most absorbing topics of conversation. Not that this is surprising, for though Glapthorn Manor was one of the smaller manor houses of the neighbourhood, upwards of twenty people sat to table three or four times a day, winter and summer, year in and year out, and all of them had to be fed. Small wonder that the most important room in the house, its very heart and hive of activity all day long, from dawn to dusk, was the kitchen, presided over by Mistress Joan Cook.

The present-day visitor to the Pavilion at Brighton is filled with awe at the sight of the *batterie de cuisine*, row upon row of gleaming copper saucepans, frying pans, omelette pans and sauté pans, stewpans and fish kettles, soufflé dishes, aspic and blancmange and jelly moulds, pudding and pastry and patty tins that line the walls beneath the Prince Regent's slender and elegant palm trees. The Tudor kitchen could hardly rival such wonderful equipment, and yet Sabine's 'battery ware' as it was called even in those days, was doubtless the best that John could procure for her in England and Flanders. The kitchen at the manor house was certainly more labour-saving in one respect than that at the Palace of Hampton Court, for there most of the cooking was done on the row of brick ovens, but at Glapthorn there was the big 'oven of metal' which John imported from Antwerp at a cost of four nobles, not counting the cost of carting the cumbersome thing half way across England. There was also, of course, an open range at Glapthorn Manor, with the inevitable turnspit for the roasts; and besides that, the brick bread oven, big enough to take the great faggot of wood that was put in, lighted and left to burn through, before the ashes were raked out and the loaves put in to bake in the warmth. Sabine's smaller kitchen utensils were varied enough, and she possessed gridirons and cauldrons, hanging kettles and colanders, brass and copper boiling pans, frying pans, saucepans and skillets of different sizes. Doubtless many of the wares that John brought over from the Low Countries found their way into her kitchen. His journal entry for October 26th, 1543, records the following cargo:

Battery ware oweth for accounts kept in Calais,
and is for the sum of £10. 2s. 2d Fl. by Henry
Southwick in the Sinxon Mart paid for certain
battery bought at Antwerp by my commission,
and sent to London in September last. To wit, for
two cauldrons and eight pans, poise together
196 lb, at 7d Fl. the lb, sum £5. 14s. 4d Fl. Item,
for six hanging kettles, poise 44½ lb. at 7d le lb,
26s; for two copper pots with iron feet, poise 23 lb.
at 5d the lb, 9s 7d; for six brazen pots, poise 127
lb at 4d the lb, 42s 4d; for six iron bands for the
six hanging kettles, poise 50 lb at 1½d the lb,
6s 3d; for charges of them, and for a rope and
maund thereto, 3s 8d.
Sum in mere sterling, accounting 26s Fl. for the
pound sterling, for so went th'exchange . . .   £7 15s 6d

Sabine also possessed pewter and horn spoons and ladles of
every description, and many different sorts and sizes of knives. We
find Otwell on one occasion sending a pair of chopping knives to
Sabine, and know that her mother once bought her two basins of
latten at Harborough Fair. In the cool larder stood deep wooden
meal-tubs and flour-barrels, salting tubs and earthenware pre-
serving jars; and in the cellars below, the barrels of wine and
rondlets of ale and beer were stored. Outside were the brew-
house, where the ale was made, and the storehouses, kept under
strong lock and key (like Mrs. Cave's), where supplies of dried,
preserved, pickled and barrelled food of every kind were kept, with
immense quantities of general provisions. If a Tudor household
ran short, there was no running down to the village shop to buy
what they wanted. Good housekeeping in the sixteenth century
required an amount of practical forethought and planning undreamed of today, except in the remoter parts of the world. It
goes without saying, of course, that to run such a kitchen, and
cook for so many people as at Glapthorn Manor, called for a vast
amount of time and energy and hard work on the part of cook and
maids. There were no labour-saving devices. Every scrap of water
for cooking and washing had to be drawn up in buckets from the

courtyard well, and every stick of wood used in the fires and ovens had to be chopped, stacked and gathered by hand.

Good food and wine were in later years the rule at Glapthorn Manor, and Christopher Breten was wont to make pointed comparisons between the 'poor fielden fare' in his own home, and the delicious meals to be had at the manor house. But it seems that during the first years of Sabine's married life she was not greatly interested in cooking. Impatient by nature, it probably irked her to have to spend hours closeted with Joan Cook, or bent over the stove, in order to produce something that was eaten in a matter of moments, and with nothing to show for the effort except a row of empty trenchers. Clearly she thought there were more pleasant things to do in life than cook. And then there occurred the incident which seems to have changed her whole approach. Early in 1545, John took a new apprentice, a London boy by the name of Pratt. A sophisticated lad, perhaps a little spoiled, the darling of his mother's heart, he arrived at Glapthorn to find that no one was particularly interested in him or his doings, and that the comforts he had enjoyed at home were conspicuously lacking, especially food. He had not been there many days before he wrote a long letter to his mother, complaining bitterly that he was not getting nearly enough to eat. The anxious lady at once rushed over to see John at Lime Street, and after what must have been an extremely awkward interview, John wrote home to Sabine.

Your young gentleman, Master Pratt, hath complained by his letter to his mother that he lacketh both meat and drink, as well his breakfasts, as also at meals not sufficient. All your menservants have been of counsel with him, for they be of no less opinion, declaring that your bread is not good enough for dogs, and drink so evil that they cannot drink it, but are fain when they go into the town to drink to their dinners. If ye know they complain with cause, I pray you see it amended: if they complain without cause, let them seek new masters and boarding. I pray you, try out this matter by examining of them each alone by themselves that ye may know the truth, and then ye may keep and put from you whom ye think good, and that ye perceive to be faulty. I shall be content, for I will keep no such servants. Some of your servants report that no gentleman's house is so evil ordered as ours. If ye examine

Jasper and Ferne well, by them I think ye shall come to the best trial of the matter.

Sabine's feelings when she received John's letter can easily be imagined. If the servants had indeed been gossiping over half the countryside, then her reputation as a good housewife was lost for ever. Human nature is frail at the best of times, and Tudor society was nothing if not provincial and narrow-minded. There was nothing better calculated to enliven conversation at the dinner-tables of the gentry and coarse jokes at the alewives' benches than the news that John and Sabine, wealthy and pious as they set up to be, were so gloriously mean with their money, so penny-pinching over food, that they well-nigh starved their servants and apprentices to death. In all the circumstances, Sabine could think of nothing better than to follow John's advice. She summoned the servants to her one by one, questioned Master Pratt and Richard Preston, and then sat down to reply to John.

As for Master Pratt's complaint, I can find nobody in fault but himself, and he doth deny that he did write any such things but lack of meat and drink. If three meals a day in winter and four in summer be not sufficient, I would his mother had him, that she might feed him every hour. I will have all my house to say with me that he had his breakfast, his dinner and supper all well eaten. Lying Master Pratt could say before Richard came home that he did know of the making of his letter, the which when Richard came home, he clear denied.

So determined was Sabine to prove that she kept a good table, that her bread was the equal of any woman living, and that no one in her household was starved of food that, when she had finished her letter, she went down to the kitchen, called for wheaten flour, yeast and milk, and baked a whole batch of new bread with her own hands. When it was done to her satisfaction, she packed the fragrant loaves in cloth and gave them, still warm from the oven, to the astonished carrier of Glapthorn, and told him to take them to London as soon as he could, so that she could prove the truth of her words to the boy's mother. Tactful Otwell, however, ate the bread himself, and did not show it to Mrs. Fisher because, as he explained, her anxiety was now quieted and the matter forgotten. But unpleasant as the affair was, it bore good fruit. From that time onwards there were no complaints of the food at the manor house, and Sabine seems to have developed a genuine interest in cooking.

Indeed there was no reason why their food at most seasons of the year should not have pleased the most fastidious palate, for all of it was fresh and home-grown, except for the occasional luxuries that came from London and abroad. Their bread was made from the wheat and rye that stood in their own fields at Glapthorn and Polebrook, stone-ground in their own mill, and risen with yeast out of their own ale-vats. Their milk and butter and cheese came fresh from the dairy, with eggs from Sabine's hens; their fish came from the swift-flowing Nene or the Fens, and much of their fruit from their own orchards. Their own herds gave them all the meat they needed; they had beef, mutton and pork in plenty, although it is true that they ate fresh meat only in summer. After the autumn killing they had to eat salt meat all winter long until the spring again, helped out by rabbits from the warren, and such game as there was in the woods. The roast beef of old England did not in fact become a reality until the eighteenth century, after Turnip Townshend had preached the use of root crops as winter feed for cattle.

Presents of food were always acceptable in the sixteenth century, and whenever there was anything specially good to eat, the Johnsons always shared it. 'Give my sister your wife hearty thanks for the puddings and pork that she hath sent us', wrote Otwell one December. A pig had been killed, and Sabine was busy helping her maids at the salting-tub, and curing the sides of bacon in the smoke-house, to provide breakfasts and dinners for the house, for even in the sixteenth century, bacon and eggs was a favourite dish. 'My wife sendeth unto Mistress Baynham a flitch of bacon for her and you', wrote John to a friend in Calais. 'I would have sent you eggs also, but for fear of making of caudles by the way.' Another dish of which they were particularly fond was brawn, for, although it was extremely indigestible, it made a welcome variation on the continual salt beef and mustard sauce of the winter months. 'Brawn of the baiting' was what Anthony Cave frequently served to his household. The unfortunate animals were baited to death with what seems unfeeling and useless cruelty; but the Tudors thought beef uneatable otherwise, and they were in any case not over-sensitive. Even John, who as we know was a most religious man, thought it no shame to attend bull-baitings (as his journal reveals), and he was probably equally addicted to the bear-ring and cockfighting. All these unamiable diversions appealed strongly to the sixteenth century, and for generations after that. Only gradually have the civilized arts taken hold of man's imagination.

Sabine often sent vessels of brawn to Otwell in London, and to Mrs. Baynham at Calais, and one of the most delightful letters in existence is Margaret Baynham's letter of thanks to John for a Christmas present of brawn and beer.

> Jesus, the 30 day of December,
> anno 1543, at Calais.

Master Johnson, in my most heartiest manner that I can, I recommend me unto you, and to Mistress Johnson your good bedfellow; very glad to hear of your good health, which I pray God long to continue to his pleasure.

And the cause of my writing unto you at this time is to certify you that I have received from Mr. Smith, two barrels of beer and a rondlet of brawn which you and Mr. Cave hath sent me, most heartily thanking you both for the same. And according to Mr. Smith's writing, I have delivered to Mr. Armigill Wade a shield of the brawn, and to Henry Southwick two rounds, for the which they do heartily thank you, and have them heartily commended unto you, and to good Mistress Johnson. There was never thing came better to pass, for it come into my house upon Christmas Even, and was delivered incontinently.

Good Mr. Johnson, I am very sorry that I have no good thing to send you, but thus you bind me to be your bedewoman and ever shall so long as I live, for I have great cause: I pray God (I may) be able to recompense somewhat your kindness hereafter; also I heartily thank you for this and many things more. I pray you, let me be commended to your brother Otwell, and to good Mr. Flecton. No more to you at this time, but Jesu have you in his most merciful keeping, and send you long life to his pleasure.

> By your own to th'uttermost of her power,
> > Margaret Baynham,
> > widow.

To the worshipful John Johnson, merchant of the Estaple at
Calais, this letter be delivered at Polebrook.

As for what Mrs. Baynham's present cost, John's journal entry
for January 20th, 1544, gives all the details:

> Expenses ordinary and extraordinary oweth for
> Thomas Smith, merchant of the Staple: and is
> for the sum of 38s 1d mere sterling paid by him for
> sundry petty parcels, as doth appear in his reckon-
> ing received the 13th in January. To wit, for a
> barrel beer sent Mistress Baynham, 4s 10d; for
> two shields and four rounds of brawn, 10s; for the
> vessel, 10d; for sousing ale and carriage to the
> ship, 2d; for Thomas Holland's horse here, 5s 8d;
> for a dozen sweet gloves, 6s; for two pair fine
> sweet gloves, 2s 8d; for brokerage of £190 by
> exchange, 7s 11d. Sum —   £1 18s 1d

Almost more than any other food, the Johnsons and their
friends loved venison, the strong-tasting flesh of the red deer that
roamed the English forests. As often as they could afford it, and
always when there were weddings or christenings in the offing, the
Johnsons would obtain a warrant for a fine buck or doe from one
of the royal parks, either employing one of the King's verderers to
kill it, or else shooting it themselves. Hunting was a favourite
sport with them. John handled the English longbow with ease and
accuracy, and, excellent marksman that he was, coached Christopher Breten, his lawyer brother-in-law, in the sport of archery,
lending him bows and sheaves of arrows to practise with. As a
good longbow could be bought for fourpence, it was an inexpensive
sport, and one to which most men were trained from their childhood. Otwell Johnson and Ambrose Saunders, on the other hand,
preferred to use their Antwerp-made handguns. They would all
go off in the early morning into the nearby forest, where they had
many a day's 'good sport' with their friends, bringing down a deer if
they could get it, or wildfowl, but apparently enjoying themselves
whether they were successful or not. And besides archery, they
hawked ('My uncle Brian Cave desires you to help him to a falcon',
wrote Sabine, when John was in the Low Countries), and coursed
the hare, 'poor Wat, far off upon a hill'.[46] They hunted any game

that was worth eating, but the red deer most of all. As Christopher Breten wrote to John:

> I kept your man long in the morning, upon trust I should have sent you a couple or two of our country bucks, or else does, but the keeper was not at home, so that my warrant could not be served. One that was in the house ye shall have by this bearer. I would it were the best stag in Sherwood.

How much they enjoyed their roasts of venison and venison pasties! 'The sweetest and best that ever I saw', were the words John used to thank his uncle Anthony Cave for a haunch of venison. In the lean years, when harvests were bad, there were always poachers busy in the forests, and the deer were hard to come by. 'Venison you should have if we could catch it,' wrote Sabine in the autumn of 1545, 'for you may believe me, I see none since you went from hence.' In the autumn of 1551, it was equally unobtainable. But the full measure of their liking for venison is best revealed in Thomas Flecton's plaintive letter to Sabine, written from Calais one miserable autumn day, when he was far from home.

> If wishing would take place for all your harvest, you should be here to take and know the fare your husband taketh here this hard season, for as now we must be content to live with poor fresh herring, French wine, sometimes woodcocks, partridges and small birds for fault of other victuals: for here we wish us some of your ale and fat venison, and of your good wine that is at Oundle.

During the sixteenth century, fish formed a great part of everyone's diet for, despite the coming of the Reformation, Friday was still a universal fast day, and throughout Lent the whole population lived almost exclusively on fish, with the addition of whitemeats — eggs, butter and milk. Only those who were fortunate enough to live by the sea could enjoy fresh saltwater fish like plaice and sole, halibut and haddock, codling and shrimps, crabs and oysters. Glapthorn Manor, in the heart of Northamptonshire, had to rely largely on the comparatively tasteless freshwater fish, the pike and tench that darted about the stewpond near the house. We find John one December ordering several wagon-loads of live fish for Anthony Cave from a local fishmonger, Rayner of Peterborough, which were to be sent in time for the Twelfthtide festivities:

> . . . In the same two or three horseload he would have of fifteen or sixteen pickrels, five or six tenches, and the rest of breams; and although some of the pickrels pass not 15 or 16 inches, he forceth not thereof, and doth not mistrust but that ye will serve him at as reasonable prices as ye may, and as he may be served of other.

There was also the smoked or salt fish that Otwell and John bought in London and abroad. Eels came down from the City barrelled in vinegar for Lent; a 'tub of conger' would be sent, sometimes ling, and the inevitable 'Aberdeen fishes' — the salt cod, stockfish, or Poor John of a thousand hoary Tudor jokes. When John was in Flanders Anthony Cave wrote to him specially to provide 'a hundredweight of such stockfish as I bought at my being there, for me'. Herrings, of course, they adored, and ate them smoked, dried, salted and soused in vinegar. Sprats were a great delicacy, like the expensive locatur and white herring from Zealand, but the favourite was the 'puissant red herring', Greene's 'red herring of red herring's Hal', their standby at all times of the year. The aristocrats of the fish world were, then as now, salmon and sturgeon, and the price was so high that it was out of reach of all save the rich. Anthony Cave, whose tastes were little short of epicurean, was prepared to pay almost anything for it. 'Remember my sugar and spices,' he wrote to John, 'and half a good sturgeon of 40s sterling price — cut not the rounds too thick.' He was willing to pay up to £5 10s. for a whole fish. Even in wartime, nothing was permitted to interrupt the supply of Cave's sturgeon and, when it was forbidden to export food from Flanders, John managed to 'pack the half-sturgeon that I have bought you in a maund, with other sturgeon of Mr. Kyrton's', and to ship it home via Zealand.

Since their food was, it must be admitted, often monotonous for weeks on end in winter, Tudor cooks did their best to impart flavour with spices and seasoning, which they used in far larger quantities than at any time since. There is the further point that their food was often not very fresh, and spices had to be used to disguise the taint. The buck that Otwell sent to Calais for Richard's wedding must have been extremely high when it arrived, after several weeks of travelling, and only the use of quantities of new black pepper could have made it palatable. Spices were fairly easy to obtain at this time. Portuguese ships were making regular voyages to the East round the Cape of Good Hope, by-passing the Turkish corsairs of the Mediterranean, and bringing home their rich cargoes to Lisbon and Antwerp. Richard once wrote to John of the varied assortment that Anthony Cave wanted for Christmas.

My master . . . desireth you to send him the particulars of all things which ye bought for him in Flanders, for he saith that he hath not received divers of those things which he gave you remembrance to buy: as rysselles worsted, hops, sugar, dry marmelade and other things; wherefore he prayeth you to advertise him if ye have not bought them, for he will himself make provision.

My master hath further willed me to write you all the parcels which he received of my brother Otwell, being 12 lb pepper, 1 lb cloves, ½ lb maces, 1 lb grains, 1 lb nutmegs, 2 lb ginger, a green carpet, a lb cinnamon, a box of dry succade, a tonnekin of succade.

John and Sabine were particularly fond of olives and capers to flavour their mutton and beef, and several times a year they were ordered and shipped home from Flanders. 'I would gladly have two tonnekins of capers of 2 lb apiece, and a quarter of olives,' he wrote to Robert Andrew, 'but I would have the capers small and fine, of 7 or 8 stuvers the lb.' For common cooking purposes, they used salt, the fine white salt from the Bay of Brouage, and the coarser grey salt, and malt and wine vinegar, and also crab-apple juice — verjuice as they called it.

Sabine, like everyone else in the country, kept ducks and chickens, both for the table and for eggs, although these only cost three or four a penny to buy, and sometimes were cheaper than that. She would often send poultry to John and Otwell in London, and her own friends and relations frequently used to send geese and fat capons to the manor house as small remembrances. Anthony Cave took a lively interest in his poultry-yard, as a letter from his servant, George Grant, shows.

Mistress Karkeke hath her heartily recommended to your

mastership; and for the chickens she says they shall be ready for you of the first brood, and by the grace of God you shall have of your hen as good if it please God, for your hen had when I was at Tickford four, the which was fair, God send them good fortune and well to come forward.

Pigeons were prime favourites. 'You shall receive by this bringer twelve pigeons', wrote Sabine to John. 'If I had any more you should have them.' They often had pigeon pie for dinner, for Polebrook parsonage, only a mile or two away from the manor, had its own dovecots. The parson, however, also happened to be fond of pigeons, and once, when Sabine was away from home, he refused to allow Richard Preston to have any. 'The priest sent word I should have none: knaves should eat none', wrote the aggrieved Preston, but eventually the parson gave in, and 'six pigeon pies, and twelve pigeons not baked' were packed in a basket and sent to London. Otwell, before he married, had cause to bless Sabine's generosity. Her thoughtful presents of food must have been a considerable help in varying the monotony of his diet, and he once wrote to John, asking him to convey his thanks 'to my sister your wife for my pigeon pasties, which Atkins this bearer now brought me, and many other things at other times'.

There were many other birds, snared in the fields and woods, which made a welcome addition to the menu, partridges, woodcocks, widgeons, wild duck, snipe, teal and plover; and, since they were so near to the Fens, the Johnsons often ate wildfowl. 'To one that brought wildfowl from Yaxley — 1s', and 'To one that brought a swan — 1s', are two entries, taken at random, from Thomas Egillsfield's account-book. A present of a couple of young crane from the father of one of John's apprentices was by no means despised, and indeed it seems that the Tudors had few qualms about eating anything, provided they could digest it. Singing birds sweet may have been admired in the springtime, but they were eaten without a pang all through the year. Larks were considered a great delicacy and used to arrive a dozen at a time at the manor house, while blackbirds were hardly less enjoyed. 'You shall receive by this bringer a dozen and a half of as good blackbirds as ever you had', wrote Sabine one December day, and implying that a great treat was in store for her husband.

But of all table birds, quail was the favourite. 'I trust I shall have quails shortly to make fat against my uncle Anthony and my aunt comen.' Sabine reminded John when he was in Calais. Taken in the early summer in the lowland country of Flanders and France, the birds were put on sale in Calais market-place, and shipped over to England in great wicker baskets, equipped with water and hempseed for the journey. All who could possibly afford to buy them did so, and never a year passed without a consignment for the Johnsons, who, however, used to give many of them away as presents for their friends. Sir John Gage and Sir John Croke, and Sir Ambrose and Brian Cave were among the chosen recipients. But Otwell was just as fond of them as the rest of the family, and he invariably reported that a dozen or so had 'shrunk in the waiting' before they arrived at Glapthorn Manor, as Richard Sandell's letter reveals.

At London, the 18th in June, 1547.

Worshipful Sir, it may please you to understand that by th'enclosed of my master's you may perceive that he wrote you that Atkins would not carry your quails. But this morning he came to my master, and he entreated him to carry them, and now by him your mastership shall receive in a cage 11 dozen and 6 quails. And my master hath kept here 7 dozen: 3 dozen for my Lord Cromwell, 2 dozen for Mr. Serjeant Saunders, and 2 dozen for Mr. Breten, which is the rest of your 20 dozen; and the other be dead and gone. With the quails there is four troughs, two long and two short, and a peck of hempseed. Thus in much haste I commit you to God, who ever send you and all yours good health.

By yours to command,
Richard Sandell.

To the worshipful Mr. John Johnson, merchant of the Staple of Calais, be this delivered at Glapthorn.

Next to bread, fish and meat, the staple articles of diet in the sixteenth century were butter, milk and cheese, and by tradition the dairy was the exclusive province of the housewife, for cows, like hens, thrive in a woman's care. As soon as she arrived at Polebrook parsonage, Sabine took over the dairy herd and, while she was still there, her brother Joseph bought her 'two kine' in return for 'say and other things for children's clothings' that she had purchased for him. During 1546, she spent £12 — no inconsiderable sum — on buying milch cows. To do this, she borrowed the money from John, promising to pay him back later. As with the egg-money, the profit from the dairy was the housewife's own, and if she could make it pay, so much the better for her.

From April beginning, till Andrew be past,
   So long with good housewife, her dairy doth last,
Good milchcow and pasture, good husbands provide,
   The res'due good housewives knows best how to guide.

Ill housewife, unskilful to make her own cheese,
   Through trusting of others hath this for her fees,
Her milk pan and cream pot, so slabbered and sost,
   That butter is wanting and cheese is half lost.[47]

The dairy at Glapthorn Manor was equipped with proper cheese presses, cream bowls, milk pans and tubs, as it was at Polebrook. Some months before they moved into the parsonage house, Parson Saxby wrote and reminded John of what he needed.

Sir, the cause of this my writing unto you at this time is to certify you that you, or some other man for you, must provide for certain implements of household as concerning your cheese-making, for the tithe day for the gathering of milk shall be the 18th day of April next. Therefore you must needs have divers things: in primis, a cheese press with many cheese vats, linen cloths for to put the cheeses in, divers pans for milk, three or four cowls or tubs, and barrels to gather all your milk in; and you must have a horse and a car for to draw home your milk from two villages that is in Polebrook parish, with divers other things that belongs unto the milk-making that I cannot write you of. . . .

. . . And you must have some wood to make the cheese withal, for straw is not good for it, as ye say. And if you do intend to dwell there, you must provide for wood this summer fair: now there is many wood bales there, and you are best to write to Richard Morton to buy you some shortly, because of the fair weather and carriage.

At the manor house there were always milk and cream in plenty, with delicious fresh butter to their bread, and for cooking. Sabine often sent a 'dish of butter' to Otwell as a special treat. She was also a born cheese-maker. Much of her time was spent in the cool dairy, making the soft curd cheeses and the hard country cheese that John was so fond of. Very often in the letters we find Sabine sending her delicious round cheeses to both her brothers-in-law in the City, and to her friends at Calais, with careful instructions to Atkins the poulterer not to break them en route. 'They two cheeses that be scraped on the oven I take for the best,' she wrote on one occasion to John, 'but I would they were better; as so good as I find in my heart to send you.'

Like the dairy, the garden was also regarded by tradition as a feminine occupation and, as Sabine enjoyed gardening, the manor kitchen was doubtless well supplied with fresh vegetables. The walled Tudor kitchen gardens possessed a fair variety of plants, though naturally nothing like that of the present day, or even the seventeenth century. But they had cabbage and lettuces, radishes, beetroot, spinach and celery, wild carrots, beans, turnips and onions. A sackful of 'onions' and a 'little barrel, which I think is samphire' is recorded as being sent down to Glapthorn from the City. Samphire, of course, is the famous seaweed, esteemed as a great culinary delicacy, which used to be gathered off the Norfolk coast until late in Victorian times. Green peas they loved, and looked forward to the first picking with as much eagerness as we do today. Early one June, Otwell wrote to Sabine: 'For novelties in your country, I send you by this bearer a peck of green peas, having none other good thing at this present to recompense you with, for your good butter sent unto me before the holidays.' Potatoes had not yet been brought from America, and bread took the place of a 'filler' at every meal. Salads they greatly enjoyed, and on the back of a piece of paper we find that one of Otwell's apprentices, sent to do the marketing one morning for Maria, jotted down on a piece of paper the money he had spent: 'For bread, white and wheaten, 8d, for salad herbs and pot herbs, 2d.' Along with spices, the Tudors used a great variety of herbs in cooking: thyme and marjoram, fennel, chives, rosemary and bay leaves, parsley and purslane, sage and sorrel, to name only a few. As the years went by, and interest in gardening increased in England, stimulated by the work of the knowledgeable French and Dutch market gardeners in 'Sandwich, and Surrey, Fulham and other places',[48] more and more delicious vegetables were added to the housewife's list, including such exotics as artichokes, cucumbers and endive.

Tudor gardens contained a variety of fruits, although these were mostly of wild stock, and not the wonderful improved and hybrid varieties we enjoy today. There were gooseberries and barberries, raspberries and the sweet wild strawberries. It is pleasant to know that even the martyr Laurence Saunders loved strawberries, for he once referred to the 'dainty dish . . . of strawberries which come but once in the year'. Tusser exhorted the good housewife never to neglect her strawberry bed.

> Wife into thy garden and set me a plot
> With strawberry roots of the best to be got,
> Such growing abroad among thorns in the wood,
> Well chosen and picked prove excellent good.[49]

In the orchards grew cherries and plums and bullaces, medlars, mulberries and warden pears, even figs and vines and apricots in sheltered spots, and, of course, apples. A man from the village brought a whole bushel of crab-apples to Sabine one autumn, which she doubtless used for jelly and verjuice; and there was also the fruit from their own great orchard. 'I have received your letter and your apples, for the which I thank you.' Anthony Cave was writing in February, when apples are normally scarce: there was probably a cool, dry apple room at Glapthorn Manor, where the fruit could be stored all winter long if it was a good keeping variety. Besides the cultivated fruits, there were also the wild ones, the blackberries and sloes in the hedges and on the commons, the field mushrooms, and the autumn nuts — filberts from the nut-hedges, walnuts from the grove, and special treats like the 'maund with chestnuts' that came down from London.

A great deal of dried fruit came in from abroad, such as raisins, figs, prunes and dates, and with it quantities of ripe lemons and oranges, which the Johnson family adored. Every autumn, as soon as the ships came in from Spain, Otwell would go down to the wharves and bargain for them, hundreds at a time. Maria once sent Sabine a great sack of 'oranges, as many as this bringer could carry', and three whole boxes were sent down in 1548, in time for Faith's christening feast. Friends and relations in Calais were also remembered when the orange season came round, and Otwell was a generous giver. 'By William Spender abovenamed

I send you a white hand-basket with 200 oranges therein, and my mark thereon,' he wrote, asking John to present them to aunt Johnson and Bartholomew Warner. 'And my baskets I would be glad to have another time, for sending of oranges grieveth me.'

All the Tudors had a sweet tooth, and loved confectionery of every kind. 'I pray you, forget not my sugar,' wrote Sabine, when John was abroad, 'for if you do, you are like to have but sour sauce!' And Otwell besought his brother in similar terms. 'When you buy sugar and spice in Flanders for my sister your wife, remember our little London household (et pour cause, peradventure!).' Most of their sugar they bought abroad, rather than in London. The finest kind was the hard white sugar, packed in chests, that came from the Canaries and Madeira; and there were also sugar loaves, and sugar candy. 'Sir,' wrote John to his Antwerp agent, 'I am written unto from Mr. Cave my uncle, to provide him a pound of the purest green ginger that may be had, and a pound of the whitest sugar candy that may be had.' Both were wanted for Christmas fare: the green ginger was a sweetmeat in syrup, like the stem ginger in blue china jars of later years. John once paid 10s. 2d. for '2 lb green ginger given my mother Chantrell'. The succade they were so fond of would seem to have been a kind of orange conserve, and 'dry marmelade' was the famous quince conserve from Portugal, which they ate for dessert. They also ate quantities of boiled and suet puddings, good for keeping out the cold in winter, and egg custards and tarts, gingerbread and puff pastry and cakes of all kinds. Marzipan, made with ground almonds, rosewater and white of egg, was a favourite sweet, and Sir Hugh Plat, in his *Delights for Ladies*, gives recipes for the comfits that the Johnsons liked so well. Round caraway seeds and the aromatic seeds of the coriander were dipped in sugar, but as they needed from ten to twelve coats apiece, one understands why Sabine preferred to buy hers ready-made. They cost about a shilling a pound, and a '2-lb box of comfits', or 'four boxes of comfits' of different sorts, made by the skilled confectioners at Antwerp, were an infinitely better bargain than three hours spent over the hot stove while the seeds stuck together and the syrup candied in the saucepan.

According to the best medical advice of the time, water was not considered wholesome, 'sole by itself, for an Englishman to drink'.[50] Ale was by tradition the national English drink, and firkins of it were downed several times a day by every man, woman and child in the country. But already beer was rivalling ale in popularity. Early in Henry VIII's reign, hops were being grown in the eastern counties, and now vast quantities were imported every year from Flanders to ferment the home-brewed ale. At a penny the quart, beer was one of the cheapest drinks sold in tavern and alehouse, and the Johnsons consumed barrels of it with their cheese and brawn. Foreigners were wont to observe that English beer soon fuddled, and with such dragon's milk to nourish them, it is not surprising that Tudor Englishmen had the reputation of being able to drink even the stolid Dutch under the table. The double beer of which the Johnsons were so fond — three-ha'penny beer, they sometimes called it — contained twice the quantity of hops to the normal amount of liquid. It must have been unbelievably potent. 'You shall receive a kilderkin of our double beer,' wrote Otwell, 'marked on both the heads with your fell-mark, and directed unto you. When both your vessels are empty, send them again shortly after, and you may have them filled.'

But the favourite drink of all, both rich and poor, was wine. To the Johnsons, no meal would have been complete without the accompaniment of wine, and they drank it on every possible occasion, at any hour of the day or night — when company came, when they had a thirst, or when they felt nervous and in low spirits. Sabine liked nothing better than a glass of red wine 'to make merry withal'. John and Otwell, as wine importers, took care to keep their cellars stocked with the best they could buy, and hogsheads of 'good Gascon wine', with puncheons of sack, went jolting over the dusty roads to Glapthorn Manor. Their first choice was always the great wines of Bordeaux, the wine of the new season's vintage, fullbodied red wine — though white wine and claret was not despised — which was drunk fresh, and not left to mature in the cask. Even in those days certain vineyards were renowned for their soil and the quality of their wine, and the English merchants made every effort to close with the owners before their competitors got there. After the Bordeaux wines, the Tudors liked 'good French wine', the lighter wines from the Orleans country and Auxerre, although, according to John, these would never sell in the north of England, where only Gascon wine was liked. Anthony Cave had a special weakness for the Rhine wines, which John used to buy for him in Flanders. The sweet Mediterranean wines — the malmsey and muscadel brought in by the argosies — were much esteemed; and even more popular were the wines of Spain, the delicious bastard wine and sack, which the Johnsons enjoyed in abundant measure. Their capacity for wine seems to us literally incredible. It was nothing for John and his apprentice to drink two quarts of French wine a day in Calais, at the delightfully easy price of twopence a pint.

When the nation ate and drank as much as it did in the sixteenth century, it is perhaps not surprising that manners sometimes fell short of perfection or even grace. Fifteenth-century books of etiquette, for example, give very serious advice against burnishing bones with the teeth at table, or using one's knife as a toothpick, together with sundry other helpful hints that would appear somewhat redundant today. Apparently they were not so then, for even in 1558 Monsieur Perrin was raising his French eyebrows at the belching competitions which were all the rage at the tables of the aristocracy.[51] Eating, of course, did present certain technical difficulties. Knives and bread did yeoman service at the table for almost every dish; and one imagines that peas must have presented an almost insuperable barrier to the polite, unless they used their spoons. Knives were always bought by the pair, the price varying with the quality. John once paid 6s. 4d. for four pairs of knives, and 2s. 6d. for six pairs of a cheaper make. Anthony Cave paid 7s. 6d. for a dozen pairs on one occasion, but one pair of very fine workmanship cost him 2s. 4d. The 'pair of knives of three in a sheath' that Mrs. Fayrey sent to Sabine were probably for different courses of the meal. It is just possible that a pair could mean knife and fork, but not very likely, as forks were not yet in general use. As long ago as the early fourteenth century Piers of Gaveston had owned three silver forks for eating pears, but he was a solitary sport among the baronial types who surrounded him, and who certainly viewed his every action with extreme disfavour. Later, in the fifteenth century, someone is known to have possessed a fork for eating green ginger with. Italy was really the home of the fork, and not until late in Elizabeth's reign did it come into common use in England. But the Johnsons were intimately acquainted with many of the Italian merchants who lived in Lombard Street, and Maria and Sabine may well have liked the fastidious way of eating à l'Italien, and introduced the fork into their own homes.

Tudor table linen was superlatively fine, almost the quality of the double damask dinner napkins of the Victorian era. The inventory at Canons Ashby, where Sabine's cousin lived, lists twenty table-cloths, damask, plain and coarse, for the tables in the parlour, five table-cloths for the hall, and upstairs in the master's bedroom, locked away in the linen chest — Sabine used sea chests to hold her linen at Glapthorn Manor — were another fifteen table-cloths, as well as dozens of napkins, and fine hand-towels for the guests to wipe their fingers on, when the rosewater ewer and bowl was carried round. Although some excellent and industrious housewives, like Mrs. Baynham, spun and wove their own napery at home, most of that used at Glapthorn Manor came from abroad, and was either bought by the yard to be cut and hemmed, or else purchased ready-made. John bought quantities of table-linen for his own house, and for all his friends and relatives, whenever he visited Flanders, varying in quality from coarse to fine. Otwell once wrote to his brother: 'I have here diaper for a dozen of napkins of yours, which John my knave forgot to put into your male. I pray you, if they be not promised, let them be for this my poor London household, for I have need of such implements. It is but very coarse stuff, but good enough for me.' Needless to say, this was before his marriage to Maria. There is no doubt that the most beautiful napery came from Antwerp at this time, and so John thought when he asked Robert Andrew to buy and send over a special order for his friend Thomas Ashley, a close relative of Kate Ashley, the Princess Elizabeth's governess.

Copy of a letter to
Robert Andrew, at
Antwerp.
Jesus anno 1547, the . . . in March,
at Glapthorn.
Beloved friend . . . I desire you to be so good to buy for a friend of mine these parcels of diaper following, and to send them to London to my brother Otwell.
First, 8 ells Fl. damask work or gillyflower work, of 3 ells broad and 26 narrow ells, for a towel and a dozen napkins.
Item, two coverpanes of some fair story, one contrary to the other.
Item, 8 ells Fl. Venice work of 3 ells broad and 26 narrow ells, for a towel and a dozen napkins.

A cupboard cloth of Venice work, 2 ells broad, 3 ells long, and a piece holland cloth of 12d Fl. the Flemish ell.

This diaper ye shall best have of the Sisters by the Linen Market, for theirs is whitest and best made in all the land. Ye shall have the damask for 4s th'ell or thereupon, and the Venice work for 3s or 40d th'ell. Thus always bold to trouble you, I bid you farewell, praying God to send you your good desires.

Your friend to his power,

John Johnson.

England in the sixteenth century was renowned for her silverware, and the Italian diplomat found that one of the most remarkable things in London was the 'wonderful quantity of wrought silver' there. 'In one single street named the Strand,' he writes, 'leading to St. Paul's, there are fifty-two goldsmith's shops, so rich and so full of silver vessels great and small, that in all the shops in Milan, Rome, Venice and Florence put together, I do not think there would be found so many of the magnificence that are to be seen in London.' The City guilds possessed a wealth of silver-gilt, even humble innkeepers set their tables with silver dishes and drinking cups, and there was hardly a private house but had its array of plate.[52] Anthony Cave's silver was so valuable that when it was sent down to his house in Buckinghamshire, he ordered it to be packed in an iron chest, securely fastened, which in turn was to be placed in a great trunk, padded round with straw and canvas 'that it be not perceived for the bruit of people'. The Johnsons themselves clearly possessed a goodly array of silver spoons and salts and wine-bowls, as well as goblets and standing-cups. Otwell coveted 'three goblets with the cover' that had belonged to his uncle William in Calais, matches of others that had been sent to John; while John himself owned a set of six silver goblets which cost him a pretty penny at Antwerp — the silversmith's bill came to over £11. This, of course, was cheap beside the remarkably fine garnish of silver that he asked Robert Andrew to order for his wealthy landlord, Sir Thomas Brudenell, the final cost of which was in the neighbourhood of £40.

Sir, I must . . . desire you to cause to be made for a friend of mine twelve drinking pots of silver, each of 6 ounces weight, and twelve round trenchers of silver, also of 6 ounces the piece; all which I pray you let be well and clean wrought, and of the best fashion. The pots would be with two ears each pot, and without cover, fashioned as ye know our English beer and ale pots be. The trenchers must be to lay a wooden trencher in the midst, as ye know the manner is, and about the round edge would be some pretty print or work. I hope ye shall be sped for 33 stuvers th'ounce, all white, and above I have no commission; and therefore if ye cannot so speed, send word or ye make a bargain, and when these things be finished, send them to London to my brother Otwell.

The loveliest drinking vessels of the time were not the silver goblets, but the wine glasses, the Venetian glass that glowed and sparkled at the merchants' banquets. They were fashioned in many ways — ruby glass and ice-glass, latticinio glass and glass that was powdered in gold-dust — the bowls as shallow as leaves, the stems blown into the delicate lion-masks or into the exquisite and fragile fantasies that only the glassblowers of Murano could devise.[53] It is very probable that merchants like Henry Bostock, who had visited Venice, and John, who knew his Antwerp so well, should have owned such glasses. They would have been among their most precious possessions, reserved for company use, and rinsed and dried by Maria and Sabine themselves, not trusted to the maids, for at one jarring touch they would have broken into a thousand pieces.

Porcelain was hardly known as yet. An occasional Chinese vase or bowl would reach England by way of Venice, to be treated with the respect its beauty deserved. Set in mounts of silver-gilt, the celadon bowl served as an ornament and a tantalizing reminder of the luxury and civilization of Cathay, still more of a legend than reality. Some majolica ware they probably possessed, and also some pottery, as a letter to John from his brother-in-law reveals.

1551, 9 September, in London.

After most hearty commendations to you and my good sister, this shall be to advertise you that ye shall receive by the bringer hereof a maund, which is directed to you upon the covering, wherein is the clock with th'appurtenances, and two stone pots which my sister delivered me, of Potincary ware; a deep basin, and sauce-pots, with a case to set them in. Other I have not to write, but I desire you to have in remembrance the tavern pots which were sent to Mr. Cooke of Oundle, which weighed 30 lb at 8½d, as the price was then: 21s 3d; and for the basket, hay and cord, 5d; totals 21s 8d. And thus I commit ye to Our Lord's keeping, with all yours, Amen.

Yours to command,
John Gery.

Brother, being very glad to hear that ye be merry.

Add. To the worshipful Mr. John Johnson, this deliver at Glapthorn in Northamptonshire.

End. 1551, from John Gery, 9 September, received at Glapthorn the 11, answered in Richard Sandell's letter, le 12 of the same.

Although the plates in Sir Thomas Brudenell's beautiful garnish were fashioned to hold wooden trenchers, probably polished beechwood, and wooden tankards were also much in use, pewter was rapidly gaining favour at this time. The 'two dozen of trenchers' sent to Sabine by Otwell were probably made of pewter, for they could be obtained at cost price from John Gery who was himself a leading London pewterer. In later years, William Harrison's raconteurs told of the change that had come over the nation since their youth, how treen platters had changed into pewter, and wooden spoons into silver or tin, until in Elizabeth's reign the country had become so prosperous that there were few farmers who did not possess 'a fair garnish of pewter' on their cupboards, with a silver salt and bowl for wine, if not a whole nest, and a dozen silver spoons to furnish up the suit, while the 'costly cupboards of plate' belonging to the wealthy Elizabethan merchants were worth at least five hundred pounds, and often more.[54]

CHAPTER 6

THE GLASS OF FASHION

SABINE had ample leisure to make life pleasant, for with so many servants to do the work, she had not always to be busy about the house. She had time to visit and gossip with her friends, to play with the children and her little lap-dog, and to sing with John of an evening to the music of the lute. But the most constant delight of her leisure hours lay in her needlework, the occupation in which so many women have found pleasure, whether they be nuns in a convent, Jane Austen, or romantic Charlotte Brontë. Sewing has a calming effect on the nerves, and Sabine was an impatient creature; it is also one of the few arts that can be pursued in company without distracting the flow of conversation. Since the days of the Syon Cope, England had possessed a European reputation for embroidery — 'opus Anglicanum', as it was called — and the Tudors proved themselves worthy heirs of a great tradition. Every girl was taught to sew as an essential part of her education, and most could work their stitches with exquisite fineness by the time they were twelve years old. Margaret Hoby relates in her diary how she and her maids beguiled the long winter evenings spinning and weaving, sewing at their embroidery, and making lace. The royal ladies gave a great impetus to the art, for Catherine of Aragon, the Princesses Mary and Elizabeth, and Marie Stuart were all exquisite needlewomen, both by reputation and from the samples of their work that have survived. Tudor embroidery is some of the most gorgeous to be found anywhere in the world, with its complex geometric designs and strange heraldic beasts, its interlacing patterns of flowers and leaves and twining stems, worked in the finest satin and chain stitch, the designs sometimes influenced by the illuminated manuscripts, but mostly created by the embroideresses themselves. Like the Victorian women, whose work is of equal beauty, Tudor women loved to work with bright jewel colours, disliking insipid shades; and they were accustomed to use floss silks, which are capable of the greatest delicacy of execution. The strands of silk would be

149

laid across the polished table, and several different shades of the same colour would be threaded into one needle to gain the subtle effects desired. The needles of this period, imported from the workshops of Germany and Spain, were incidentally of far better quality than the drawn-wire needles which had been available in earlier years.

Silk in the sixteenth century was a luxury article, imported into Europe from the Levant, which alone held the secret of the beautiful Eastern dyes. A list drawn from the Wardrobe accounts of Queen Elizabeth I in 1600 includes the following colours: gold, silver, black, white, carnation, watchet blue, ash, crimson, orange or marigold, red, clay, pink, purple, blue, straw, murrey, tawny, yellow, Isabella-colour, bear's ear colour, dove-colour, Drake's colour, lady-blush, peach, green, pound citron and brazil, to name only a few.[55] It was bought in skeins, so many to the pound, and it was extremely expensive. John once paid five-and-fourpence for 'Cologne silk, four ounces' for Sabine, and three-and-twopence for 'two ounces blue silk' for her. Ordinary linen thread was not much cheaper, and we find him ordering '$\frac{1}{2}$ lb of the whitest and evenest thread at 4 gildons the pound, $\frac{1}{2}$ lb of 10s the pound, and $\frac{1}{2}$ lb of 6s. 8d. the pound'. Women naturally love to have everything as perfect as possible, and they were sometimes difficult to please, as Otwell's letter shows.

> The things recited in Robert Andrew's letter I have received; and also, by the ship that brought the Haarlem frizado, divers other small parcels with their prices: viz. white thread, 4 lb at 28 stuvers the pound; 3 several pound more of 8s 4d, 6s 8d and 5s; a painted story of the Scripture, cost 7s Fl.; two small tonnekins of capers containing $4\frac{1}{2}$ lb, cost 4s 6d; and a third, containing a stoup of olives, cost 6d. I pray you, send me word if you can before my coming down to you again, what shall be done with these things. Mistress Smith would gladly have some of your thread, but she liketh not the coarsest sort — and yet I suppose all that sort was bought for her. Let me know if you can shortly of what sorts she shall have any.

The very finest quality silks came from the Low Countries and, whenever John went abroad, it was his task to buy not only what Sabine wanted, but also to make purchases for her friends. One

autumn we find John sending 'samples to buy silk' to Robert
Andrew at Antwerp and following up his first request with another
'lady's commission . . . the providing of white silk for her'. Within
a month, the first order was delivered by the carrier at Glapthorn
Manor. 'Your letter by the poulter I have received,' wrote
Sabine, 'and also six skeins for my cushions.' The white silk took
a little longer for, although Robert Andrew and his friend ransacked the silk warehouses and the Linen Market, they could find
'no silk here so white as your pattern'. The friend indeed
obligingly offered to let her have as 'fair and good' from his own
warehouse in the City of London, but John, preoccupied with
business, forgot to send word to Otwell. 'I trust I shall have thread
shortly', wrote Sabine. 'If you have not sent it, I pray you send
it as soon as you can, for I will provide of New Year's gifts . . .'
But November came and went, and the weeks passed by, and still
there was no sewing silk. 'I marvel you do not send me thread',
wrote Sabine again, more than a little vexed at the delay. When
eventually John arrived home for Christmas, he brought the silk
with him, but it was far too late to begin embroidering presents,
and Sabine left him in no doubt of her feelings. Next time John
put in an order, he was careful to ask his agent to buy only the
best.

I pray you, buy me ½ lb white thread of 15s Fl. the lb;
½ lb of 13s the lb; and ½ lb of 10s. the lb. But I pray you, get
some help to choose it to be of the best, and that which is white
and well twisted, or else I shall be shent of my wife! The
Sisters' thread is best, and if ye be acquainted with some fair
maid in the pound, such one can best help you to choose it.

Sabine's gift for sewing had an immediate practical use, for she
made many clothes for herself and the children, and also most of
John's nightcaps, nightgowns and shirts. These could be bought
ready-made for about eighteenpence each, but she preferred to
cut and stitch them herself from the bolts of fine lawn and linen
sent down by Otwell. With the help of the maids, she made shirts
for the apprentices as well, from the 'coarse linen cloth' that was
considered suitable for hard wear by growing boys. The shirts
were sometimes cut with the boat-shaped neckline seen in the
Titian portraits. But the classic turned-down collar was becoming
increasingly fashionable at this time, and also the small stand-up

collars — bands they were called — with full sleeves gathered at the wrist. 'Your ruffs shall be mended', wrote Sabine one November. 'If you send me cloth I will make you three new shirts, for the bands and ruffs be made already.' Doubtless both collars and ruffles were edged with fine black or russet-coloured buttonhole stitching, and embroidered in a running pattern of formal flowers and leaves, such as appears in the Clouet portrait of the *Man with a Petrarch*, or the swaggering *Young Man in Red* at the National Gallery.

The hallmark of masculine fashion in the Tudor age is really the doublet, that magnificent garment in which even Henry VIII became twice the man he was. Contemporary portraits of the king and the young nobles are monuments as much to the creative genius of the tailors as to the splendour of their masters. There was literally no end to the inventiveness of the tailors where the doublet was concerned. They were cut and slashed in a hundred different ways, sometimes quilted, sometimes strewn with pearls, the fine lawn of the shirt showing through, or with the rich brocade and satin stuck with jewelled aglets. Doublets were always made by professional tailors, for only they had skill enough to manage the elaborate padding and slashing that were necessary, and the huge separate sleeves. The contrast in the price of clothes was then, as now, enormous. A quilted yellow silk doublet, made in Antwerp for a friend, cost John 33s. 6d. Against that, Thomas Tailor of Glapthorn village was paid 8d. for making a plain canvas doublet, which only took an ell of material. And while the worthy merchants may have lacked the diamond-sewn glitter of the Court, they made up for it in the sober richness of their attire. John had many doublets in his wardrobe, made of silk and satin, bombasine and damask. In 1545, three new doublets were made for him, one of them from 'tawny unwatered camlet', which must have been admirably suited to his auburn colouring. Frequently, lengths of 'caffa damask and russet satin, clean packed in a piece of canvas' were sent abroad to be made up. 'Your new jacket of satin is in the trunk', wrote Richard Sandell in the summer of 1547, and it was one of several that were ordered that year. The tight-fitting jacket, the 'doublet jerkin-ways' was beginning to be popular, gradually replacing the great skirted doublet of previous years. Often the doublet was open to the waist, and the gap filled in by the stomacher, with a partlet or yoke attached. Hans of

Antwerp wears a velvet partlet in the portrait which Holbein painted; it was a fashion that John himself followed, for it was warm in winter, and indispensable to the wearing of a ruffled shirt.

One of the most curious features of this period is the way in which the English seem to have looked abroad for the best fashions and craftsmanship in men's tailoring. The influence of France as the arbiter of woman's fashion was just beginning to make itself felt, but it is clear that England was still far from being the acknowledged leader of masculine attire. Certainly the Johnsons and all their friends preferred Antwerp tailoring to that of any other city in Europe. John once forwarded the following request to his Antwerp agent:

> Sir, Mr. Cave hath written to me to have a doublet of bombasine for winter made him, quilted, the sleeves as the pattern in the margin, and a doublet of canvas of the prettiest ye find, which may not be cut. Spiershon the tailor hath his measure. Let him make them, I pray you, but ye must will him not to make them too large in the bodice.

Indisputably, the sixteenth century was an age when men were men. They all had a leg, and every muscle of their fine manly thighs and swelling calves was revealed by their brilliant-coloured hose. A yard and a quarter sufficed to make a pair in kersey for John, price 3s. 4d. These were made to measure but, since they were not knit on the round, and the material was thick, it is possible that the fit was none too good, and that they were not very comfortable to wear. Certainly they were far more difficult than knitted socks to mend. 'Item, paid for lining a pair of hose of my master's at heels, and a pair of my mistress' — 1d' wrote Thomas Holland in his little account-book. And Otwell: 'In my wife's malle, which this bearer carrieth back again with him, are your hose that you sent up, new mended in every point to your just measure, as I suppose, for I declared all the faults of them to the maker.' Their breeches, called impartially stocks or slops, were generally made to match the colour of their hose, and fustian was a favourite, hard-wearing material. 'Item,' run the entries in John's personal expense-book, 'at London I bought a pair of stocks to my hose, cost with mending — 2s 6d.' 'Item, for fustian to make me slops, and linen cloth to line them with, and for the making, to Henry Butler — 3s 2d.' 'Item, in Calais paid unto Robert Lake for three sticks fustian for a pair slops, 3s 2d sterling, for linen cloth to line them with, 10d sterling, for making 8d. Sum — 4s 8d.' The breeches were made with the inelegant cod-piece, that article of attire which, as James Laver has remarked, has been viewed with mingled surprise and horror by every suc-ceeding generation, and which the eighteenth century found so indecorous that they eliminated it from their engravings after Holbein.[56] Slops were fastened to the doublet by corded tags with metal ends, threaded through eyelet holes. John's apprentice, Thomas Holland, once bought 'a dozen of points' for a penny in Calais.

Among merchants and the soberer sort of men the long gown had not yet gone out of fashion and John seems to have liked wearing one. When he worked in the counting-house in the mornings, he used to wear a buff jerkin, that 'most sweet robe of durance',[57] with a row of leather buttons down the front, and over it a 'work-day gown'. The gown was dignified and stately on ceremonial occasions, and John also owned a 'best gown' with fur trimmings and a 'single gown of black . . . with a tippet'. For Richard's wedding in the autumn of 1547 he had a new gown specially made. It was fitted with 'powettes', which, said Otwell, who was negotiating with the skinner,

> . . . becometh the garment very well, and the cost thereof is very little more than cat's would have been, and better cheap than budge of any goodness, for thole face, with workmanship and all, doth stand you in but 13s 4d sterling, which is reason-able enough for the goodness of the thing; and also, if you like it not, the skinner is contented to receive it again, to do me pleasure, so small gains he hath had in the sale and doing thereof.

John liked fur trimmings and he sent another of his gowns to be furred that year, which cost him 16s. 8d. Like many other things, fur was scarce and dear during the winter of 1551. John's friends made a 'general search' through all the streets and markets of Antwerp for marten skins, but they found 'none of any goodness, and yet at unreasonable price', and John had perforce to wait until better and cheaper could be obtained.

In place of the gown, a surcoat was sometimes worn over the

doublet and was apparently *de rigueur* for formal occasions in their Companies. Both John and Otwell possessed silk livery coats. Cloaks, of course, were the normal protection against wind and rain, and they were very necessary in the English climate. It was about this time that the Spanish short cloak first became popular, a sign of the Spanish influence on fashion which was later to be predominant. In 1538 John had a Spanish cloak, which was sent to be 'dressed', while another 'cloak and coat' were ornamented with parsemano work. In 1545, he left his 'Spanish cape of frizado' behind him when he went to Calais, and it had to be packed up and sent after him. Otwell was also fond of the Spanish style.

I would be glad to know (brother) by your next letter in anywise whether you will occupy any of the black cloth that was sent hither out of Holland for either of us a gown, for if I may know that you will not, I intend to put it into a Spanish cape and coat for myself, before my going over.

Where hats were concerned, John was evidently something of a dandy. He owned numbers of flat caps and a lace-trimmed hat, and his brother-in-law, Christopher Breten, once paid him the supreme compliment of imitation, asking him to buy 'such an hat as ye wear, if there be any better cheap there (in Calais) than here'. Great stress was laid on the importance of gloves in the sixteenth century. They were often superlatively beautiful and heavily perfumed, and were favourite gifts among men as well as women. John once purchased eight pairs of gloves to give away to his friends, and himself thanked Henry Southwick for them: 'My wife and I have received your gloves, and do right heartily thank you for your gentle remembrance.' They could be bought for as little as fourpence a pair, but the elegant Anthony Cave once paid 5s. 4d. for 'a fine pair of gloves'. The shoes they wore were of the type seen in contemporary portraits, made of leather, with exaggeratedly wide slashed toes, that seem to balance the enormous width of sleeve and doublet. On the average, John used to pay about a shilling a pair for his walking shoes. Inside the house he wore slippers, which cost only a few pence. For riding, they wore high leather boots. 'Item,' runs an entry in the account-book, 'for setting laps to my boots to make them wider, and for mending them, 6d. Item, for a pair of spurs, 6d.' Besides the other gear that John possessed, the 'purse malle of leather to carry my apparel in', the wallets and purses in which he kept his money, there was also the one thing which makes us sharply aware of the age in which he lived. John never stirred abroad without his sword and sword-belt, considered indispensable for the traveller. For a blade of Antwerp making, John paid 3s. 4d. in 1547, and a 'sword girdle' cost him 4s. 8d. Even the young apprentices carried their swords. 'Item,' runs Thomas Holland's account, 'paid at Calais for a scabbard for my sword, and for making clean my sword, and for a new chap, 10d.'

Feminine to the core of her being, Sabine naturally loved clothes, and she would doubtless have echoed with all her heart the cry of Madame de Sévigné, 'Dieu, comme j'aime la mode'! Sabine, however, was English, not French. Moreover, the ideal held up to the English housewife in the sixteenth century was so unalluring as to leave positively no room for fashion. Her wardrobe was to be 'comely, cleanly and strong, altogether without toyish garnishes or the gloss of light colours, and as far from the vanity of new and fantastic fashions as near to the comely imitation of modest matrons'. It is a relief to turn from pompous old Gervase, and to find that in real life, despite the complete absence of great couturiers and dressmakers, some Englishwomen were passionately interested in dress and fashion. All the sixteenth-century writers, Shakespeare, Dekker, Ercole Tasso, tilt at feminine extravagance. The English Ambassador to Scotland once wrote a delightful account of the way Henry VIII's sister behaved when she lay ill with rheumatism at Morpeth Castle.

It would pity any man's heart to hear the shrieks and cries that Her Grace giveth when she is removed or turned, and yet for all that, Her Grace hath a marvellous mind upon apparel for her body. Her Grace hath caused the gown of cloth of gold and the gown of cloth of tissue that Your Grace did send unto her by me to be made against this time; and the fashion liketh her so well that she will send for them and have them holden before her Grace, once or twice a day, for to look on them, though that Her Grace may not wear them; and Her Grace hath within the said castle twenty-two gowns of cloth of gold and silks, and notwithstanding, Her Grace hath sent for more silks in all haste to Edinburgh, and thus the silks is this same day brought unto her; and Her Grace will have in all haste a gown of purple velvet lined with cloth of gold, a gown of right crimson velvet, to be furred with ermines, and three gowns more and three kirtles of satin, and this five or six days Her Grace hath had none other mind but ever to see her apparel. I pray God that it may be all for the best![58]

Naturally no merchant's wife could aspire to such lovely clothes, nor afford to have twenty tailors dancing attendance at her bedside. John was well-to-do and doubtless liked to see her well-dressed, but, even so, Sabine practised the economy of making many of her own clothes, and spent hours round the parlour table, cutting, pinning, pleating and sewing her own patterns. It was, of course, John who bought all Sabine's clothes for her and, as she had no money of her own, she was entirely dependent on him. But right from the beginning of their married life, John made her a small yearly allowance for pin-money, and this she could spend as she pleased, without giving him any account of where the money went. The journal for April 2nd, 1544, has the following entry:

Expenses ordinary and extraordinary oweth for Otwell Johnson: and is for the sum of 40s mere sterling assigned him to deliver to my wife, which is for her necessaries this year that I do allow her.
Sum —   £2 os od

The lingerie that Sabine wore was of the simplest kind: a lawn or silk chemise in summer and a flannel shift in winter; and no doubt she made her own. At this date she would also have worn nightgowns, although it was not so many years before that every-one had gone naked to bed, even in winter. The nightgowns of the Court ladies were embroidered in silk and gold thread to match their nightcaps; and they threw dressing-jackets, called waistcoats, over their shoulders when they got up in the morning. Sabine's London tailor, John Mell, once sent her a length of 'satin for her waistcoat, unmade', which she was going to sew and finish herself. Over the chemise, Sabine probably wore a vasquine, a kind of primitive *guêpière*; at all events, it is to be hoped that she did not have to struggle into the hideously uncomfortable steel corsets that were then in vogue, and which resemble a suit of

armour more than anything else. Silk stockings did not come into
fashion until late in Elizabeth's reign, and Sabine's were made of
woollen material, dyed in brilliant colours. We find Otwell sending her a special pair of Flanders dye, and on another occasion, 'a
fine pair of hose for yourself, which cost 16d.' Like every other
woman, she wore garters to keep her stockings up, and made
them herself. 'I send my sister your wife 4 yards Cologne silk
riband for garters,' wrote Otwell, 'which cost 6d a yard.' At
that price, the ribbon was evidently of the best quality, and far
prettier than the twelve yards which John once bought for her,
costing only half a crown. Sabine's petticoats were made sometimes of light silk and sometimes of wool. Several lengths of
petticoat material were included in Margaret Mattrys's wedding
trousseau, and one length was of scarlet cloth, warm and service-
able for a winter morning. John once imported five knitted
petticoats from the Low Countries, and one of them was sent to
Sabine, evidently to see if she approved of it.

> From Calais by Spender's ship (wrote Otwell) the day of
> your departing hence, I received your maund with stuff, and
> other trinkets out of the master's chest; but of your harness
> and other artillery from my brother Lake, I hear nothing.
> Of the five knit petticoats mentioned in your remembrance
> to be in the maund aforesaid, I have delivered four as you did
> appoint me. The fifth I send you by this bearer the goodman
> Atkins, your poor neighbour, with the four boxes of comfits,
> the say for an apron, and the two new shirts, all trussed to-
> gether in a piece of canvas, with your fell mark thereon.

The magnificent gowns that we see in contemporary portraits
were, on the whole, fairly simple to make, with their plain, square
necklines, and long, straight, undraped bodices — the inspiration
of the Christian Dior line of 1954. The kirtle or skirt was put on
first, over the *verdugado* — the Spanish farthingale — that carried
the weight of the material. Above the kirtle went the upper gown,
with its skirts falling heavily on either side. Tudor gowns took a
great deal of material. Six and a half yards went into Margaret
Mattrys's second day gown, not counting the spare bodice or the
kirtle, and the gown itself was lined for warmth. While Sabine
sometimes made her own gowns, her best dresses came from a
London tailor named Robert Allen, who was, it seems, highly

temperamental about delivering them on time. One spring, John had to break the news that Allen had disappointed her of her new gown. She bore it philosophically. 'As for Robert Allen,' she returned, 'I did never know him other than you do write.' In winter, Sabine wore a stomacher to keep her warm. 'I pray you, husband, bring me a gray cony's skin of the largest, to line me a stomacher withal.' The sleeves of a Tudor gown were made separate from the rest. The charming Eworth portrait of Princess Elizabeth shows how the outer bell-sleeve, made of the same material as the bodice and gown, partly concealed another full sleeve that matched the kirtle. This second sleeve was elaborately slashed so that the fine silk of the third and innermost sleeve was revealed, with the delicate ruffles falling over her wrists. Mell the tailor made two pairs of just such separate sleeves for Sabine one year; and on one occasion Otwell wrote: 'My wife sendeth unto my sister a pair of linen sleeves that she forgot.' It is clear that Sabine, as the wife of a wealthy merchant, possessed an extensive wardrobe of gowns and kirtles. In a journal entry of 1543, John recorded the following:

> And trussed in a malle sent by the carts to London, a single gown of black of mine with a tippet, my wife's gown of black, two partlets of russet velvet and a purple, two partlets of black velvet, three partlets of black velvet, a tawny camlet gown, a body of a gown of black camlet, a buck's skin, a pair of women's hose, certain remnants of black cloth, my black coat, a gown of black worsted pelted with velvet of my wife's.

Sabine was fortunate in living in an age when mediaeval sumptuary legislation was a dead letter, and when she was free to buy and wear whatever she could afford. Gold and silver tissue, 'cloth of silver and tabine, that like beaten gold doth shine',[59] was of course only for the luxurious rich. Shimmering bawdkins (the metal threads shot through with silk of a different hue, like lamé) and brocades from the Venetian warehouses were also far beyond the reach of a merchant's wife, however much she might desire them. Velvet, however, she could afford, and it was a favourite material with Sabine. It was made in many different ways: there was plain silk velvet, figured velvet and raised velvet, cut Genoa velvet, even worsted pelted with velvet, of which one of Sabine's gowns was fashioned. Half a yard of 'tawny velvet for a stomacher

for my wife' cost John 7s. 6d. one year, but a cheaper kind was on
sale at 12s. 8d. a yard. Like everything else, the price of velvet
soared upwards during the chaotic winter of 1551, and when
Sabine sent her samples and patterns to Antwerp, the agent wrote
back to John: 'The like of the velvet which I received of Mistress
Johnson, unto whom it may please you heartily to commend me,
is not here to be had', and she had to wait until 'better and
cheaper' could be found. Satins and opalescent taffetas, muslins
and sarcenets she delighted in, all the 'soft wind of whispering
silks',[60] but these were expensive to buy. John once paid £8 for
'two pieces satin of Turkey', the real silk satin from the Levant
and not the imitation variety that was made in Bruges. Damask
caffa, at 5s. 2d. the ell, was a fairly inexpensive material and
widely used. Anthony Cave once bought a length of green silk
camlet, and one of Dornick camlet for 38s. These were probably
dress lengths for Mrs. Cave. Otwell once chose six and a half
yards of orange-tawny camlet for Robert Saunders's wife, when
she wanted a new gown to go to a wedding in, and could not get
up to London to buy the material. The obliging Otwell apparently
chose the right thing, and received the 17s. 4d. in due course from
the grateful Mr. Saunders.

Since the English climate was no different in the sixteenth
century from what it is today, woollen fabrics were much favoured,
and they could be bought in a fairly wide range of colours: pearl,
peach, palm, sops in wine, celestial, cinnamon, turtle and willow,
violet and azure, carnation, ruby, crane, sea-water, brazil, sand,
marigold, and popinjay green.[61] The fine Flemish materials were
much sought after, the bayes and says, perpetuanas, mockadoes
and frizadoes (as cheap as 5s. 6d. a yard), for they were attractive
to look at and the dyes were the finest in Europe. Otwell searched
Blackwell Hall one afternoon with patterns of say that Sabine had
asked him to match for her without being able to find the exact
shade, although the '4 yards of green say and as much of red'
that he managed at last to obtain were as 'like of colour to your
pattern as can be found in London'. How much the piece of
'finest black ryselles narrow worsted' — bespoken by Otwell and
Maria when they were engaged — cost, it is not possible to say,
nor yet the price of the 'remnant of blue narrow ryselles worsted,
containing 5 yards' that was sent down to Sabine. That it was
expensive is certain, for Otwell paid more than 17s. a yard for the

MRS. PEMBERTON

worsted for Margaret's wedding gown; pure woollen materials were dear, even in those days. One material that Sabine liked for gowns was Naples fustian, and John asked his agent to send over a gown length 'the soonest ye can, for else I shall have my wife's displeasure'.

For the trimming of her gowns, Sabine liked lace better than anything else, and John often used to buy 'knots' of lace for her in Flanders, while Otwell hunted the shops in London. Once at Christmas time he sent her three yards of round red lace, adding 'If she like it well, she shall pay no money for the same lace: but if she like it not, she shall pay as it cost me!' Sabine was inclined to be critical, and it was with a sigh of relief that Otwell handed over the task of pleasing her to his gentle fiancée. 'Maria doth send my sister your wife 6 yards russet lace for her belly; other could not be gotten this solemn day (it was Epiphany). If she like it, let the same Maria be her provider of more necessaries hereafter.'

The Holbein portraits and drawings reveal that Tudor women wore their hair plainly dressed. It was drawn back from the forehead and braided, the plaits held in place by ornamental pins, 'a fine sweet little delicate dressing, with a bodkin',[62] such as the one Mrs. Fayrey sent to Sabine as a present. Always, whether inside the house or out of doors, their hair was covered; sometimes with a coif of white linen, and at other times with hats. Sabine used to buy her hats from William Street, the hatter of Lombard Street. Hats of all shapes and styles were fashionable at this period: little flat saucers worn over a lawn cap and openwork snood, the pretty whelk-shell headdress, the 'lettice cap' of soft grey fur, and the 'velvet cap for a gentlewoman'. Philip Stubbes's bewilderment is evident at the end of Elizabeth's reign. 'On tops of these stately turrets . . . stand their other capital ornaments, such as French hood, hat, cap, kerchief and suchlike; whereof some be of velvet, some of taffetie, some (but few) of wool, some of this fashion, some of that, and some of this colour, some of that, according to the variable fantasies of their serpentine minds. And to such excess is it grown, as every artificer's wife (almost) will not stick to go in her hat of velvet every day, every merchant's wife and mean gentlewoman in her French hood, and every poor cottager's daughter in her taffetie hat.'[63] During the years of the Johnson Letters, the most fashionable shape was perhaps the

French hood, which had crossed the Channel early in Henry's reign, and remained a fashion favourite for many years; some of the portraits of Marie Stuart show her wearing the French hood. It was a pretty, bonnet shape that suited almost every type of face. A close-fitting lawn cap covered the hair; over that, a goffered frill of golden gauze framed the face, and on that was set the small stiffened crescent-shaped bonnet, with its edging of gold, and sometimes pearls as well. Three French hoods were once specially trimmed for Sabine, and on another occasion, Otwell asked John to order a gold filigree edging from Antwerp for Mrs. Cave.

> Mistress Cave of this house desireth you to buy for her now at Antwerp, an edge of gold goldsmith's work for a nether habillement of a French hood, without amell, of the valeur of 40s sterling, and not above, which shall be like the great one that you bought for her the last year, and to have the same the soonest you may. . . .

Sabine must also have possessed a considerable amount of jewellery, although we know almost nothing of this. But the letters and accounts reveal that John once gave her a 'pensée in a ring', that he paid £3 10s. for two bracelets for her, and that a quantity of silver was once melted down and fashioned into a hundred and fifty silver beads for a necklace. It seems to have been customary for them to give the goldsmiths coins to melt down for the jewellery they wanted made. The ring which Sir Ambrose Cave asked John to have made in the following letter was actually fashioned from 'two old crowns put to a light royal broken,' the whole thing costing £1 18s. 1d.

> In my most hearty manner, good cousin, I commend me unto you, and to my good niece your wife, and so thank you for the many travails you have taken for me, eftsoons praying you to cause my brother Croke's arms to be graven again, in the compass of half an angel or of a single ducat or thereabouts, for that that is made is so small that it is hard to be perceived, either in the print or in the colours. And for anything, let not the posy (which is *virtutis amore*, and the letters above the scutcheon) be forgotten to be graven in the stone as well as in the arms. And if it may be, I would the arms were graven in such a scutcheon properly, as is the same that

you have painted in paper, and the letters that stand above the scutcheon, which is JK.JC, or JK.C, to be likewise graven and divided with a title or such a thing, for that they signify two names. And though this cost 3 angels the doing, or more, I pray you cause it to be done as gallantly as the workmen can do it, and at your will you shall be requited for the same with thanks, as knoweth Our Lord, who give you health, and your good desires. Written at Ingarsby, the 22 day of July, 1545.

Per your loving uncle,
Ambrose Cave.

Voluminous cloaks, soft leather shoes, and 'fine sweet gloves', perfumed with almond or civet, such as John often bought for her, completed the basic essentials of Sabine's wardrobe. The Tudors loved perfumes, and used lavender and orange-flower water, musk and heady Arabian perfumes in large quantities. Philip Stubbes wrote that it was a 'certain sweet Pride to have civet, musk, sweet powders, fragrant pomander, odorous perfumes, and suchlike, whereof the smell may be felt and perceived, not only all over the house or place where they be present, but also a stone's cast off almost, Yea, the bed wherein they have laid their delicate bodies, the places where they have sat, the clothes, and things which they have touched, shall smell a week, a month and more, after they be gone . . . And in the summer-time, whilst flowers be green and fragrant, ye shall not have any gentlewoman almost, no, nor yet any droye or pussle in the country, but they will carry in their hands nosegays and posies of flowers to smell at; and which is more, two or three nosegays sticked in their breasts before, for what cause I cannot tell, except it be to allure their Paramours to catch at them'.[64]

Sabine made many of her own perfumes and cosmetics. The art of distilling was already a fashionable pastime, and one to which Sabine had early succumbed. Otwell had originally bought a still for his cousin John Helierd in Calais, and laughingly told him to 'gather his herbs ready' when the glass vessels and retorts had been carefully stowed away on board a Calais-bound ship. So successful were John Helierd's efforts that Sabine could not resist copying him, and in due course Otwell was commissioned to buy another 'stillitory', which duly travelled down to the manor house, accompanied by quarts of vinegar. After that, much of Sabine's leisure in summer must have been spent in the stillroom, busy with her 'spice mortar and pestle' (also bought by Otwell), among fragrant heaps of petals and leaves, making lavender water and rosewater, and lotions for removing freckles and whitening the complexion, much after the manner set out by Sir Hugh Plat, the writer of the first popular Beauty Book in the English language.[65] Tusser also was lavish in his praise of distilling.

> The knowledge of stilling is one pretty feat,
>   The waters be wholesome, the charges not great,
> What timely thou gettest, while summer doth last,
>   Think winter will help thee to spend it as fast.

> Fine basil desireth it may be her lot,
>   To grow as the gillyflower, trim in a pot,
> That ladies and gentles for whom she doth serve,
>   May help her as needeth, poor life to preserve.[66]

The reason that perfume was so widely used lay, of course, in the fact that most people did not wash regularly. Except among the unusually fastidious, cleanliness was by no means regarded as being next to godliness. Indeed, it could hardly have been otherwise, for they had no modern conveniences of any kind, none of the manifold aids to elegant living that are available today, from chlorophyll to constant hot water, and there was no social pressure urging people to be clean. Few things give a more vivid picture of life as it was lived by some people in Tudor England than Sabine's own picturesque description of the company she and Maria found themselves in on the way back from Gravesend, where they had been seeing Otwell off for Calais.

I pray you, commend me to my brother Otwell, and so does my sister, and you may show him that on Thursday when we came from Gravesend, we were at the least four or five hours coming three miles a' this side Gravesend, and in such a company that I had rather five shillings for a telt boat than I would come amongst such a company again. For there was cuckolds by their own confession, and both whores and bawds, with so much knavery that it was too abominable, and such a lousy company that they had work enough to pick off lice one off another's clothes. My sister was as well sped as the best!

And yet, in spite of that cheerfully lousy boatload of people, it would be a mistake to imagine that no one was clean, for those who wanted to make the effort could always be so. In London there were public bath-houses; most houses had big wooden tubs in which they bathed before the fire; and there were plenty of servants everywhere to do the work of fetching and carrying hot water. Certainly at Glapthorn Manor there was never any lack of soap, for white castile was one of the wares that John used to import from Flanders. A letter from a friend, asking him to buy a 'box of soap', costing 2s. 6d., suggests that it could be bought even then in solid tablet form, as well as liquid in barrels. Plat's *Delights for Ladies* gives elaborate recipes for scented washballs and perfumed washing water. Most people cleaned their teeth with toothpicks and soft, peeled wands, and Plat mentions 'sweet and delicate dentifrices'. Bath-tubs are spoken of as commonplace in his book, and there was even a sort of Turkish bath for those who dared to try one.[67] John himself, we know, was scrupulously clean in his person, and he bought and used a twopenny sponge — a price that was well within the range of most people. And the account-book of one of the apprentices reveals that John's magnificent auburn beard was washed and trimmed by the Calais barber at 8d. a time. As for Sabine, it is impossible to imagine that lively young woman as anything else but spotlessly clean and fastidious, both in her person and in her home. The tart remark she made about poor Mrs. Hosse is too revealing for anything else to be true.

This day (she wrote to John) hath Bartholomew Hosse wife been here, who came afoot, as like a slut as ever she was. She would have money, but I had it not for her.

PART THREE

L

CHAPTER 7

GENTLEMAN, MERCHANT, FARMER AND HUSBANDMAN

GLAPTHORN MANOR was part of that district of Northamptonshire, near the ancient market town of Oundle, which John Leland in 1542 described as 'marvellous fair corn ground and pasture'.[68] It lay in undulating, upland countryside, a great island of cleared land where the earth gave a rich yield of grain, and the fat sheep and cattle grazed in lush meadows. Beyond the cleared land on one side were impenetrable woods, the spreading oaks and beeches of Rockingham Forest, where for hundreds of years the hart had roamed free, and the wild boar started up in the thick undergrowth. On the other side, beyond Peterborough, the land was channelled and dyked and flooded by the waters of the Fens, a part of England where men lived strange and separate lives, cut off from the industry and comparative civilization of the towns, their occupation the snaring of wildfowl, fishing in the reedy waters, and grazing their herds on the islets; it is related that when they burned their stubble in the autumn, it seemed for miles around as if the marshes were on fire.[69]

Compared with the vast estates of men like the Cecils and Brudenells and Spencers, Glapthorn Manor was only a small property, and yet it was large enough for a young and inexperienced merchant to begin his farming career, and it was capable of considerable improvement. The principal lands — originally the demesne land of the manor — consisted of a hundred acres of arable and pasture 'lying scattered in all the fields of Glapthorn and Cotterstock'. Besides this, there were a number of large and valuable enclosures in Glapthorn itself — Willow Row Close and Bodger's Close, the Great Close with its thirty acres of arable, and Caies Stybbing, the forty-acre meadow where the horses were put out to graze — and various smaller closes in the neighbouring village of Cotterstock. John was also able to lease from Lord Cromwell, the actual owner of the manor (the

Brudenells only rented it), the Lord's Close, Clark's Close, a
meadow and a mere. There were also, of course, the customary
rights in the woods and on the village commons. In all, with the
land he rented from Parson Saxby at Polebrook, John farmed a
comfortable estate of well over two hundred and fifty acres. The
one disadvantage — that the demesne lands were scattered in the
form of open fields — was more than offset by the large number of
enclosures. And whatever hardships the enclosure movement
inflicted on the evicted tenants, there is little doubt that it did in
fact make for more efficient farming. There can be no comparison
between the agriculture of enclosed land and the old unthrifty
ways of champaign farming. The mediaeval system had guaran-
teed fair shares for all, within limits, but it had also meant the
virtual stagnation of agriculture for centuries. Both the leading
Tudor writers on farming, the shrewd Fitzherbert and the popular
Tusser, sang the praises of enclosure in no uncertain strain.

> The country enclosed I praise,
>   The t'other delighteth not me,
> For nothing the wealth it doth raise,
>   To such as inferior be.
> More profit is quieter found
>   (Where pastures in several be)
> Of one silly acre of ground
>   Than champion maketh of three.
> Again what a joy is it known,
>   When men may be bold of their own.[70]

Arthur Young's words, 'The possession of land makes amends
for everything' were just as true of the Tudors as of Hanoverian
England. There was a land hunger in the sixteenth century, an
urge to put money into land, and to acquire property and respect-
ability in one go. The thought that he might one day be able to
purchase an estate was never far from John's mind and, while as
yet he could not afford to do this, he was determined to rent as
much land as he could. Indeed, he had not long been settled at
Glapthorn Manor before he began negotiations. Early in 1546 he
learned that 'my Lord Cromwell's lands, meadows, leas and pasture was offered to be letten for fines for term of years', together
with the woods on the lordship, to whoever 'would give most for
fines for the same'. John at once begged his uncle Brian Cave and

Sir Thomas Brudenell to help him, and though for a while, owing to the indiscretion of a too-talkative servant, the issue was in doubt, John eventually had his way, and by Lady Day 1547 the rent he paid to Cromwell had risen to £5 a year.

Even while these complicated negotiations were in train, word reached him of a large enclosed pasture that was to be let at Benefield, a few miles westward along the Glapthorn road, belonging to George Zouch of Codnor, in Derbyshire. As he had to travel to Calais that autumn, John left everything in his agent's hands, and Richard Harrison succeeded in getting a year's lease of the close, on payment of a premium of 20 marks, and the option on a twenty-one year lease if it was desired. When John returned home at Christmas, he was suffering from the ague. There was no question of his being well enough to travel north, and all the details had to be settled by an interchange of letters. It seems that John was not the only man after Northawe Close. Zouch's kinsman, the eccentric, rabbit-breeding Sir Thomas Tresham, had offered £40 in goodwill, a rent of £10 a year, and 'a velvet gown to my wife'. But since John finally decided on a long lease of thirty years, all was well. 'I hope ye will be contented therewith,' he wrote to Zouch, 'and the rather if ye consider the great cost I must be at in stubbing, which with the money that I must pay you now beforehand, will be a great minishing of my small stock for a thing of so small profit.' As for the rent, John, after taking the precaution of having the agreement perused 'by one that is learned', i.e. his lawyer brother-in-law, Christopher Breten, was apparently content to leave this to Zouch's 'gentleness and liberality'; it was probably about £10 a year. What he particularly desired was to 'receive benefit at your hands, as other your tenants do'. Chief among these advantages was the right of common for three hundred sheep, 'and some reasonable number of beasts'. 'If it be your pleasure to make me a commoner in Benefield fields, by virtue of the occupying of your close, it might do me some ease; and your mastership should have no hindrance by it, nor yet your tenants, for (the Lord be thanked) there is commons and large fields enough.' One wonders, however, what the villagers really thought about this invasion of their common land by a wealthy merchant; so far as they were concerned, it was almost as great a usurpation as if John had proposed to enclose the land outright.

Significantly enough, John's principal object in renting

Northawe Close was to keep more sheep, and this type of enclosure was one of the great problems of the Tudor age. As the price of wool and cloth had risen in the fifteenth century, it had become ever more profitable to farm sheep on the enclosures, instead of tilling the soil for grain. Sheep meant big profits, even while they needed few men to care for them, and there was no stopping the movement once it had begun. Despite the attacks launched year in and year out against the 'caterpillars of the commonwealth' by preachers and statesmen from Sir Thomas More to William Cecil, despite the activities of the Enclosure Commissions, Acts of Parliament, the Pilgrimage of Grace, and the rebellion of Robert Kett, despite the beggary and despair of the evicted peasantry, nothing could shake the hold of the landowning classes. Every farmer possessed enclosures, and most of them kept flocks of sheep within the hawthorn hedges. 'An husband cannot well thrive by his corn without he have other cattle, nor by his cattle, without corn. For else he shall be a buyer, a borrower, or a beggar . . . Sheep in mine opinion is the most profitablest cattle that any man can have.'[71]

It was impossible that John, already a stapler, should not turn sheep-farmer as well, like Anthony Cave and many other members of his company. During the months before the move to Glapthorn Manor, John was busy making preparations for the flocks there, commissioning his Oundle agent, Richard Harrison, to buy rams and ewes, hoggets and bell-wethers, ordering tar and sheepbrands from London. As the years went by, the size of his flocks steadily increased. The enclosure at Northawe was turned into a sheep-pasture, just as soon as the ground could be cleared of thorns and briars. This was a lengthy process, as John had foreseen when he asked George Zouch to put his rent as low as possible.

> For truly, being at charge to stub it, as I must needs be if I will have profit thereof, the rent is great, and so much as no man is able to save by it, the ground being more than three parts overrun with thorns; and besides that, an hundred marks will scant clean the ground of thorns, and the ground where the thorns shall be stubbed will bring no grass that cattle will eat in four or five years after the stubbing.

At last, in 1550, Northawe was under pasture, ready for the

flocks. John had also sought permission from Zouch to lop and top all the oak, ash, survey and crab-apple trees that lay inside the hedges, 'so the same be to employ on the ground for the building of a house, sheep-cot or hovel . . .', and in the spring of 1550 two of the local carpenters were called in to build a small, thatched hut for the shepherd's use. Also in that year, John laid out a considerable sum of money — nearly £40 — on sheep, buying them from two Essex breeders, William Tendering and William Sandell. The latter handed over the flocks to John's servants in London, and with them a long letter giving details of the hundred odd 'sheep in the wool', the ewes and lambs and hoggerels destined for the Glapthorn pastures, some marked with 'a little tar newly-blotted upon the loins, or between the horns on their faces'. Unfortunately the drovers were so careless that many of the sheep were injured on the way. Anthony Cave, who had bought sheep at the same time, was so furious at the condition in which the animals arrived that he thought the drovers should be forced to pay for the damage they had done.

By this time, John owned flocks of well over a thousand sheep. In the spring, he employed as many as 'sixteen sheep washers for washing of new sheep', besides two extra hands, who dipped a hundred wethers between them. Some of the sheep were kept exclusively for wool, some for breeding purposes, and some for meat. The surplus animals were sold in the market, and one of John's chief buyers was the London dealer Cooke, who used regularly to make the rounds of the country fairs and farms. Sabine often dealt with Cooke while John was away. Several times, however, the dealer complained of a bad bargain at their hands, and, finding that poor sheep fetched poor prices, John evidently determined to improve his stock, for in the autumn of 1551 he implored Cave to send him 'cullings, ewes so they be young, or lambs that be good . . . desiring you to spare me so many as ye can, for that I would fain mend my breed. I have none but good in a pasture I pay rent for'. Anthony Cave agreed willingly and, when the shepherd and Ralph Collyshoe arrived at Tickford House, they found a good flock of a hundred sheep waiting for them. 'Sergeant did beg of Master Cave for you one ram, and for Evangelist a ram lamb, and he hath given them.'

To the sixteenth century, there was no more romantic figure than that of the shepherd, the incarnation of goodness, living a life of rustic simplicity, far from the temptations of evil and ambition. 'Sir,' said Colin, 'I am a true labourer; I earn that I eat, get that I wear, owe no man hate, envy no man's happiness, glad of other men's good, content with my harm, and the greatest of my pride is to see my ewes graze and my lambs suck.'[72] And no wonder, the twentieth century might add, when the shepherd, like all labouring men, earned so little money. John employed his own shepherd, William Sergeant, at a wage of four nobles a year. Almost alone among the servants at Glapthorn Manor, Sergeant received no allowance for boots or livery; and it seems that in many parts of the country it was customary for the shepherd to clothe himself. His flocks, as a later writer said, 'afford him raiment, outside and linings, cloth and leather, and instead of much costly linen, his little garden yields hemp enough to make his lockram shirts'.[73]

> This shepherd ware a sheep-gray cloak
> Which was of the finest lock,
> That could be cut with shear.
> His mittens were of bauzon's skin,
> His cockers were of cordiwin,
> His hood of miniver.
>
> His awl and lingel in a thong,
> His tar-box on a broad belt hung,
> His breech of cointree blue,
> Full crisp and curled were his locks,
> His brows as white as Albion rocks,
> So like a lover true.[74]

Drayton's picture of the young shepherd is doubtless a highly romantic one, but none the less charming for that. Of all the workers on the land, the shepherd's job was the most skilled and the most difficult. 'All goes to the devil where shepherd is evil', said Tusser.[75] The shepherd was out in all weathers, in the soaking rain, as well as in the warmth of summer. The lambs fell in the time of greatest cold, when the snow was on the ground, and the sheep had to be got into shelter. And always they had to be pastured on dry ground, for footrot set in if they were allowed to graze on damp grass, and they also suffered frequently from scab, the reason for the shepherd's tar-box. The most terrible disease, however, was the dreaded murrain, which decimated the English flocks during the 1540s, in a succession of rainy springs and autumns. 'We have so much wet weather', wrote Anthony Cave in the autumn of 1544, 'that a great murrain of sheep will be again this year.' In the spring of 1545, he predicted that, apart from the London yield, not sixty thousand fells would be dried in all the counties of England, because of 'these murrain years'. It was long before the flocks were back at their full strength, and the acute shortage of wool and fells was almost certainly one of the factors contributing to the meteoric price-rise of the time. The murrain coincided with the war with France and the debasement of the coinage and, as wool prices rose steadily higher, there resulted a competition between clothier and stapler that could only have one end.

The letters reveal just how acute the price-rise was. In April 1545, John refused to pay 12s. a tod for his neighbour Mr. Belcher's wool, saying that it was far too much to give; but by the autumn he was thankful to have it at 13s. Cotswold wool, selling at £10 a sack in 1544, was fetching £12 a sack in the autumn of 1545, when Anthony Cave was talking of having to pay £5 a hundred for fells that had cost under £4 in 1543. In 1546, prices rose higher still. Christopher Breten, scouring the countryside for John, found that wool was 14s. a tod in Rutland, and 16s. about Northampton. Mr. Belcher, who had promised his wool to John, eventually sold it to a clothier for 15s. a tod, and a tierce of wine. 'Well, the loss of the not having of it is not much,' was John's comment, 'for I think ye shall hear that clothiers have burned their fingers in buying of wool: but yet, when opportunity serveth thereto, let him know how glad he is for every trifle to shift his merchant, and when I meet him, I will say also no less to him.' High as this price was, it had not reached the zenith, for Mr. Humphrey of Boughton demanded 18s. a tod, 'a pretty butt me-semeth to shoot at'. Even the usually obliging Christopher Breten decided to ask John for more money, in view of the general price-rise, and John had perforce to agree.

My very singular good brother . . . even as you do write, I do think that few men have bought so much wools about Northampton so reasonable priced as ye have done for me. I have both thanks to give you for it, and also am content to make you such recompense for it as yourself shall think reasonable: howbeit, out of doubt the gains that will come of it in the Staple will not be so much as it was wont to be, and our charges be as great as ever they were, which will cause other men and we also not to be so liberal as else we would be. If the raising of the price of your own wool from 10s 6d the tod unto 14s may do you pleasure (because ye would sell like your neighbours), I am content therewith, although I would not have disbursed my money so long unto one that had not been my special friend, for so small a profit as I have done to you. Well, that is not the matter: £7 or £8 between you and me is not the thing that I greatly esteem, and therefore am content ye do as ye will, and consider it to me-wards again another time, as ye write me ye will do.

The staplers and clothiers did make an attempt to regulate the prices that were paid, but to little avail. 'I have not bought you much wool above 17s', wrote Breten in the autumn of 1547. 'For 18s I might have had Holwell wool, Haldenby wool, and the rest in Ralensthorpe that I have refused, and now it is good for 19s.' In 1548, Leicester wool varied between 8s. 8d. and 19s. a tod, Bucks wool was 20s. a tod, and Cotswold wool '24s and under'. In 1550, Mistress Elmes asked 24s. 3d. for her fleeces, while William Dormer, who lived not far from Anthony Cave, was offered 25s. a tod, cash down, by the rich clothier, John Winchecombe. But the climax was not reached until 1551, during the period of dislocation caused by the devaluation of the coinage. Lady Brudenell was then getting 24s. a tod; John himself offered one man 26s. a tod for Cotswold wool; and as for aunt Croke, she would look at none of her relatives' offers, for she had been promised 30s. a tod by a clothier, the money to be handed over immediately. Thirty shillings is the highest price recorded in the letters. As the economic situation began the slow process of readjustment, commodity prices began to fall, although they never reached the low level of the years before the war.

Sheep were part of the time-honoured ritual of English country life, woven inextricably into the fabric of existence. Sheep-shearing was one of the great country festivals in which everyone took part, coming from village and farm in the mild spring weather.

When the new washed flock from the river's side,
  Come in as white as January snow,
The ram with nosegays bears his horns in pride,
  And no less brave the bellwether doth go.[76]

When the flocks were sheared, and the great mounds of wool
rose white in the barns, then thoughts turned to entertainment
and feasting. For this one time in the year, nothing was be-
grudged, no expense spared, and, from highest to lowest, all ate
and drank their fill. 'Let me see,' cried Perdita's brother — and
things were the same all over the countryside, from Glapthorn
Manor to Romney Marsh — 'what am I to buy for our sheep-
shearing feast? Three pound of sugar, five pound of currants; rice
— what will this sister of mine do with rice? But my father hath
made her mistress of the feast, and she lays it on. She hath made
me four-and-twenty nosegays for the shearers, three man songmen
all, and very good ones; but they are most of them means and
bases; but one Puritan amongst them, and he sings psalms to
hornpipes. I must have saffron, to colour the warden pies; mace —
dates — none; that of my note; nutmegs, seven, a race or two of
ginger — but that I may beg; four pound of prunes, and as many
of raisins o' the sun.'[77] In many parts of the country, and Northamptonshire among them, the housewives baked special tarts and
cakes and pastries for the sheep-shearing feast.

After the shearing came the winding, often carried out by
parties of itinerant woolwinders who travelled among the farms
and villages seeking work, under contractors such as Dunkerley
of the letters. Woolwinding was one of the busiest times of the
year; depending on the amount to be wound, the men would live
on the farm for weeks together, cleaning the wool of grit and dirt,
and packing it into the great canvas sarplers that held about
1000 lb. of wool all told. At Glapthorn Manor in 1545, winding
went on throughout September, October and November.

Commend me to Harrison, I pray you (wrote John to
Sabine), and desire him that the woolwinders lack no work.
Ye may show him I make reckoning to have no less than 2000
stone of wool at his hand. If it be 100 or 200 more, I shall
provide him money for it shortly after Michaelmas. If he need
any about Michaelmas, let him send for some to my brother.

177

And I pray you, let as much of my wool be carried up as can be, while the weather is fair. When ye do pack any wool, in anywise let it be as fair handled for breaking the fleeces as is possible, and remember that there be three sorts made in the packing, as was the last year: to wit, one of th'end wool, which is that is wound in the lock; another of the fairest of the clift wool; and the third of the darkest colour of the clift wool; and in anywise keep remembrance what is packed in every cloth, and let them be surely marked that we may know one sort from another. If ye mark the end wool with three pitch brands, the best of the clift with two pitch brands, and the worst with one pitch brand, besides marks and numbers with red stone, it shall be no hurt.

When Sabine replied, she told her husband that the men were working hard enough, but that they were dissatisfied with the wages they were getting.

You have eight woolwinders of work, the which woolwinders be appointed to go their ways, saying that they will not work no more for 2s a sack, for they do not get 4d a day. Dunkerley did set them all a-work, and doth ride about himself, for he was not here this eight or ten days. Wherefore I pray you send word so shortly as you can what you will give them, for Harrison would not that they should go away, for they handle your wool as it should be. They do ask 4s for a sack, as they have in London, and to find themselves meat and drink.

In his answer, sent haste, post haste from Calais, John refused to give more money than Dunkerley had contracted to pay, and eventually the woolwinders gave in, knowing most likely that it would be difficult for them to find work elsewhere. By the middle of November the winding was all done, and seventy-seven sacks lay stored in the Glapthorn barns.

This shall be to certify you that this day your woolwinders have made an end of winding your wools, and I have reckoned with them. They have wound you 77 sack and 10 tod, and packed 27 cloths. Their winding comes to £4 15s 8d, and their packing 27s, so is in all £9 2s 8d, of the which I have given them 40s; the rest my brother must reckon with

Dunkerley and pay him. A reward they do say that you did promise them. You did write me that I should give them 10s, and if they would not be content with that, that then they should stand to your reward. I have taken upon me to give them 12s, wherewith they be content.

Wool alone was not John's sole source of income from the farm, nor were sheep his only livestock, for he went in for mixed farming on a big scale. There were plenty of pigs on the farm, and they were profitable animals to raise; kept in warm, clean sties in winter, they could be put out in the woods in summer, and left to fatten on acorns and beechmast in the autumn. John employed a special hogherd to look after his swine, at a wage of 1s. 5d. a quarter. Besides these, there were the poultry and the dairy cattle, and the oxen, essential to the sixteenth-century farm, both as beasts of burden, and as fat cattle to sell in the market. John's oxen were kept both at Polebrook and Glapthorn, and he had a neatherd to care for them, paying him 3s. 9d. a quarter in wages. One of the cardinal points of good husbandry that Tusser was always urging on farmers was that pennypinching did not pay where cattle were concerned. 'Who abuseth his cattle and starves them for meat, By carting or ploughing his gain is not great.'[78] It was a saw that John was to experience to his cost, for at least once in his farming career, when his steers were driven to Salem Fair, he could find no buyer because they were so miserably thin, and it took weeks of expensive feeding before they were at last sold. On another occasion, he sent up a drove of cattle to Smithfield Market, and asked Otwell to find a buyer; but again the same thing happened. The servant, Jasper, returned almost empty-handed.

At the writing hereof (said Otwell) he had dispatched but a couple of them here, which he sold yesterday in Smithfield Market, after four nobles apiece. The rest, being a score, no man offered him above £21 for them, and so he drave them homeward again. Howbeit, at the receipt hereof from me, he had with him certain butchers of the suburbs about London to look on his said cattle, being at Newington: whether they shall agree or not I cannot here ascertain you. But truly, most of them were unreasonably bought by your providers, and now with their driving up unfoddered before, their bellies are clean washed away, so that I doubt much that you shall be a small gainer by them. God send you more profit by the rest that you have at home to sell, and make yourself sure (if you can) of wiser buyers of your young ware hereafter, than Richard Preston and your shepherd have showed themselves in most of these.

Winter was always a difficult time of year, for the cattle pined for food, and were given to losing their teeth from lack of nourishment. Even so, John's cattle must have been in poor shape for the buyers to offer only 26s. 8d. apiece for the best. That same year as much as 39s. was paid for a single ox, and when shortly afterwards the prices of stock began to soar, like everything else, 70s. 4d. is one of the prices recorded in 1549. In 1551, the year when Sabine wrote that 'Cattle was never so dear, and so is all things else', as much as 82s. 6½d. was given. 'You would not believe how dear are all kind of cattle waxen of late, as well lean as fat', wrote Anthony Cave.

No gentleman's household was complete without its stables in the sixteenth century. Horses were indispensable as the sole means of swift transport, and many were the journeys that John made on horseback through the countryside between London and the manor house. Whenever he arrived in London from Calais, his horses would be waiting for him to ride home; and horses were always available for his brother Otwell and other of their friends who came to visit them at Glapthorn. John's favourite animal was his prized white gelding and, beside that, he reserved the 'great horse' especially for his own use. Sabine had her own 'little black mare', for she loved riding, and had too much spirit to sit tamely behind the groom. By the year 1550, there were a good many horses at Glapthorn Manor: Otwell's two horses, John's and Sabine's, a sorrel mare and another mare, the grey mare and the grey filly, and horses for the use of the servants and apprentices.

One of John's horses earned Ambrose Saunders's praise, when he rode him down to the manor house, as being 'very good of labour as for his easy trot. Praise him as ye find him, but I can very well away withal. He doth lack a good bit, which I think will make him go much the easelier'. Some were not such amiable creatures, and it must be admitted that John was occasionally a bad judge of horseflesh. The 'dull nag' he bought from the parson was one such animal, and Don another, whom he later sold. 'Mr. Dunne your horse hath a new master this day in Smithfield for 50s sterling', wrote Otwell. Bawird, the horse he purchased from Henry Southwick, was a 'pretty horse, but he is fair unrid in the head . . .' But the biggest mistake of all was perhaps the horse he bought from Dunkerley, the local wool dealer, who rode it round the countryside for a fortnight after the deal was made. Sabine duly upbraided the man for the 'knavish part' he had played, but she was also a little amused at John's idea of a bargain. 'Dunkerley's horse shall be well kept,' she promised her husband, 'and one of his eyes, for the other eye is out. Goodnight, good husband, with all my heart!'

It was during this period of the sixteenth century that the rival merits of ploughing with horses or oxen were being hotly debated, and Fitzherbert's conclusion was inevitable in an age that seldom had food enough and to spare for both man and beast. Horses, he said, were well enough on heavy clay soils, but they had to be fed all winter long on hay and fodder. The ox, on the other hand, even if he had to be left out to pasture all night long, was the more economical proposition, for, if there was not enough fodder to go round, he could be slain and eaten.[79] The winter feeding of horses and cattle was one of the greatest problems that sixteenth-century farmers had to face. Grass does not grow for five months of the year, and until root crops and artificial grasses began to be cultivated at the end of the seventeenth century, followed by the pioneer work of Coke at Holkham and Turnip Townshend, the shortage of fodder meant the annual autumn killing of beasts that could ill be spared, and endless salt beef for the farmhouse in winter.

John was one of the fortunate farmers who had pasture in plenty. He sometimes wintered cattle for his neighbours, charging them for the 'hay and pasture' the animals consumed, and several of his friends used to make a practice of sending their horses to graze in the Glapthorn meadows until they were in 'honest plight'. 'This bearer doth bring with him a stoned horse of my brother Bartholomew Warner's', wrote Otwell, early one February, 'which he saith you promised him meat for: but once in his life he will recompense you for the same with some other pleasure.' Those horses for whom there was not enough fodder in the stables were put out in the closes, or even in the woods, where they could be recaptured in the spring. 'Keep no more in the stable than needs must', was John's instruction to Sabine one autumn. 'The rest let be put into the closes, and let the mares and foals be put into the forest. If ye keep in the stable Don, Dunkerley's gelding, your mare and Curtal, it is enough for our occupying this winter.'

Every bale of hay and straw was of vital importance. Haymaking was only second in importance to harvest, and one of the most eagerly awaited and enjoyable tasks of the farmer's year. When the mowers had finished with their scythes, the haymakers went into the fields with their hayrakes and hayforks, tossing the fragrant bundles on to the wain. 'Leave never a dallop unmown and had out',[80] was Tusser's advice, for the coarse stuff could be fed to ox and cow, and the finest reserved for the sheep and horses. The whole village used to turn out at haymaking, men, women and children.

> Go muster thy servants, be captain thyself,
>   Providing them weapon and other like pelf,
> Get bottles and wallets, keep field in the heat,
>   The fear is as much, as the danger is great.

> With tossing and raking and setting on cocks,
>   Grass lately in swathes is hay for an ox,
> That done, go and cart it and have it away,
>   The battle is fought, ye have gotten the day.[81]

In the sixteenth century, as from time immemorial, the farmer's year began in the late autumn, with the ploughing of the fields and the Michaelmas sowing of winter wheat and rye. The sower walked behind the plough, scattering the seed, and afterwards came a bevy of small boys, 'armed with sling or with bow, to scare away pigeon, the rook and the crow'.[82] Throughout the months that followed, the farmer turned anxious eyes on the weather, and on the crops that were ripening in his fields. Wheat was the most important crop, although the yield was uncertain and barley, oats, rye, peas and beans were more widely grown. In many places a mixture of wheat and rye — blendcorn, or maslyn — was preferred as 'the surest corn of growing', according to Fitzherbert, 'and good for the husband's household'.[83] John's own chief crops were wheat and barley, and it is interesting to see how late the harvest was gathered at least one year in Northamptonshire. In his letter of October 1544, Thomas Flecton wrote to Sabine.

This ten days, thanks be unto God, we have very fair and dry weather, trusting in God that ye have the same with you, the which is comfort for all England: for now I trust ye shall have home your harvest in good season, trusting in God that both you and the good parson shall lose on time to labour sore, so long as the time doth last. Howbeit, ye must take heed that ye take not too much pain in nowise, nor yet specially the good parson.

When the harvest had been got in, every sheaf scythed by hand and stooked in the fields, and the sheaves piled on to the wagon, the grain was stored in the barn until it was needed for household use, for bread and malt, or stover for the cattle. The surplus grain, whatever was not used at the farm, was sold at Oundle to the grain-dealers and corn-bodgers. Thomas Tusser stressed the necessity for 'good market and nigh', and that a farmer must know the price of all his wares.

This lesson is learned by riding about,
The prices of victuals the year throughout,
Both what to be selling and what to refrain,
And what to be buying, to bring in again.[84]

Oundle was the nearest market town to Glapthorn Manor, and there John's grain was sent on market days, and displayed to the local grain-dealers and corn-bodgers. Like the other farmers, John tried always to wait for the best prices, and held back his grain as long as possible. 'As yet your wheat will not be sold,' wrote Thomas Saxby in 1543, 'and it will not be your profit to sell any malt before Lammas Day, for you may buy the best malt in Oundle Market for 4s a quarter.' That year, grain prices were still fairly low, but soon they were to go sky-high, forced up by bad harvests and the effects of the debasement of the coinage. During 1545, when the harvest almost failed after a wet summer, wheat prices reached famine level. John wrote from Calais to tell Sabine to sell their beans and malt in Oundle market 'whiles the prices be good. Wheat is dear in many places in England, above 20s a quarter: I trust therefore ye shall sell our wheat well'.

Sabine replied: 'As for selling of any corn, I will not (by your leave), for seeing I have but little to sell I would sell it at the best, for it is like to be dearer than it is (the more pity); for wheat, if it be of the best, is worth 18s 8d, malt 12s, barley 12s, paye (peas) 8s and above.' The shortage continued until the following year, when the good harvest of 1546 brought prices down a little. In the spring of that year Richard Preston wrote to his master: 'Harrison told me that malt fell; in every place where he came it was at 10s 8d, and some better cheap at Oundle of Saturday. Your beans will not be sold at the price ye left word: they are in Oundle at 8s 10d, and better cheap.'

The harvest of 1547 was excellent, and wheat prices lower than they had been for a long time. But in the succeeding years the harvest grew steadily worse: in 1550, for example, John's malt was fetching 12s. 8d. a quarter, and rapeseed in Norfolk could not be bought for much under 13s. 4d. a quarter. Even this, however, was nothing compared with the situation in 1551, when the coinage was devalued, and prices reached a level they had never attained before. There was everywhere a 'great dearth of most things, specially of victuals'. That year the average price of wheat rose to 20s. 4d. a quarter, and in June, before the harvest, Sabine wrote that 'grain is risen 3s or 4s in a quarter, and poor people can get none for money, Our Lord amend it'. Despite the ban on the export of grain, and price-fixing measures taken by the justices, prices continued high, and in February 1552 John paid 24s. a quarter for grain that he bought to ship to the garrison in Calais. Fortunately the harvest in 1552 was good, and prices dropped to a level that compared favourably with those of the previous year.

In a century when grain was the people's staple food, long before potatoes had been introduced, there was considerable profit to be made not only in growing and selling corn, but in grinding it as well. The very first addition that John tried to make to his property was in this direction. In the neighbouring village of Cotterstock the two divided streams of the river Nene met to flow as one. Watermills had been erected there, and whoever owned the mills possessed also a secure income, for fair weather or foul, good harvest or bad, the millers must grind their corn. Early in 1545, Otwell was trying to get for John 'the farm of three watermills there situate, and with two leas holmes, one barn, and all the fishing waters, and other appurtenances and commodities to them belonging'. But other people were also after the mills, notably one Hugh Lawe, and, though Sir Ambrose Cave exerted his influence, they were not to be had. A ray of hope came through their friendship with Thomas Ashley, whose kinswoman was governess to the young Princess Elizabeth. The manor of Cotterstock had been left to the princess in Henry VIII's will, and Kate Ashley promised to deliver John's letter to 'my Lady Elizabeth's grace', and to help his suit. But either her memory was short, or else she had more important fish to fry, for in November 1548, John was still without his watermills, and Otwell was writing:

> For brief answer to your letter to Mr. Ashley, know that his advice is (which I do not dislike) that you shall resort yourself, or some witty person for you, unto my lady's surveyors that are now in your quarters, and require their grant of the mills and other parcels that you desire to have: which if they deny, or say that some other grant is passed them before to some other man, it may briefly and gently be said unto them, that my lady's grace's promise was unto you by your friend long since for the same, etc., as you think best, and the truth thereof may be learned of Mistress Ashley her woman by them; and upon your certifying of Mr. Ashley how you sped with the said surveyors, he will further put the said Mistress Ashley in remembrance of you, or else my lady's grace herself, if need require, and before to do it, it were superfluous....

It is to be feared that Kate Ashley had now far graver things to occupy her mind than John's three watermills. For months past she had encouraged the young Elizabeth to set her heart and affections on handsome Thomas Seymour, all unaware that the Council were merely biding their time. Within a few weeks of Otwell's letter, Kate Ashley was hailed before the Council for her part in the dangerous flirtation, Thomas Seymour was under arrest, and Elizabeth herself received a bitter lesson in discretion that lasted the whole of her life. Before the spring came round, Thomas Seymour died on Tower Hill. The watermills at Cotterstock became a thing of the past.

At Glapthorn Manor, John employed a number of servants in husbandry. They lived, ate and slept at the manor house, earned a regular wage, wore John's livery of grey frieze, and helped to run the farm. Their status would seem to have been far more highly regarded than that of the farm labourer of later years, for in the sixteenth century agriculture was still recognized as a skilled occupation. First came Lucas and Ralph Collyshoe, both of whom earned 30s. a year, and in addition the former received 6s. 8d. for his livery, and the latter 2s. for his boots. The account-books show them riding round the countryside to the various cattle fairs, or journeying to London with messages, and doing all kinds of farm work generally. Their wages are very nearly those allowed a decade later by the Justices of Northamptonshire and Buckinghamshire to 'chief servants in husbandry of the best sort, which can eire, sow, mow, thrash, make a rick, thatch and hedge the same, and can kill and dress a hog, sheep and calf'.[85] Another of the men, Saunders, was paid sometimes monthly and sometimes fortnightly. He received the comparatively high wages of 5s. 4d. a month, with the yearly allowance of 3s. 4d. for his boots, but it is possible that he was not regularly employed. Jasper the groom received 'four nobles a year and his livery', and Friar also got the same sum of money, together with 3s. 4d. for his boots. There was also a man named Thomas, although we know very little about him, apart from glancing references in the letters.

Some of the men, like Lucas and Ralph Collyshoe, probably helped with the indoor work as well, assisting John's factotum, Richard Preston, where they could, and serving as footmen on occasion. We know that John was accustomed to keep a butler, for there is a letter from Anthony Cave offering the services of a man he knew.

> My wife hath her recommended unto you, and she hath offered her service by William Molynes, which was my butler two years; and because I have one honest man ready, but partly I doubt of his continuance with me, therefore if this William Molynes' service may do you any pleasure, I would ye had him for a time, though I bear part of his wages, for I know him true and honest. I pray you, write me your mind if ye like him. Unless I put this I have from me for some urgent cause, ye shall be sure of William Molynes and it be for a whole year. And so bid you farewell.

For field work at times of great pressure, such as haymaking and harvest, extra hands were always called in, mostly the day labourers from the village. At Glapthorn in 1550, a certain John

Thelbie mowed seventeen acres of meadow 'at 8d the acre', and, when he had finished, he mowed the Great Close (twenty-six acres) for 17s. 8d. In due course, he wended his way to Northawe, mowing nine acres of it for 6s. 9d., while five other men tackled the rest for 11s. 8d. As the labourer was paid then — the Buckinghamshire Justices in 1561 allowed a man 7d. an acre without meat and drink, and 5d. with meat and drink[86] — Thelbie can be said to have earned fairly good money. At Polebrook a man named Patchingham was nearly always employed. 'For 4½ days' mowing at 7d the day, 2s 7½d', runs a journal entry, and evidently he was a slower worker than Thelbie at Glapthorn.

At haymaking time even the women helped. Mistress Jankinson, the carpenter's wife, earned 1s. 4d. for working four days in the manor fields at Glapthorn. Bess Dewesborough did six days work, also at 4d. a day, and so did the Goodwives Carter and Gye; while Rose Elam joined them with Simon Dewesborough's maid, although the young girl was only paid 3d., since she did less work than the others. Over at Polebrook, it seems that Patchingham's household turned out in full force, for he collected 10s. for 'three women for ten days' making of hay', and 4s. 4d. for 'his wife's wages in harvest'.

Patchingham did all kinds of odd jobs at Polebrook throughout 1550, and probably in previous years as well, although there is no record of this, since the account-books have not survived. If ever the grain needed to be threshed and winnowed, Patchingham was sure to be called in. Between April and October he threshed 29½ quarters and 3 bushels of barley, and a quarter of wheat for the house, and John paid him 4d. a quarter for the barley, and 6d. a quarter for the wheat. It was a task that had to be done all the year round, to keep the household in bread.

> When rain is a let to thy doings abroad,
>   Set threshers a-threshing to lay on good load,
> Thresh clean ye must bid them, though less they yarn,
>   And looking to thrive, have an eye to thy barn.[87]

Threshing, like everything else before the coming of the machine age, was hard work. The grain was flailed with short clubs fixed to staves by cords, and the grain was winnowed out into great baskets with the help of a draught raised by goosewings. It was then stored in the 'cistern', and taken out as needed, to be ground in the mill. Many kinds of mills for grinding were in favour in the sixteenth century, 'some with small wheels, some with great, and some otherwise', but John preferred the largest kind, which were much easier to operate because of the compass of the wheel. During the winter of 1543, he shipped one home from Flanders that weighed nearly six hundredweight. Anthony Cave was most interested in the samples that John eventually sent him. 'I thank you for the meal of your milne's grinding which ye sent me. I have provided you a man for it, so that ye will let him take toll of your milne's getting.'

Much of the barley that was grown at Polebrook and Glapthorn was dried and made into malt, to ferment the strong ale that they drank. 'To Patchingham for his wife for 20 quarters of malt making — 3s 4d' runs one entry in Egillsfield's little book. More malt was produced than even John's large household could consume, and the surplus was always sold. Once a local man named Laurence Bailey came to the manor house to buy forty quarters of malt, and many were the instructions that Parson Saxby gave to Sabine.

> The cause of my writing to you at this time is to desire you to deliver to this bringer, Laurence Bailey, 40 quarters of malt ready dressed; or else he must have it in the dust, 9 stricks for 8, and he must have horse meat for himself and his man. And if he do take his malt ready dressed, he must pay half the charges for the dressing of it, and you must find the carters hay for their horses. I pray you, let him be honestly served, because he hath paid his money unto you before the receiving of the malt, which was but at his pleasure so to do.

Winter and summer alike, all the year round, there was work in plenty to be done on a farm, and not only at harvest and haymaking. There was ditching and digging and raking, ploughing and sowing, carting dung, spreading muck on the fields, weeding — 'mowing of thistles', the cutting back of the threatening brambles and undergrowth, and the clearing of the farmyard ponds. Another essential task was hedging, already a symbol of the enclosure movement, and a valuable improvement to the farmer's land, for they kept the cattle from straying, and gave shade in the summer heat. Whitethorn and hazel trees, crab-apples and holly were all advised as the best plants for hedging, and at Northawe Close, John bound himself from

> . . . felling, lopping or topping in your close other oak, ash, survey, or crab-tree; howbeit I desire it to be lawful to me to lop and top any of them within the hedges as often as I shall plash the hedges, whereunto I mistrust not but ye easily agree, forsomuch as the dropping of them would mar the quick, and so lose all my cost and destroy your hedges.

Plashing was a back-breaking job: the hedges were carefully thinned of their wood, and then the remaining branches were bent double and intertwined, so that in the spring the growth would be twice as thick as before. 'To Pollard and his son for seven days' felling of thorns and hedging in Batesman's Close, 7s' runs one item in the account-book for October 1550, and they were actually employed for another two weeks on the same work about the manor. Anthony Cave had the same problems at Tickford House, as his letter to John reveals.

> Touching our business at Tickford, I pray you, show Sir Richard that as soon as Premer hath done plashing that hedge he is in hand with, let him afterhand make an end of that at the Long Close end unto the watergate; and let Sir Richard in anywise cause the bank besides the hedge to be cast by Clark and two of his fellows, and quickset next the brook: I mean two or three places which I showed both Pawley and Sir Richard. This I think is not in the remembrance, but in anywise let it be done this next week if the water will serve; for it must be done shortly or it will not serve to do any good this year . . . And let him hire no day's men more than needs must, for I am content they take more leisure; and let mine own folks do it, unless the mending of all the hedges about my woods and closes about Thickthorns, which I 'pointed both Solme and Williamson should do. But I mean for all my things to be done about home, both in the garden and else-where, except the quicksetting and hedging of the leas, and scouring the rest of the ditch behind the barn, which things let Clark and his company do, other agreed or by the day, as ye think most for my profit.

There was then, as there is today, an unending succession of jobs to do. Repairs were often needed to the stables or the barn door; the tinker came every so often to mend the pots and pans, and the local blacksmith was called in to shoe the horses. Thomas Egillsfield's account-book shows that the Polebrook cart needed frequent repitching, and Patchingham used to do it at fourpence a time. Often too, the haywain needed repairs at Glapthorn, and the carpenters Kett and Jankinson would come up from the village to work on it, earning fourpence or sixpence for their labour as the case might be. Indeed, the carpenters were constantly employed, for many implements were made entirely of wood in the sixteenth century: the wooden wheels and the yokes for the oxen, the ladders and wheelbarrows used on the farm, the cheese presses, butter churns and deep wooden cream bowls in the dairy. Enormous quantities of wood were used as stakes for fencing, for bean-poles and pea-sticks, rails and hurdles and gate-posts, to say nothing of the great stacks of logs and split kindling that were consumed in the open hearths. 'To the sawers for two days — 1s 8d' runs one of Egillsfield's entries. John was fortunate in that he could rent the woods at Laund, and also at Cotterstock, for timber was scarce and highly prized in the sixteenth century, when it was reckoned that one acre of woodland properly managed was as good as an acre of corn or grass.

It is clear from the entries of wages paid to the servants in husbandry and the labouring men, that the gulf in the lives of rich and poor yawned deeply in the middle years of the sixteenth century, when prices were high and rising steeply, while wages lagged far behind. It has been estimated that while at the end of the fifteenth century a man could provision his household in grain and malt by dint of fifteen weeks' work a year, it took forty weeks' work by the time of the Statute of Artificers. The cost of board and lodging, put at a shilling in 1542, had risen to three shillings a week by 1552.[88] Those who were best off were the regular servants like Lucas and Preston, for their food and livery was found for them. The hardest hit were the labouring families in the village, the Patchinghams, Pollards and Elams. Admittedly they had their own little plots of ground to cultivate and keep a few hens and sheep on, but they could never count on steady employment, and such money as they did earn was attuned to the principle that the masters should have 'skilful servants to till the ground without unreasonable wages'.[89] Egillsfield's account-book reveals that Patchingham's slender earnings with John over five months totalled 21s. 2½d.; his wife earned 7s. 8d., and the other women of the family 10s. Even if Patchingham earned as much again working for other farmers in the district, while the womenfolk took in spinning, he would have been lucky if he could count on a steady wage of 3s. 6d. a week all the year round.

For such humble folk as these, the struggle to live must have been unbearably hard, and it is no wonder that so many in that age took to vagabondage and crime as the only way out. Not that John and Sabine would have allowed their poor neighbours to starve, for charity was a Christian duty to them, and many baskets of food and firewood must have found their way from the manor house during the long, hard winters. Often gifts of clothing are entered in the account-book: shoes and hose, a jerkin or a doublet for someone with no recognizable claim on John's goodwill, like the 'coat for Goodwife Samson, and a pair of sleeves — 6d'. There was poverty in plenty to be seen on the streets in those days. When Sabine was riding through Northampton one day she checked her horse and gave 2d. to 'two poor men', a gift which Egillsfield duly entered down in his little book, as he did the alms that John gave to the poor in Calais. It is also on record that John paid the rent of Goodman Atkins's — the poor poulter's — field for seven years and more at Glapthorn Manor, while the poulter presumably rendered him such services as he could by going back and forth to London with messages, parcels and the like. The standard of living of these poor husbandmen and 'peasants', as Ambrose Saunders called them, was miserably low. They lived in cottages whose floor was bare earth, with walls of mud and reed-thatched roofs. Their furniture was equally simple: a trestle table and rough forms, a bed with a mattress of plaited straw, a coverlet of 'dagswain or hopharlots' and 'a good round log under their heads instead of a pillow', as Harrison wrote in the reign of Elizabeth I. Perhaps the most vivid picture of their way of life comes in Arthur Golding's translation of the *Visit of the Gods*.[90] In place of the classic Philemon and Baucis, there emerges a vignette of Patchingham and his wife.

Philemon, bringing each a stool, bade rest upon the same
Their limbs; and busy Baucis brought them cushions, homely
gear.

Which done, the embers on the hearth she 'gan abroad to stir,
And laid the coals together that were raked up overnight,
And with the brands and dried leaves did make them gather
might,
And with the blowing of her mouth did make them kindle
bright.
Then from an inner house she fetched sere sticks and clifted
brands,
And put them broken underneath a skillet with her hands.
Her husband from their garden plot fetched coleworts, of the
which,
She shredded small the leaves, and with a fork took down a
flitch
Of resty bacon from the balk made black with smoke, and cut
A piece thereof, and in the pan to boiling did it put.
And while this meat a-seething was, the time in talk they
spent,
By means whereof away without much tediousness it went.
There hung a bowl of beech upon a spirget by a ring.
The same with warmed water filled the two old folk did bring
To bathe their guests' foul feet therein. Amid the house there
stood
A couch, whose bottom, sides, and feet were all of sallow wood,
And on the same a mat of sedge. They cast upon this bed
A covering which was never wont upon it to be spread,
Except it were at solemn feasts; and yet the same was old
And of the coarsest, with a bed of sallow meet to hold.
The gods sat down. The aged wife, right chare and busy as
A bee, set out a table, of the which the third foot was
A little shorter than the rest. A tilesherd made it even
And took away the shoringness; and when they had it driven
To stand up level, with green mints they by and by it wiped.
Then set they on it Pallas' fruit with double colour striped,
And cornels kept in pickle moist, and endive, and a root
Of radish, and a jolly lump of butter fresh and soote,
And eggs rare roasted. All these cates in earthen dishes came.
Then set they down a graven cup made also of the same
Self kind of plate, and mazers made of beech, whose inner side
Was rubbed with yellow wax. And when they paused had a
tide,

Hot meat came piping from the fire. And shortly thereupon
A cup of green hedge wine was brought. This ta'en away,
anon
Came in the latter course, which was of nuts, dates, dried
figs,
Sweet-smelling apples in a maund made flat of osier twigs,
And prunes and plums and purple grapes cut newly from the
tree,
And in the mids a honeycomb new taken from the bee.

It was of course inevitable that John should exercise a great
deal of authority and influence in the neighbourhood of Glapthorn. He was a wealthy and learned merchant, known to be
deeply attached to the Reformed Religion, and connected with
the local gentry; the tax-collectors now assessed him as 'John
Johnson, gentleman, of Glapthorn' in the subsidy rolls, where
once he had been recorded as the yeoman of Polebrook; and last,
but by no means least, he was Lord Cromwell's duly appointed
bailiff on the estate. This was an office which involved him in
many local affairs. In the letters, we find him collecting the rents
from the tenants and husbandmen, attending the manor court,
inquiring into the lord's 'rights and customs', distraining the goods
of villagers convicted of felony, helping the deserving poor, dealing
with stray horses that wandered in and out of the parish boun-
daries, and even trying to secure the action of the ecclesiastical
authorities in a case of suspected witchcraft. In everything he did,
and in all his beliefs and prejudices, John was completely a man
of his time.

In return for his assistance on the estate, Lord Cromwell and
Sir Thomas Brudenell did much for John, exerting their influence
where it would help him, and ensuring that his contribution towards the subsidy and benevolence was never heavier than he
could afford to pay. Sometimes, however, John aimed rather too
high, as in the spring of 1548, during that final wholesale plundering of chantry and church property. The dissolved monastic
estates of Fotheringhay had been granted to the Lord Admiral,
Thomas Seymour, who was the brother of Lady Cromwell, and
John was trying hard to obtain some part of the property. It was
through Lady Cromwell that Otwell hoped to urge his brother's
suit, and he waited upon her every other day in the hope of seeing

her, though with little chance of success, for, as he wrote: 'My lady is very sore grieved with the toothache, in suchwise as she went not forth of her house these ten days, nor yet can without further displeasure.' The suit failed, and eventually Fotheringhay passed into other hands. John was discouraged, but he decided to try another line of approach; he asked Otwell to try to secure for him all the moveable chantry property, the lead and timber, pewter, bellmetal and plate, which were even then going under the hammer in Northamptonshire. Otwell thought the idea hopeless, as indeed it was.

To compass to get all your chantries' stuff in your shire at the price it is praised for, passeth my capacity to attain to, not knowing to whom I may resort to speed thereof. And besides that, I think it is in the country as it is here in London, viz., there be men at hand to snatch up things of any profit before the Visitors can praise them.

Candlestick metal and such other like stuff is sold here (saith my brother Gery) but for 20s a 100 lb, which is 2¼d a pound, and that amongst pewterers and founders, one to another of them, and therefore to pass 14s or 15s for a 100 lb in the country you shall do no great profit, saith he.

Harrison's chantry must be sued for at Mr. Mildmay's hands, but it must be done with plainer instructions than you have now sent, and also diligent attendance to be given upon him, etc.

With so much competition against them, the result was a foregone conclusion. Richard Harrison obtained a quantity of bell-metal, which Otwell was commissioned to sell in London, while John received such a minute amount of pewter that it was hardly worth the trouble of carting it to London. 'My brother Gery hath your pewter,' wrote Otwell, 'which weigheth just 50 lb scant weight, for I see the weighing of it myself.'

The history of any Tudor manor would hardly be complete without its tale of argument and altercation between squire and parson. The severance of the tie with Rome, the creation of a national church under the authority of the temporal sovereign, and the spread of learning through all classes of society, were already tending to lessen the authority of the clergy, even though the reputation of the great Protestant preachers was at its height, and the struggle of Mary's reign had yet to come. The parson had not yet sunk to the position of dependency he held in the eighteenth century, but already the seeds were there. The wealthy and well-educated Tudor landlord saw no special reason to feel humble before his impoverished parish priest. However often the squire went to church on Sundays, he was more likely than not to be at loggerheads with the parson during the week, particularly over the vexed question of tithes. The church in the sixteenth century took as her due one-tenth of all the fruits of the earth. As the sheaves of wheat and barley, rye and oats, stood in the fields after harvest, every tenth sheaf was cut out and given to the parson. A tenth of the eggs and milk, calves, ducks and chickens were also yielded, and a tenth of the harvest of beans and peas, apples and pears. Tusser advised the farmer to pay up cheerfully. 'Tithe duly and truly with hearty goodwill, that God and his blessing may dwell with thee still', he wrote, at the same time warning the priest to keep a sharp lookout for his rights.[91] Tithes were exceeding profitable and worth having, and in the sixteenth century the parish priest frequently found it worth his while to farm them out for ready money, as did Parson Saxby, who leased the tithes as well as the parsonage of Polebrook to John, and was himself to a great degree dependent on John's goodwill.

There was thus no reason for John to suppose that the parson of Glapthorn would be less amenable to his wishes than cousin Saxby. But no sooner did he and Sabine set foot in the manor house than trouble began. The little church of St. Leonard at Glapthorn had always served as a chapel of ease to the fine neighbouring church of Cotterstock, where a great college had once stood, like that of Fotheringhay. In Henry VIII's reign, however, the College fell on sad times, and it was dissolved like so many other ancient foundations. The fine building was pulled down by John Norwich, a local landowner who eventually rented the manor and its lands. Two of the former provosts of the college were still living when John came to Glapthorn; and one of them, Dr. Edward Artewyke, was even then resigning the living into the hands of the other, Edmund Oliver.

It was the elderly Dr. Artewyke whom John so mistakenly approached about leasing the tithes. Oliver hotly resented this move, and the more so because the previous farmer, Nicholas Walker, had already made him an offer of £23 10s. a year to continue his lease, while John was only offering £20 10s. So vexed were the relations between the parsonage and manor house, despite all that Sir Thomas Brudenell could do to keep the peace, that in the spring of 1545 both sides met at Lincoln's Inn to air their grievances. Otwell, representing his brother, found himself at an acute disadvantage that afternoon. All the lawyers of the family were either ill, down at their country houses, or too busy to be bothered, and he had no legal counsel to help him. The preliminary discussions all went in favour of the parson. In fact, so certain was Oliver that he would win the case, that as soon as he got home to the village, he seized all the tithe milk and several calves. John was abroad at the time, and Sabine could do nothing except urge that the matter should be settled quickly, 'for the longer that you tarry, the less profit you shall have of it'. During the summer, the parson and Nicholas Walker went up to London again and, by a deliberate piece of deception, managed to engage John's unsuspecting uncle Croke, one of the Six Clerks of Chancery, to act as their lawyer. Sending the news down to the manor house by a shifty and unreliable messenger, nicknamed Sir Evank, Otwell told his brother what had happened.

A like gentleman unto this, the first letter of whose name is Nicholas Walker, is come to London, and yesterday put up a supplication against you unto my Lord Chancellor, Mr. Croke your uncle being retained of his counsel, but he not being ware that you were any party of the same. For the crafty child Nicol Walk-a-Knave hath left out of the said supplication your dwelling at Glapthorn, your being a gentleman, merchant, farmer or husbandman of the country, and saith singly, one John Johnson, of no place, faculty, nor occupation, but a man that is rich and greatly friended hath done and doth great wrong about the farm of the parsonage of Cotterstock (not once naming Glapthorn) unto one A. B. C. (for I know not this name), now parson of the same and successor to Edward Artewyke, clerk, etc., requiring process against you in the Chancery (for that he is not able to contend with you at the common law) and also against Artewyke, for to cause him to appear and to be examined and sworn upon certain articles that he hath devised interrogatories for, etc.; which Artewyke hath already been examined upon the same by Mr. Croke, and his examination put in writing before that I had knowledge of any part of the matter.

Otwell went to see John Croke as soon as he heard the news, but to little avail: he was told that matters would have to take their course. In one sense, Parson Oliver had shrewdly cut the ground from under John's feet, for the Court of Chancery in the sixteenth century existed mainly for the poor petitioner, who could hope there to obtain the impartial justice which was seldom to be had by process of common law. In his petition to the Court, the angry parson alleged that not until after he had been presented to the living did he discover that Artewyke had made over the tithes to John, and that the lease had been deliberately back-dated to January 1544. John, of course, strongly denied all the allegations, and countered by offering to produce the lease, which, he said, was dated in the September of 1544, and was perfectly in order. However eager the two contestants were to get the matter over, the law's delays were proverbial in the sixteenth century, and it was months before the hearing took place. In the country, village sympathies were all on the parson's side, and, when a local court was held in the summer, the presiding justice ordered Sabine to hand back all the tithes she had collected. Much against her will, she did so, except for two cows which she decided to keep. 'I pray you, take no displeasures with me for it', she wrote to John. 'Our priest is a very K., as our last was.'

The hearing was scheduled for November 1545, in Westminster Hall. Otwell was confident that they would win the case without any difficulty; he considered that John was in the right of it and, besides, they had solid legal backing. Sir John Croke was now on their side, together with Serjeant Saunders, and also Christopher Breten, 'whose diligent solicitation shall not be missing thereunto'. It came, therefore, as a great shock when all their hopes were suddenly dashed to the ground. Otwell himself could scarcely believe his own eyes.

In my former letters ... I did certify you at large of all your business then known. But since that time, viz. on Monday last, my Lord Chancellor himself made a decree against you in your parsonage matter, which Mr. Walk-a-Knave carried down into the country yesterday with speed, as I am informed, and there will put the parson in possession of all things that belong thereunto, with no small brag I am sure. To declare the circumstance of the ordering of this matter, neither time nor paper doth serve me now. The truth is, that the manner of such a decree-making hath not been known, seen, nor heard of before: that is, th'one party only spoken with by my said Lord, and th'other never called thereunto, nor any day given for the hearing thereof, or to make proofs. But my Lord, being thoroughly and privily incensed by Mr. Griffin, very suddenly and in a day (in a manner) extraordinary, pronounced the decree aforesaid; Mr. Croke, Mr. Serjeant, nor none other of your Counsel being heard speak therein, but rather commanded to silence, and the decree being ready drawn before my Lord sitting down in Westminster Hall. This judgement is to be taken in worth at my Lord's hands, for it can in nowise now be changed. . . .

Justice had been done. Lord Chancellor Wriothesley may have been moved by the facts of the case, convinced beyond a shadow of doubt that a great wrong had been done to a poor and unfortunate parson. However, the most reverend and approved good judges at that time had a fondness for rich gifts, and a man's innocence depended more often than not on how much he could afford to pay for it. There is unfortunately no record of the interview between Wriothesley and the parson's Counsel, Edward Griffin, so recently made Solicitor-General. What actually happened we shall never know. But, arbitrary as the decision was, the Johnsons had perforce to accept it. The parson took immediate advantage of the decree. He rode home post-haste to Glapthorn Manor, and demanded the corn and other tithes that Sabine had received. Sabine pretended valiantly that she knew nothing of the matter, but that same evening she wrote to Calais, begging John to come home, 'desiring you with all my heart to make all the speed that you can; and consider, good husband, how I am troubled with a Sir Priest, and have great need of help'. Three or four times did the parson hammer on the door, and each time she managed to fob him off. At last she was driven to write to her landlord at Deene for help, but Sir Thomas only replied that the lawsuit was over and done with, and that if she held on to the tithes any longer, 'then the parson upon malice might set both you and me in the Fleet. I had as lief the parson were there as other you or I'. Sabine was no sweet and clinging vine, but the thought of still more visits from the wrathful parson was driving her to desperation.

In most loving wise, well-beloved husband, with all my heart I commend me to you. This shall be most heartily to desire you to make all the speed home that may be, for if you come not home before Saint Thomas day, I shall not know how to behave myself to the parson and Walkerer, for as that day they will come to receive at our hands all such things as we have received, as wool and lamb, hay and other things; for I am sure if you be not at home they will be extreme with me. Wherefore if you come not home, I intend not to be at home all that day, but other I will go to Mr. Brudenell's or to Polebrook, because I will not be troubled with them, for two enemies against one woman is too much. You and my brother have small thanks to give the parson and Walk-a-K. for the report they give you, for I think there is nother my brother nor you that nother have done nor said as they say you have done. At your coming home you shall know more, and many lies I think.

Realizing at last how difficult things were for her, John decided to return home immediately. He took the next ship for England and rode straight into Northamptonshire, making up his mind that under no circumstances would he part with the tithes. When the parson and Walker came to demand them, he flatly refused to hand them over, and when a writ of imprisonment was issued against him, he took the matter to Sir Ambrose Cave and Sir John Croke, asking them to intervene personally with Lord Chancellor Wriothesley on his behalf. Thanks to his influential connections, the affair was smoothed over, at least for a time, and no more was heard of his being put in prison. Obstinately, John continued to collect the tithes. Here he met with considerable local opposition. Public opinion was now solidly behind Parson Oliver, and once, when John's servant went to collect the corn tithes, all the villagers stood round about him and threatened violence. The local court even made Sabine pay '£3 to the good parson of this town' for the tithes she had received. This state of things was very wearying to John. 'Fain I would be at quiet in the matter', he wrote to his brother-in-law, Christopher Breten, and yet, with both sides determined not to give way an inch, there seemed no prospect of agreement. But eventually a way out did present itself. The King made a grant of the advowson of Glapthorn to a certain Sir Robert Kirkham, and from a much-torn letter of Sabine's, written late in 1546, it appears that an amicable solution was reached between the new landowner, John and 'our wise Mr. Parson' that satisfied all parties to the quarrel.

John was perhaps inclined to be a little cavalier in his disregard of village opinion. This was not to be the only time that he met with opposition. John took his office as bailiff very seriously indeed; he was also an ardent Protestant in his religion, and the two together made it certain that he would alienate those who liked neither his authority nor his beliefs. And so it happened that during the spring of 1548 there was a disturbance over the mass at Glapthorn church, and an attack was made (or at least threatened) on John himself. 'Your neighbours' foolishness about the mass and sacrament, tending to a kind of seditious uproar', Otwell called it, when he was asked to forward letters to the Lord Protector from Sir Thomas Brudenell. This he did through his friend Armigill Wade, the Clerk of the Privy Council, and received word that while the Council was 'busy with matters of a more importance than this', yet the Duke of Somerset had himself found time to read the letter.

This day Mr. Wade hath declared unto me my lord grace's pleasure to be that this said bearer should repair home to his master, and shortly the Council's mind shall be sent after him in writing; he further saying unto me that (per adviso) I might certify you that my lord, have read over Mr. Brudenell's letter himself, took it in very good part, and very much commended his wisdom and your soberness in the pacifying of the matter so honestly, willing both him and you to keep the thing at that stay still, with all quietness and modesty, until ye be further written unto from his grace and the Council; me disant plus autre secrement, que puis que leur Dieu est bas, qu'il demeure bas, sans faire semblant de rien, et tout ce portera bien, au plaisir de Notre Dieu venant. This is it that I have to write you of for this matter.

The affair itself is shrouded in mystery. But it is clear that the disturbers of the peace were Catholics, poor adherents of the Old Religion, whose deepest feelings had been roused over the changes so recently instituted in the ritual of the mass. The Protector had ordained that Communion should now be given to the laity in both kinds; private masses were abolished; and a new evangelical Prayer Book was published for use throughout the realm. It was against this Prayer Book that the whole of the west of England rose in rebellion, to be followed later by Robert Kett in Norfolk, and the abortive rising in the north. Disturbances were common everywhere; there was fighting in the churches in many places, and a proclamation was actually passed forbidding assaults on the clergy. The degree of feeling in Glapthorn village can be seen from the Protector's reply to Sir Thomas Brudenell, which Otwell copied out carefully, in his large, tranquil handwriting, for his brother's benefit.

Copy.

After our very hearty commendations, we understand your diligence with good wisdom in the proceedings of the King's Majesty for the quiet of the country there, to have been such that we must needs render to you hearty thanks, praying you to continue. And whereas of late in the town of Glapthorn there hath and is great disturbance and disorder, in such sort that the bailiff there remaineth in much unsurety by the lewdness of divers there, whereof we understand John Broughton, John Desborough and Richard Trusse be ringleaders: we would ye should repair thither, and to examine the whole truth thereof, committing the offenders to prison for a season, until they be taught to study and apply to quietness and godliness, for such is the obstinacy of many people that without sharpness they will not amend. So fare ye heartily well, from the Westminster, the 21st of June, anno 1548.

Your loving friend,
Edward Somerset.

And so to prison they went. It says much for John that he now did everything possible to secure their release, writing letter after letter to Armigill Wade, imploring him to petition the Council to get the sentence quashed. Otwell, ever helpful, gave all the assistance he could towards 'the delivery of the poor men, because I know that the longer they lay in durance, the greater displeasure they will conceive against you, which is already too much; and I am heartily sorry that the things have so sharply passed against them (so knoweth God), for doubt of the continuance of their evil against you alway hereafter'. Otwell was a far more subtle and tactful person than his brother; he was adept at personal relations, and sensitive to the reactions of others. It is impossible to imagine Otwell in the awkward situation in which John now found himself, having provoked, however unwittingly, the hostility of the neighbourhood where he lived. But John tried hard to undo the damage that had been done, and with perseverance all the difficulties were gradually overcome. At the beginning of July the prisoners were released, though whether they were ever again able to feel charitably towards the manor house must always be doubtful.

Deeply involved as he now was in the affairs of manor and farm, and in every aspect of country life, whether work or pleasure, John never really forgot that he was a merchant by profession, and shortly after he had secured the release of his poor neighbours from prison, he turned towards trade in the country itself, shipping cargoes of wares to King's Lynn, and selling them there and at St. Ives, Peterborough, Oundle and Glapthorn, where he actually opened a shop. People came from miles around, as far away as Kettering and Market Harborough, to buy iron for their anvils and wine for their cellars. Richard Preston was kept busy delivering goods, collecting money, and even committing debtors to jail when he had to. 'He is but poor man,' he wrote of Simon Trundle, 'nevertheless he was in purchase when he had the wine of me.' There is a pathetic letter from Trundle begging John to release him for the sake of his wife and children, and promising to pay what he could. Occasionally there was trouble of a serious kind, when the customers complained of the quality of the wares. One citizen of Peterborough went round the town swearing that he would never have bought the wares if he had known they came from John Johnson, and refusing to pay for them. Nothing could conciliate such a man, as John explained to the merchant who was acting for him in the dispute.

Your Customer Lively of Peterborough ceaseth not to provoke me to think him to be mine enemy, as himself if he list to declare his stomach unto you will testify, your wife also knowing partly the same by his words and writing. I know myself in conscience clear that I bear no hatred toward him nor his occupying as he doth toward mine, for though it pleaseth him to misname me and my merchandise with doggish terms, yet I will not learn of him to be a merchant who can better teach a boy in the school, than such one as I am that have all my life been trained in the feats of merchandise. But seeing his malice is such as it is without cause, that he reporteth and writeth that he buy none of that ware he knoweth hath been mine, for to make him to know his good stomach the better, I shall heartily desire you not to let him have any wares of that ye have of mine, and then he shall not only have his own desire, but it may teach him to know himself the better, to bear malice toward them from whom he receiveth commodity.

The reason for the undoubted hostility of the Peterborough merchants (they once threatened to 'come into the cellar and lay your wine for the sobsides') may have been due to the fact that John was a Londoner, trading in their territory, and on privileged terms. The merchants of King's Lynn were hardly less hostile, although more law-abiding. When they discovered that John lacked an official certificate proving that he was a Freeman of London, and thus automatically exempt from paying butlerage dues, they seized their opportunity. One fine day, Richard Preston found the door of John's wine cellar sealed against him, while the customs officers threatened to make John pay £16 on the wine on board a ship in the harbour, and to have a cast at last year's money if a certificate was not immediately forthcoming. 'In this labour,' advised Preston, 'for if ye pay that, ye shall pay more customs that belongs to Lynn, and not suffered to sell anything but to a freeman.'

As John well realized, his whole existence as a merchant was now in jeopardy, for while in the provinces he was attacked as an intruding London capitalist, the City, jealous of her privileges, might well decide to treat him as a provincial merchant, domiciled in the heart of Northamptonshire. This they had already done to a merchant from Boston, taking away his cherished Freedom of London, and forcing him to pay the local dues. Accordingly,

John appealed first to the High Butler of England, and then wrote a classic statement of his case to one of the Wardens of the Drapers' Company, the wealthy and influential Edmund Calthorpe.

Laus Deo.

Anno 1552, the 6 in February, at Tickford.

After due commendations unto your mastership, so it is Sir, being here with my uncle Cave (who is sick, God comfort him), I am informed by letters from my friend and partner Bartholomew Warner, that Mr. Elderton, the High Butler of England, is put in doubt of my freedom of London because I am sometime resident at a house I have in Northamptonshire; wherefore, being troubled at Lynn for butlerage of wine (whereof all freemen of London are free cleared by charter, and ought to pay none thorough the realm), I cannot get Mr. Elderton's discharge for the same, unless he be otherwise satisfied than by my own saying.

This shall be therefore most heartily to desire you to be so good master unto me that it would please you, being one of the Wardens of the Company, to declare unto the said Master Elderton how I am used and taken amongst the Company of the Drapers, not doubting, considering I have and intend to use myself as an obedient citizen in paying and doing all that is my duty to do, if need shall be, the rest of my masters the Wardens will also be so good as stand with me, that I may enjoy that which I have served for, and borne charges for. And although during my brother's life my house in London seemed to be rather my brother Otwell's, God rest his soul, than mine, yet I assure you, as I am a true man, the charges was mine as much as his, and part of the house I always occupied for a wool-house, and at many times the most part I used for the same purpose. And now, since my brother's decease, my charges will not be borne in London for a hundreth mark a year; and therefore, bearing such charge in a City, methink I should have much wrong if I should not be permitted to enjoy part of the profit.

Besides all this, Sir, my case is not alone, for a great many worshipful men of the City is in my case, and therefore if they should lose their freedom because other for their pleasure, health, or commodity they lay or keep house in the country, a great many should lose it, and it were such a bondage as it behoveth none of us all to grant unto. Thus Sir, I am troublous unto you, but your accustomed gentleness hath boldened me, requiring you in my absence to be so good as help my said friend Bartholomew Warner in that he shall need in this matter; and within this month by God's grace I will be at London, and shall give you most hearty thanks for the same, and at all times be glad to recompense you with any pleasure or service that may lay in my power.

When next one of John's ships docked at Lynn, the cellar doors were open wide to receive his wine, the customs officers smiled on him, and there was no more talk of freedom and butlerage. The inference is clear. The Worshipful of the City, with their magnificent country houses and vast estates, were in no position to debar John from their midst. The decision was a victory, not only for John, but for all merchants everywhere. Go where they would for pleasure or for health, their liberty and livelihood were safe. A man could make his fortune and build his country house; he could lay out his charming gardens with their fountains and lawns and flowers; he could farm his land, breed cattle and sheep, and invest his spare capital as he pleased throughout the realm, sure that his rights and privileges in the City would be unimpaired. A precedent was set, a custom established that later generations were to enjoy to the full, until it became rooted as part of the English way of life. The prosperous Cit of Stuart times, the fabulous Nabob of the Hanoverian age, the millionaire railway magnate of the Victorian era, all returned at last to the land as John Johnson once had done. 'See', wrote Cobden to Bright, 'how every successful trader buys an estate!'

PART FOUR

GEORGE GISZE

CHAPTER 8

JOHNSON & COMPANY

No more delightful and intimate study of a sixteenth-century merchant has ever been painted than the Holbein portrait of George Gisze. 'The picture you see here records the features of George', reads the billet on the wall. 'Such are his lively eyes, such is his face.' 'He sits alone in his accustomed room,' wrote Ruskin, 'his common work laid out before him; he is conscious of no presence, assumes no dignity, bears no sudden or superficial look of care or interest, lives only as he has lived — but for ever.'[92] Thirty-four years old, he stands in his counting-house as John or Otwell might have stood, the sombre black of his flat cap and surcoat acting as a perfect foil to the flame-coloured satin of his doublet.

Before him is a small, square table covered with a Turkey carpet, and on the soft pile lies a chased silver timepiece, with the hands pointing to half-past twelve o'clock; nearby is a seal and a signet ring, a large pair of scissors, and a round money-box with coins in it. There are two slender pewter inkwells with the worn quill pens still in them, and a sandbox ready to sprinkle over the wet ink of the letters. To one side of the table is a delicate glass vase, filled with pink-and-white carnations; and on the other side, propped up against the wall, is a leather-bound ledger, stitched with criss-cross vellum, buckled with leather straps, and clasped with a steel clasp. The young merchant himself has just broken the seal of a letter, which is folded as the Johnson Letters are folded, and addressed, 'Dem erszamen Jergen Gisze to Loundon in Engelant, mynem broder to handen.' Other letters have been hooked carelessly into the narrow laths that run round the panelled walls, serving as letter racks. On one of the carved wooden shelves lies a second ledger, a thin book — perhaps of Latin verse, to while away the leisure hours — and just such a 'box with writings and letters' as was once sent down to John at Glapthorn Manor. Strongly made of spruce and pinewood, hasped with steel, these standing-boxes, as they were called, were used for filing all kinds of documents, and they were proof against both dust and vermin, unless the careless owner left them open, as Henry Southwick did on one occasion.

As yet (he wrote to John) I hear nothing from Marcus Backlier, whose bills by a great misfortune are chawed with mice or rats so that they are no more than legible. It is no danger, considering the men to be honest, and if they were otherwise, the bills be pleadable enough. I never perceived mouse nor rat to bear my compt before, but now am I warned to keep my boxes better shut!

From another of the shelves in the counting-house hangs a heavy seal on a crystal ball, and from a hook on the opposite wall swing a great bunch of maze-cut keys, and a stringholder (Ruskin's 'ball of gold, chased with blue enamel') with a length of sealing thread still dangling from it. Here also is that indispensable item of a merchant's equipment, the delicately strung triangular scales, fashioned so that they could be held in one hand while the gold and silver was weighed in the balance. We find Anthony Cave asking John to find his gold weights, and the leather bag with his touch-stone, by which the fineness of the gold was assessed. Another time, Otwell asked John to buy 'a small pile and balance' for him in Flanders, of which he was much in need. The best of these intricate precision instruments came from the Antwerp workshops. They were expensive to buy, and merchants used to set great store by their favourite weights and scales.

In any wise (wrote Anthony Cave to John) I pray you remember my cousin Haddon for the hourglass, and that it may be very good and cleanly; and I pray you, let be sent in my chest and handsomely trussed, my two balances and pile. I lent your brother Otwell one: whether it were that I had in Calais in a case, or that in London I am uncertain; but I pray you seek or know where the balances in the case that I had at Calais be, for I saw them not a great while. I would not give them for 20s and more money.

It was in just such a counting-house as Holbein painted that the firm of Johnson & Company had established their headquarters by the year 1542, in a house on Lime Street belonging to Anthony Cave. It must have been a good-sized house with plenty of room in it, for although the owner stayed there only on his rare visits to the City, it could comfortably accommodate Otwell and Maria, and their apprentices; John or Richard if they happened to be passing through London; and the caretaker and housekeeper, George Grant and his wife. There was the counting-house where the firm's business was transacted, a woolhouse where the great sarplers of wool and fells were packed, and deep, stone-paved cellars where the wine and salt were stored. Lime Street itself was situated in one of the best parts of town, with 'divers fair houses for merchants and others' set among charming gardens.[93] One of the Woodrofs, the wealthy stapler family, lived at the Green Gate, a house which had once belonged to the Frenchman John Meautas, and which had been attacked in the Evil May Day riots of 1517. Nearby stood Stephen Kyrton's great house and, not far off, the mansion belonging to Richard Whethill, the merchant who built himself a lofty tower — one of the first of its kind in London — from which he was accustomed to admire the view over the City streets, across the masts of the ships in the river, to the woods and hills beyond.[94]

The firm of Johnson & Company developed naturally out of the circumstances and events of the 'thirties. Having no son, Anthony Cave looked on John much as if he were his own flesh and blood, and his willingness to take him into partnership increased as he realized how intelligent and ambitious the young man was, and that Otwell showed as much promise as his brother. When John married his master's niece, the link between them was forged still closer. Together they embarked on joint trading ventures, and eventually, despite the fact that Anthony Cave was wealthier and many years older that John and Otwell Johnson, the firm was established as Johnson & Company, continuing under that name for more than a decade. The three men were the senior partners of the firm. Richard Johnson and Ambrose Saunders were apparently not taken on until 1547 and 1550, when their Staple apprenticeships came to an end, and then only as junior partners. The firm was a predominantly family concern, like the majority of other firms at that time, a self-contained organization which was yet capable of almost limitless expansion, and which was the nucleus from which the great capitalist firms of the future were to evolve. It was a system which called for immense shrewdness on the part of the men involved in it, for cool judgment and an eye to the main chance, loyalty to the common interests, and an enormous capacity for sheer hard work. It was an age when businesses could be built up from nothing, but when their independence and fortunes were bound up in every move they made. One man's success must help them all, but let him slip up on the job, and the smooth working balance was destroyed and all their prospects were ruined. •

The Johnson Letters afford many examples of such family firms, both English and foreign, into which not only sons, but also sons-in-law, brothers, nephews and cousins had been absorbed. We read of Thomas Appenrith and his son, Pierre Artus & Company, Sir George Barnes and his son, John Branch and his son-in-law Robert Dunne; the three Brinklows; John and Edmund and Martin Calthorpe; Bernardo, Guido and Tomaso Cavalcanti; George and Thomas Eton; Cornelis, Francis and Quirin Peter Garbrantzon; the four Mahiews at Lille; Sir Andrew and John and William Judde; James, John, Richard, Thomas and Walter Leveson; Matthew and Thomas Lok & Company; the elder and younger John Lyons; Jois and Leonard Schorer et Frères at Antwerp, to name only a few. Of these firms, many were to succumb in the course of time, but others, like the Loks and Levesons, were to survive the crises through which they passed, and achieve great wealth in succeeding generations. Through it all, the merchant's attitude was one of faith tempered by patience and resignation. As John wrote to a friend whose firm was in temporary financial distress,

> I beseech God send you better tidings of the rest of your adventure, and that it may please him to send you gains to recover your losses. Ye are wise, and can consider that the chances of this world is not always alike, and therefore to confirm your will patiently to abide that which God knoweth is best.

The framework and organization of sixteenth-century firms like Johnson & Company were curiously casual. It was really an association of merchants linked together by the need to serve certain common interests, while at the same time each member of the firm was left completely free to follow his own line of trade, embark on joint trading ventures with one or more partners of the firm, or with English and foreign merchants outside it, and even to act as agent for other merchants if he chose so to do. Inevitably, the interests and functions of the partners of Johnson & Company differed widely. Although a member of the Livery of the Drapers' Company, Anthony Cave's chief trade was in wool and fells to the Staple. Never in very good health, he spent much of his time at home in the country, occupied with farming and local affairs, and contenting himself with sending reams of prudent advice to the younger members of the firm, and to Thomas Smith, who handled the money side of his affairs in much the same way as Otwell did for John, but who played only a minor part in the firm's trade. It was John who did most of the hard work for himself and Cave, riding round Northamptonshire buying up wool and fells, sharing in joint ventures with his master, and travelling on the Continent between Calais, Bruges and Antwerp. And while John occasionally shared in trading ventures with other merchants, all his major ventures were undertaken in partnership with his brother Otwell, importing and exporting grain and herring, cloth and wine. Both of them shared in ventures with the Flemish firm of Mulier, Garbrand & Company, but at the same time Otwell traded on his own account and with other merchants, besides acting as agent for several foreign firms.

All the members of the firm played their part and did their share of the work, and yet the letters make it clear that much of the responsibility and most of the decisions lay with Otwell Johnson. No better person could have been chosen, for Otwell was an unusually gifted and able young man. Possessed of keen intelligence and shrewd judgment in all practical matters, he was one of those outstanding men who are able to do several jobs at once, all of them well. Until his master retired from the Court, Otwell was required to be at his beck and call, at Greenwich, Hampton Court, or anywhere else that Sir John happened to be — the post was no sinecure. Otwell was also extremely active in the affairs of the Drapers' Company. He was among those who assembled in 1545 for the election of the Master Bachelors. Held at Drapers' Hall, until recently the residence of Thomas Cromwell, it was altogether a splendid affair. There was a ceremonial banquet attended by the leading merchants in the livery, and after their departure the 'Bachelors sat at the high table, and were served with spice bread, pears, filberts and damsons. The old Master Bachelors sat with Master Wardens at the upper end of the west

side table, and after the midst of their recreation, the old Master
Bachelors came out of the great parlour with minstrels and their
cup-bearers before them, and went down by the west side table
and about the hearth, and returned up by the east side table . . .
each drinking to the others'. Only two years afterwards, Otwell
was himself one of the chief actors at the feast, when he was
elected one of the four Masters Bachelors of the Yeomanry. It was
Otwell, always sociable, who led his colleagues in a petition to
hold an annual breakfast or dinner for the yeomanry, so that 'each
of us should get a loving acquaintance of the other, as it becometh
all honest men to wish for, and as men of other fellowships do'.
Permission was granted, and so the custom of the annual dinner
began, with the merchants being free to bring their wives (but no
other ladies) along with them.[95] Otwell continued his interest and
activity in the Drapers' affairs, and in the year 1550 he was
admitted to the livery.

The greatest part of Otwell's time was of course devoted to his
own and his brother's business, for he managed all John's affairs
at the London end. Twice a year, in spring and autumn, the
wool and fells came up by cart from the country, and he had to
supervise the weighing and packing in the woolhouse, the sale of
the inferior sorts to the Kentish and Suffolk clothiers, and the
lading of the ships destined for Calais. Sometimes he himself rode
into the country, negotiating wool and fell deals with the men of
Lewes. Otwell was also responsible for receiving the cargoes of
wares that John or their various agents shipped from the Continent, for cellaring and warehousing the goods, and selling them
at as high a price as they would fetch. He settled the bills for
wares that John contracted, called on their debtors, and paid
their creditors. The arrangement was a necessary and convenient
one for John, since he was often in the country or abroad, but it
involved Otwell in a great deal of work, and there were often
times when he worked into the early hours of the morning, until
'perforce of sleep compelled to make an end'. John and Otwell
were joined in partnership together far more closely than with any
other member of the firm. Their stock of money was apparently
kept in common, and used freely by both of them without any
question of interest being paid. This was sometimes to Otwell's
disadvantage. Once he wrote and told his brother that he could
keep 'no store' of money by him, but had always to 'put it forth

to furnish your commissions', and on an earlier occasion he found that he had not so much as forty shillings in ready money to lay his hand on. During the slight contretemps with Sabine which has been related in an earlier chapter, John evidently suggested that he should pay interest to his brother, a suggestion that Otwell utterly refused to consider.

> Where you note unto me our determination of profit for disbursing of money about your affairs, I trust you did understand my writing that I should not esteem my doing too much, but that thereby I meant only the declaration of the small store of money that I had by me to furnish my sister your wife's request that she sent unto me for suddenly, and else nothing. For would to Our Lord that I had so much money of mine own as would serve your purpose continually, without taking any by exchange, and then you might be assured thereof without any reproach . . . and so continue in supporting your affairs as you do mine, with right goodwill, God to friend.

Such a generous attitude was possible only between merchants in close partnership, for the payment of interest was a normal factor of commercial life. It is true that up to 1545 it was illegal to lend or take money at interest, but there was a wide divergence between out-of-date laws and modern merchant practice. Merchants needed credit and capital to finance their businesses, and they could not wait until conservative opinion moved with the times, even if it meant that they were on the shady side of the law. The Protestantism that was so widespread among the merchant class probably helped to account for their attitude, for those who were most deeply imbued with the doctrine of the Calling were almost certain to be the most advanced in mercantile ideas. Indeed, it was said that usury 'took with the brethren like polygamy with the Turks'.[96] While Luther had condemned usury more severely than the mediaeval doctors, the more realistic Calvin and Bucer gave it their moderate approval. Anything else would probably have been useless. World trade was opening up to an extent undreamed of by mediaeval society; there were new opportunities for commerce which had never existed before, and merchants were determined to take advantage of them, with or without the approval of the Church. England was among the pioneers of this new business world, and as early as 1500 the Italian diplomat had remarked that the English were 'so diligent in mercantile pursuits, that they do not fear to make contracts on usury'.[97] John himself had no objection to doing a little pawnbroking on the side; he was always willing to lend money on silver plate, or a 'fair and lusty gelding'. But it is clear that neither he nor Otwell was mean and miserly, or that they exacted the last drop of money from impoverished debtors. They were merely willing to help out where they could, as in the case of John's carrier, William Wedd of Tickford.

This bringer, William Wedd (wrote Otwell) hath not agreed with Jackson the grocer for that he oweth him, but privily hath kept himself out of his sight, and so is come homeward: but at your coming to London next, we shall devise some way for the poor fellow.

In 1545, interest up to 10 per cent was made legal. But once again the Act merely emphasized the wide gap between the statute book and what John called 'th'order of merchants' — the unwritten code that governed the behaviour and regulated the practices of the estate of merchants, both at home and abroad. Clearly, as John remarked, it was 'folly to pay interest without great need', but, since they needed capital to finance their businesses, pay it they must. In 1544, the three partners borrowed a thousand pounds from Edward Wilmot, paying interest at 12 per cent. In 1545, the year of the Act, their uncle Tanfield tried to borrow money; the lowest rate that Raymond the broker could arrange was '£16 on the hundred for a year'. And when John's brother-in-law, Christopher Breten, offered to pay John the legal 10 per cent on a loan in 1546, 'I may not stay my occupying for such interest', came the reply. 'If I should, it might be a great hindrance to my credit.'

Their attitude to the exchange was equally advanced, for, while even in Elizabeth's reign old-fashioned theorists might condemn exchange transactions out of hand, the merchants themselves could not have existed without it. Careful calculations in one of John's account-books show that between September 1544 and January 1545 he made a profit of £25 11s. 3d. on the exchange. Not the least of Otwell's tasks was dealing with the exchange business of the firm. Only a stone's throw from the Lime Street house, and where he and Maria actually went to live in 1548, was Lombard Street, the centre of the Italian merchant colony in London, and the very heart of the business world. Lombard Street was to London what the Rialto was to Venice and the Bourse to Antwerp. Several times a day, at known and appointed hours, the merchants gathered in the 'Street' (as they called it) to transact their business, talking over all the international news, negotiating loans, meeting with their brokers, and learning the latest rates of exchange between London and Antwerp, which would often vary considerably between the morning, noon and night streets. There they discharged their bills of exchange, which must be dealt with to the very minute, otherwise they were publicly 'protested in Lombard Street', a catastrophe which would mean irreparable damage to a man's credit. The merchants met in the open air, whether it was fine weather, deep in snow or pouring with rain, a disagreeable state of affairs that continued for many years. The attempt of 1534 to turn the Leadenhall, used as a wool warehouse and storage depot for the City's pageant props, into a 'Bourse for the assembly of merchants' had failed lamentably, largely because the elder merchants insisted that what had been good enough for their fathers would be good enough for their sons, and it was not until 1576 that Sir Thomas Gresham's Royal Exchange was opened. As might be expected, Lombard Street was a miserably old-fashioned and uncomfortable place, compared with the magnificent pillared courtyards of the Antwerp Bourse, and it was the subject of many bitter complaints, '. . . considering what a city London is, and that in so many years they have not found the means to make a Bourse, but must walk in the rain when it raineth, more liker pedlars than merchants. . . .'[98]

Antwerp at this time was still the commercial centre of the world, and the great clearing-house of European trade. It was the headquarters of the millionaire banking houses, the Fugger, Deodati and l'Affaytadi, merchant princes to whom the kings of Europe owed more than they would ever repay. Antwerp was the home of every luxury and industry that the genius of man could devise. 'Il n'y a chose en laquelle n'aparoisse la richesse, la puissance, pompe et magnificence de ceste excellent et illustre Cité', wrote Ludovico Guicciardini, and the people were 'grands trafiqueurs et fort riches . . . courtois, civil, ingénieux, soudain a scavoir imiter l'estranger, scavant parler de trois ou quatres langues . . .'⁹⁹ Here at Antwerp four great marts were held every year, Cold mart in winter, Pasche in spring time, Sinxon in summer, and Balms in the autumn, lasting weeks at a time, while half Europe cleared its bills of exchange, paid its debts, bought new wares, and made its money home at the most favourable rates. The Bourse at Antwerp was as indispensable to the merchants of the 1540s as Lombard Street would soon become, and as Wall Street would be in the distant future.

Johnson & Company was not a rich enough firm to have a permanent Antwerp branch, although the volume of their business was sufficiently heavy for them to employ an agent there, a representative of a bigger firm who had time to handle other men's affairs. Their first agent, William Gifford, went on a journey to Venice in 1544, and his place was taken by another man, Robert Tempest. This appointment, however, was not successful. For over a year, he sent John no word of how his affairs stood. 'I have received no letters from you,' was John's oft-repeated complaint, 'and therefore but by guess I know not how my business proceedeth.' So unsatisfactory was the position that John gradually began to place the firm's affairs in the hands of another merchant, Robert Andrew, a young man who lived permanently in Antwerp as the representative of his master, the wealthy Stephen Kyrton. He was extremely efficient and capable, as John told Anthony Cave. 'Ye shall not need to doubt but Robert Andrew will see from time to time your bills and business answered, for he is a very honest young man, and painful.' To Robert Andrew himself, John wrote his grateful thanks, and informed him of the salary that he proposed to pay.

> I do perceive by . . . your letter in what estate all my business standeth, and in effect I am certified fully from you of all things needful at this time, for the which your great pains and gentleness I do yield unto you thanks, accounting myself no less than bound to recompense you for the same. And I heartily pray you, if there be any manner of thing that I may do you pleasure in, to advise me thereof, and ye shall be as assured of me so far as my power will extend, Yea, and something further too, if I may do it by any of my friends.
>
> Of the continuance of your gentleness I do nothing doubt,

for I have found you much readier in all things than I might honestly require you. But because I do purpose to be bold to charge you with my business from henceforth (if it please you to give me leave that I may so do), I shall desire you to accept £8 Fl. a year, which Mr. Cave and I together will allow you towards part of your charges . . . I am now bold to require you right heartily that ye will at all times hereafter answer and accept all such bills as shall come from Mr. Cave, Otwell Johnson my brother, Thomas Smith, or myself. . . .

For months after that, as long as Robert Andrew received the necessary bills, money and information, the firm's business was handled smoothly, efficiently and with dispatch at the Antwerp end. But the price that had to be paid for solvency in the sixteenth century was eternal vigilance, and trouble invariably began with the first signs of neglect. Such difficulties first befell the firm in the spring of 1547, when John was at home in the country, recovering from the ague. The 'dregs' of his sickness made him 'slothful', as he said, and since he had sent Richard to take charge in Calais, there was no crying need for him to go abroad until he was 'perfectly recovered'. It was spring at Glapthorn Manor, and every week brought fresh delights to orchard, wood and field. Leading an idyllic rural existence with Sabine and the children, John felt less and less inclined to exert himself over business. He decided, with Otwell's willing help, to conduct his affairs by letter. Unfortunately, remote control was useless in the sixteenth century. The personal touch meant literally everything. Otwell could take on just so much, but he could not be responsible for every single one of John's commitments. Soon the inevitable bills began to pile up: the wool custom, the payments on the Wilmot loan, the fell payments, and particularly the exchange transactions between Calais and Antwerp. John was so far from the head and source of news, the City, that, when letters at last reached him, all the quotations were several days old and therefore completely out of date. And when Otwell warned him not to overshoot himself, John sent a long and reproachful letter back, charging his devoted brother with 'irksomeness' in the performance of his duty. Otwell was a patient man, but he now became understandably annoyed. In a long and crystal-clear letter, he analysed all his brother's mistaken calculations, and while he promised to continue his 'diligence (as I am bold to name it) about your affairs, to the best of my power and cunning', he ended with the significant remark: 'I am sure you should have made mo voyages to London, and longer abroad there, with larger costs than you have hitherto done, since I could do anything for you.'

That same week, John went down with another attack of ague, leaving Otwell no doubt ashamed of his hasty words, though unable to resist the suspicion that his brother was not as ill as all that. But John made no move to come up to London. At the end of June he was still resting at the manor house, and 'still', wrote Otwell, 'there cometh payments of money unto me from all sides for you, and I always empty-handed, God send a good end of all'. At last the situation became too much even for Otwell. The letter he then wrote to John makes it clear how imperative it was for Tudor merchants to keep in the closest possible touch with their affairs in London and Antwerp.

As opportunity and messengers have served (brother), I have from time to time certified you of the course of th'exchange here in London, and yet now again I am (as it were) compelled to repeat that matter again, for that you cease not daily to charge me with great and sudden payments, which (you know) I cannot furnish but by the said exchange, and that is now so much risen above the prick of your calculation, that hitherto you have made in your letters to me, that herewith I must needs let you know mine unableness to perform your appointments, in suchwise as you seem to limit them to be done.

And therefore I beseech you, weigh all things better with yourself ere you charge me any further, for if you do, in good faith you shall work much against your own honesty and profit, for that it layeth not in my power to answer your business as you do appoint. Note, I pray you, that your extreme overcharging of me already against and before the payments of this Pasche mart, hath brought Robert Andrew too short of £100 sterling (at least), which he must recharge you shortly with the repayment thereof here in London (as you have already willed him to do), shrewdly to your advantage, as th'exchange is altered. But well, if that now again you will continue to do the like unto me (as indeed, you go handsomely about it), you shall double your own disprofit, and also force me to say nay to th'answering of all your things.

The much occasion of this my vehemency herein riseth of the payments now in hand of £100 sterling to Mr. John Cope, and £60 to Mr. Breten, etc., besides your often writing to have money sent unto you this week and that week, to Tickford or to Glapthorn; and so in a manner weekly, one great payment or other followeth in each other's neck, so as I am in nowise able to furnish money sufficient for all (so suddenly as you do appoint your payments) for my life, th'exchange so much differing from your reckoning thereof, as indeed it doth. Stay therefore (I pray you) for God's sake your hands in time, lest all be turned into the dust, and remember the French proverb, 'Qui trop embrasse, peu retient, ou retraint'.

Somehow or other, Otwell managed to tide things over. Indeed, he was forced to do this, as, except for a brief excursion to Calais on the occasion of Richard's wedding, John did not set foot outside Northamptonshire. And when he returned home, he stayed there the whole of the following year, with the same dire results to the business. All the time Robert Andrew was complaining incessantly that he was being overcharged, and Otwell in London was hard put to maintain their credit. 'This I say and I have said,' he urged his brother, 'use you your discretion, in God's name'. And in another letter he told John straight out: 'You have kept the country too much this last year.'

It was not entirely John's fault that things went wrong. A contributory cause was undoubtedly Richard, who had taken John's place at Calais in 1547. At first, John entertained great hopes of his youngest brother, of whom he was very fond, and as proof of his confidence, he instructed his agent to open a joint account in both their names. 'I desired you (in a previous letter) to make up in your book my account, and the rest to set in a new place on the name of John and Richard Johnson; and desired you to accept such business as my brother shall assign unto you, even as (I thank you) ye have done for me.' To Anthony Cave, John wrote that the sales were so good that even a child could handle them, and saying how hopeful he was of Richard's ability. But the older man was a shrewd judge of human nature; he had seen the sulky boy grow up into an uncertain-tempered young man, and he had great misgivings about the future. Cave's fears were justified by events, and John and Otwell were to find to their cost that Richard could never be trusted to do anything on his own. They had always to watch him and nag him into some semblance of work and efficiency.

And yet some of the things that did go wrong were due, at least in part, to the way that John was feeling. He had conceived, during these years, a growing distaste for the world of business. He desired only to live the life of a gentleman-farmer in the country, forgetting that the greater part of his income came from trade, and that without it he could do nothing. Had anyone accused him of neglecting his business, he would undoubtedly have been much annoyed, and would have pointed out that he was much occupied in the counting-house at Glapthorn, that he had a great deal of wool and fell-buying on his hands, as well as his dealings at Peterborough and King's Lynn. Besides all this, there was the training of the young apprentices to be considered, and this was a duty that John took very seriously indeed. The manor house during these years sheltered a succession of boys and young men, for whose welfare and education John was responsible. Some of the lads were promising and intelligent, like the boy at Antwerp, 'so apt to do all things as I never look for his like', wrote Ambrose Saunders. 'A good servant is the blessing of the Lord.' Others were rather different, like poor Clement Smith, whose 'lewd fashions' would never amend. The Johnsons came to know all sorts and conditions.

John's first experience with apprentices was a sad one, for capable young Thomas Holland died tragically of the plague in 1544. It was in the winter of the same year that John Master of Sandwich, an old friend and trading partner of the Johnsons, brought his son Peter to London. The lad was almost eighteen years old and, because he had been at 'his learning for to have language' since Midsummer 1543, the father wanted the indentures to date from that year, for 'he would not his son to have lost so much time as to begin his years now'. Unfortunately for the father's wishes, John proved adamant, arguing that it would be 'agin conscience to take his oath or he be made free', before he had served the nine years out, despite the fact that the boy had been set to further study at his own request. The earlier indentures which had been drawn up were cancelled in the Drapers' books, and new ones made out in 1545. Peter Master proved an excellent apprentice, and he was granted the freedom of the Staple in 1548.

The premium paid for training an apprentice varied considerably. It was probably difficult without influence to place a boy in a really well-established house, under famous merchants like Sir William Chester or the Greshams, and it was certainly beyond the means of a man from the provinces, who was only moderately well-to-do. Even so, Peter's training cost his father over a hundred pounds sterling, and it seems that John had acquired a sufficiently good reputation to be able to pick and choose the apprentices he wanted. For another year or so, he was content to have Peter Master as his sole apprentice, but during the spring of 1545, he began to negotiate for a second boy. While he was doing so, he received a letter from an acquaintance in Calais, asking him to take young John Long, the son of a man to whom John had already made a half-promise, and who had 'learned the French tongue well this twelve months at Saint Omers, and doth both write and speak the same very well, and I assure you he is a fair penman . . .' Since the negotiations for William Pratt were almost complete, however, and Staple regulations forbade John to have more than two apprentices at once, he was forced to turn the offer down. Soon, Master Pratt was on his way to Glapthorn Manor, and there, as has been related in an earlier chapter,[100] he proceeded to make as much trouble as he could.

'God make him an honest man!' exclaimed Otwell after the indentures had been signed, hoping that the boy would improve. Time, however, did not sweeten their relationship. 'Your book of copy of letters is not to be found in my house,' wrote Otwell some months later, 'and therefore let Master Pratt remember himself better thereof. The story of his life shall be sent you shortly, with beer, cheese and brawn.' But there was more to it than just an unwilling boy. Young William was clearly miserable with John; the two disliked each other, and there was no turning their antagonism into such a friendship as John had himself enjoyed with his own master. So bad were relations between the two of them that at Christmas Master Pratt was left in London with Otwell, and it was then that he confided how unhappy he was. Otwell thought it was high time such a state of affairs was brought to an end. He went to visit the boy's mother and stepfather, at the same time writing to John.

> Master Pratt, your man that was, will dwell no more with you, unless you will be his servant, for he can in nowise find in his heart to serve you, nor never did hitherto with any good-will, as he hath now plainly declared to me, and I have done the same again in his behalf to his father and mother. All that he hath done heretofore hath been counterfeited, and without any manner of love towards you or your wife, being in fear of his friends' displeasure. But now my child's gentle thoughts are thrust abroad, and like one altogether void of grace (Our Lord help) requireth nothing but his own liberty, and most especially to be rid of your service, for thereunto he will never return with any good mind towards you or his own profit, become of him what shall, and so therefore you left him in a good season, for better lost than found.

Not long afterwards, a new master was found for William, still the same 'lewd boy' they had known all along, whose mother's 'foolish love', wrote Otwell, 'will coke (cosset) him still. You are well rid of him'.

Otwell never seems to have had as much trouble with his apprentices as John did, perhaps because he was more genuinely fond of young people, and knew instinctively how best to handle them. Only one of them, John Kele, proved to be a sore trial. 'John very knave, my man', as Otwell called him, was a born forgetter of everything, from letters and table napkins to front door keys, and he was really not the stuff of which a good merchant was made. Eventually Otwell decided that the indentures had better be cancelled. 'I trust to be rid shortly of John my man,' he wrote to his brother, 'for I have written very earnestly to his father in the matter; and therefore, I pray you, if you can espy some proper boy for me amongst any of your friends, wish him unto me, for I will in no condition keep this lubber that I have.' Soon afterwards, John Kele went home, much to his master's relief. In Calais, John looked out for a suitable boy, choosing Henry Johnson, who was no relation, but who seemed promising. But young Henry's fate was as tragic as his life was brief. He died in Otwell's arms late in the autumn of 1545, of suspected plague. After such sad and discouraging beginnings, Otwell may well have been hesitant about the next apprentice that he took. He was singularly fortunate, however, in finding Richard Sandell, the son of an Essex sheepfarmer, and a good, intelligent, lively boy of whom both Otwell and Maria grew very fond. Richard lived with them for years before setting up in business on his own. In 1548, Otwell decided that he could afford to take a second apprentice, Walter Paget. We know little of him, except that Richard Sandell did not like him very much. The Lombard Street house was next door to St. Anthony's, the famous Tudor school that was the home of the ceremonial disputations with St. Paul's School each year. There was great rivalry between the schools, and every day the streets of the neighbourhood resounded to the insults bandied between Anthony 'pigs' and Paul 'pigeons', while schoolboy satchel fights were carried on at a furious pitch.[101] At some time, a schoolboy's copy of a work of the Early Fathers, a stray sheet of paper closely written in Latin, must have drifted over Otwell's garden wall. Richard Sandell picked it up, and in an idle moment drew on it a unicorn and an elaborate twisting scroll. Being little more than a schoolboy himself, he also could not resist writing some choice remarks.

> O Jesu Christ, Son of God.
> William Shor and butter and milk,
>   Robert God send us.
> Thomas Stokes hast maize and matins.
> Horrible good Master William.
> William Shipe is a knave sheep, and
> Walter Paget is a very loutish lowker.

As for John, his experiences with Master Pratt were not such as to make him in any hurry to choose another apprentice. Finally, he decided to select, not the son of a rich City merchant, but a boy from the provinces, William Tupholme, the son of the Mayor of Boston. If John thought, however, that simplicity of manner and sweetness of disposition would come with the country-bred boy, he was to receive a rude shock. William Tupholme was, if possible, even more of a problem child than Master Pratt, judging by his father's letters. He was the only son, and the Mayor anxiously besought John to 'keep him under, that he run not to follow his own swing and mind. I pray you, be unto him a father in that matter, as I doubt not but you will'.

But for all the apparent sternness, the father loved his son dearly, and when John was sending a shipment of fells to Boston he begged to see the boy if it was convenient, sending him back with much earnest advice — 'my poor counsel for to leave all slothfulness, uncleanliness and all other naughty vices. I pray God give him grace so to do, for I would be as glad that he should do well as any man living would be for his child, for I have no more'. His father's advice was to good effect, for William turned out well after his wild oats had been sown. He became a prosperous merchant in his home town, and married a Boston girl. In the light of his future career, it is pleasant to read one of the anxious father's letters; indeed, it is surely one of the most delightful letters ever written.

William Tupholme, I commend me unto you, and I send you my blessing, etc. And your letter written at Glapthorn the 18 of July I have received, whereby I did perceive that your master and mistress were in good health at the making thereof, thanks be unto God.

And where that you do write me that you will be no more sluggish nor slothful in writing unto me, but that you will be a new man, and order yourself otherwise than you have done in times past, I pray God give you grace for to be his servant, and that you may apply yourself in all your affairs for to please your master and mistress, the which would be a great comfort unto me. To see you do well, it is the chief care that I have in my mind, wherefore endeavour yourself in all your master's business, that I may once have a loving letter from your master (in your praise), the which were a great pleasure to me to hear of, for then you should wind my heart for ever. Ho! What a pleasure it is for a man for to see his child go forward to be praised of his master! It is above a great deal of riches!

Well, let this matter pass, and if there be anything amiss, let it be amended for the love of God, and then doubt not but that you shall find me a natural father unto you, and it shall also be a great occasion for your master for to put you in trust with part of his substance, the which I doubt not hereafter but that he will, upon your deserving. And Robert Bryan has promised me for to buy you a load of wool, the which I intend for to ship for you, with God's grace: it costs above 8s a stone. And I send your master by Gannoke my servant, a couple of young cranes, desiring him for to take them in worth for a poor token. And thus fare you well. Written at Osbornby, the 5th day of September, anno 1548.

By your natural father of your deserving,

John Tupholme.

The apprentice was an essential part of every Tudor firm. He was the junior, but his position was in many ways more fortunate than that of the later wage-earner, for, if his father was moderately well off, he could hope for 'somewhat to begin with', and would eventually be taken into the family firm, to become at last an independent merchant. At first, boys like William Tupholme would have been too young to be very useful, but as they grew older and more experienced they were trusted with responsible work, though always under their master's eye. A letter from the Muscovy Company to their agents at Colmogro in 1560, copied carefully by Richard Hakluyt, shows how an experienced apprentice was expected to occupy his time. 'We send you Nicholas Chancellor to remain there, who is our apprentice for years', the Company wrote. 'Our mind is he should be set about such business as he is most fit for: he hath been kept at writing school long: he hath his Algorism, and hath understanding of keeping of books of reckonings.'[102]

Essential to a merchant was the keeping of accurate accounts, for, as a later writer remarked: 'The entire prosperity and lucrativeness of a merchant's business depends (after the blessings of the Lord) upon the regular and accurate keeping of his books'.[103] The first thing the apprentice learned was the keeping of the petty cash-books. 'Thomas Holland, to him delivered in money to keep reckoning of, to pay petty parcels, 10s mere sterling' runs an entry in John's journal, and a fragment of Holland's little octavo notebook, written in his miniature handwriting, has survived. In it he entered the costs of his own and Richard Preston's breakfasts and suppers when they rode to town, the stabling of their horses at the Cock and Star, the searching of the mare's foot, and the price of two wooden tankards they bought for their ale. On one occasion he rode to London with John and Sabine, and noted carefully the money he laid out on lozenges for his master, and the packets of pins he bought for Sabine, and the sherry that she drank at the wayside inns.

When they had thoroughly mastered simple accounting, the apprentice was instructed in the system of double-entry book-keeping, the wonderful method that had originated in Italy, and which was spreading far and wide through Europe. Although the first English work on double entry was not published until 1543, English merchants were most of them familiar with the method. They had extensive contacts with the Italian merchants living in London, Southampton and Sandwich, and during their long spells of residence on the Continent they had frequent business dealings with the big international banking houses of Antwerp, where the latest accounting practices were employed. According to an eighteenth-century Scottish writer, the first folios of the account-book were to begin with a statement of assets and liabilities, and then the merchant's stock 'dissipates and scatters, spreads, sprouts, and shoots out into a variety of accounts, and these again into others, proceeding in a constant succession and continual flux, till by this propagation a whole ledger, consisting perhaps of 200 or 300 folios, be replete, and ripened as it were into a harvest'.[104] It was on this plan that John kept his own beautifully written ledgers at home and in Calais.

The double-entry system depended on the keeping of journals and day-books, and several of John's have survived. Day by day he entered his expenses under the headings to which they were later posted, as Debtor and Creditor, in the ledger books.

Otwell Johnson, my brother, oweth for Accounts kept in Calais.

Expenses Ordinary and Extraordinary oweth for Chest of Ready Money.

Herring of th'Account of me, John Johnson & Partners in Accounts in Calais, oweth for Account of Expenses and Small Parcels.

Wools oweth for Mistress Margaret Chantrell.

Chest of Ready Money oweth for Accounts kept in Calais.

Frizadoes oweth for Otwell Johnson, my brother.

and so on, and so forth, through the money paid out for wool and fells, for canvas and holland cloth and battery ware, even Accounts for the Household at Polebrook, and with his own wife Sabine, all meticulously entered and every last farthing accounted for, in preparation for entry into the ledgers as opportunity occurred. One of the regulations enforced by the great Russia Company was that 'at every month's end, all accounts and reckonings shall be brought into perfect order, into the ledger or memorial'.[105]

The great leather-bound ledgers were among the most valuable of a firm's documents, and were most carefully preserved, for they provided a complete record of business transactions over a period of years, and were accepted as evidence in the courts of law. Most of the details of the early Mediterranean voyages which Richard Hakluyt obtained came from 'certain ancient ledger books' belonging to the Greshams and the Loks — books which were then almost a hundred years old.[106] References to their ledgers are a commonplace of the Johnson Letters. John kept one set of books in Calais, and another in London, but even so the ledgers were far too bulky to carry around. Instead, they used special books in which they entered details of money they had spent, or which had been spent on their account, such as the 'memorial' with the beautiful merchants' marks drawn on the cover, which John kept for 'accounts partable with Mr. Anthony Cave, to write therein all such business as shall be done for our joint occupyings, in my absence from the great books kept for the same accounts'. Most useful of all, perhaps, were John's 'Abstracts of Reckonings to carry with me from my books'. These were slim folios of account, entered in debtor and creditor form, giving brief details in date order of the sums of money owed to and by the merchant with whom the account was kept; those kept with Otwell have survived between 1542 and 1546. Light to carry, these memorials and abstracts were often sent by post from one merchant to another when it was time to settle their accounts, so that each could see how he stood in the other's books, and a 'good, perfect, and true reckoning' be made. Such were the abstracts that John once left behind in Calais, and which he asked a friend to send him.

In the middle cupboard of the press, in the chamber where I lay at Thomas Houghton's, did I leave a book that I have need. It is upon a six or seven sheets of paper sewed together, and upon it is written 'Abstract of Accounts and Reckonings kept in Calais in anno 1544'. The key of the cupboard ye shall have of Mistress Baynham. I pray you, take out the book and send it to my brother, and deliver the keys again to Mistress Baynham.

Although January 1st was accepted as New Year's Day by most people, and the season's greetings were exchanged at that time, the official New Year did not begin until Lady Day, March 25th. For weeks before Lady Day, John was busy checking over memorials and abstracts, and making trial balances, not only for himself, but for Anthony Cave as well. John was a good book-keeper, and it was his practice to try and set his master's books in order by Candlemas Day if he possibly could, although this was mostly wishful thinking, as Cave's accounts were very complicated.

I send you George Grant's reckonings of the last year's and Mr. Smith's, which have gone once through your hands as ye shall perceive by them, and how Mr. Smith's stood the 18th in March anno 1544 at my going to Calais, which I think ye have entered; and George Grant's until Christmas last I send you now, since the which I suppose there is few payments made by him. The last of Mr. Smith I will send by him that shall come upon Friday or Saturday next, which shall not be failed with God's help. And on his horse the next week by Wedd, I would have my books sent down, and would ye could appoint to tarry here three or four days after Palm Sunday to set our things in order. Ye shall find most of Mr. Smith reckonings entered in my memorial, and until his last abstract sent me in February last.

The sheer number of the firm's accounts with English and foreign merchants, and the enormous variety of wares in which they dealt, meant much hard work for John and Otwell. The problems of currency and exchange rates also complicated matters. They had to be familiar with ducats and pistolets, crowns of the sun, francs, sous, philippus, carolus and lewes gildons, postulates, crusadoes, hornadoes and many more. For the accounts kept in England, John generally entered the items in Flemish money, and the totals in sterling. In Calais, it was the other way round, and there the official sterling table rate had to be calculated as well, so that the greatest possible accuracy was essential.

The calculations involved in routine accounting were in fact so complex that it was no wonder if, overcome by pressure of other business, a merchant occasionally overshot himself in his accounts, and behaved 'as one half robbed of his wits', as John Gery did, who, however, was very careful to correct his errors, 'lest it should hereafter be prejudicial or hurtful either to me, or any other for me hereafter to come'. There is the feeling throughout the letters that accountants were born, not made. Otwell, dealing continually with money and the exchange, was impeccably accurate in all his calculations, and a masterly hand at figures. Good as he was, he paid tribute to his brother John's bookkeeping.

At the deliverance of your abstract of Mistress Fayrey's reckonings to her, she showed me Anthony White her son's account last delivered to her, and therein he chargeth you with £660 sterling at this present, whereas the foot of your account abovesaid doth mention her rest to be but £118 sterling and odd money, besides the £500 for this year's employment. Whereupon I showed her that you were able and will at all times defend the perfection of your accounts, to Anthony White's contradiction or any man's else, and therewith she, being content, required me to take pains in your absence to accord the same your abstract with Anthony's declaration before her in his presence, if it could be done, whereby she should not be too much deceived of him; which thing I have promised her to do at her pleasure.

Richard was the only one of the three brothers to find bookkeeping difficult. This was not for lack of good advice, for John positively deluged his youngest brother with instructions. 'You shall have my advice to make you two books for journal and ledger, and keep all your reckonings in Flemish money, without the line, for that shall agree best with other your accounts. And keep apart your master's reckoning, Mistress Fayrey's and mine.' Richard duly followed the advice, but somehow everything always went wrong. He never could add up, and his accounts were so 'very mystical' to everyone that in the end it was decided that all his reckonings must go through John's hand. It was John's fortune to be called in every time anyone's books went wrong.

I most heartily thank you for the pains taken with Clement's books (wrote Anthony Cave), which I trust shall yet the lesser while trouble you at your coming, though they be not clearly finished, hoping to prepare my books to the shortest way that I can for you, but I reckon by reason of my cousin Ambrose's reckonings being raw we must take the more leisure, for I would be very glad at our meeting for both our quiet we might set all things in good order, wherein I shall most heartily desire your help, and heartily pray you bring my cousin your wife with you.

Equally with accurate accounting, the key to the organization of their trade lay in their correspondence. Detailed and regular information was vital to success, and they realized this to the full. The partners of Johnson & Company were often to be found writing far into the night by guttering candles, like Ambrose Saunders, whose letter was 'scribbled hastily at three of the clock this morning, before mine eyesight was comen down — as appeareth', and they sometimes wrote so hurriedly that the men who received their letters could 'scant make English' of the writing. Besides their wide correspondence with merchants in the City and the country, with the agent at Antwerp, and merchants at Calais and abroad, John and Otwell wrote to each other several times a week, and often as much as twice in one day if the occasion justified it. And, despite the fact that the writers say their letters are 'hastily finished', or written in 'extreme great haste', the letters are most of them long and full of news. John in particular was a diligent correspondent. Sometimes, indeed, as one thick packet from Glapthorn Manor followed on the heels of the last, Otwell wondered whether John was not inclined to be over-anxious.

To answer all your letters (brother) at length that I have received from you since my last writing . . . a whole sheet of paper written fine on all sides would scantly suffice. I mean to do it, as both I have done the like heretofore in matters of as small importance as this is, and also as (perchance) you do now look for it at my hands. But Sir, for divers considerations and impediments I cannot do it presently, and therefore with the few words that shall follow I pray you content yourself, until a better opportunity be ministered, etc.

In contrast to his hard-working brothers, Richard was not fond of writing letters, and the standard complaint is that no one has heard anything from him. Otwell did try occasionally to persuade him how important it was to write regularly and often. 'I pray you, write to me perfectly from time to time, for else (perchance) for lack of knowledge often of each other's proceedings we may enter into a confusion of our things, and so thereof may follow much displeasure, and not without dangering of our credit, peradventure.' But neither Otwell's coaxing nor John's threats could 'stir him thereunto', and the news from Calais, or wherever else he happened to be, was always thin and long overdue. Richard, of course, invariably blamed the post — so much so, indeed, that John grew suspicious of the 'evil messengers' who always happened to be carrying Richard's letters, and he eventually accused his brother of feigning to send them.

The Johnsons always wrote their letters themselves, for handwriting was a proof of the writer's identity, and a pledge that trade secrets had not been revealed to outsiders. To look at, the letters are modern in appearance, and the paper on which they were written has the finish of fine, handmade papers today. It is deckle-edged, thick to the feel, and ivory in colour. They used it in quarto or double quarto size, the large sheets being folded in half. Much of the paper is watermarked with the hand and flower, some with a jewelled orb, and yet another watermark is the beautiful and elaborate shield and crown, with the maker's name below, SPINELI. An immense amount of paper was used in their correspondence. 'Fine Lyons' was their favourite quality, and most of it came from Antwerp, the centre of the European book trade. 'I pray you', wrote Anthony Cave, 'help me to a ream of handsome paper for my servants and common business, though it be not of the greatest volume.' John accordingly ordered not a ream, but a 'quire of paper of mean price, but let it be such as will bear ink'. Paper was expensive even by modern standards, and cost about four shillings a ream. Quill pens were used to write with, and these were cheap enough, for a handful could be bought for a penny. Their ink was originally black, although it has now faded to sepia and cinnamon. It was made from imported Italian oak galls, and the Johnsons carried it about in inkhorns when they travelled, though small lead bottles and pewter inkwells were used in their counting-houses. Their letters were sealed with scarlet sealing-wax dropped on to sealing thread, and sealed with their rings. Anthony Cave used a fine intaglio of Janus, the two-headed Roman god, and it can still be seen on many of his letters, as fresh and clear as the day he used it. Envelopes as we know them were not used; instead, the letters were folded in such a way as to make it impossible to read anything from the outside once the paper had been folded and sealed, and the address clearly written on the thin oblong packet.

Extraordinary care was taken over their correspondence. Letters are accurately dated and signed, and the receipt and dispatch of previous letters is acknowledged; occasionally writers number their letters in a series 'No. 1, No. 2, No. 3 . . .' or 'A', 'B', 'C', 'D', so that their correspondent would know at a glance what order they had been written in, and whether any were missing. Whenever John received a letter, no matter whether it was from Sabine or a merchant friend, he endorsed it with a note of the date, place and writer, with brief details of his own reply. The writing of business letters was terribly hard work in the days before the invention of the typewriter. To speed up the writing time, a great deal of shorthand-writing crept into sixteenth-century correspondence, and words were often drastically abbreviated. L° for London, pnt for present, rec. for received or receipt. lre for letter, st. for sterling, are a few of the abbreviations in constant use, besides the normal sixteenth-century signs for -er, -es, and strokes over the top of words for doubled or omitted consonants and vowels. The practice of shortening words continued well into the nineteenth century, and the letter which Esther Summerson received from Messrs. Kenge & Carboy, in *Bleak House*, is a direct descendant of the letters which Johnson & Company dispatched every day from their counting-houses.

The writing of letters took up a large part of every day, and the task was made even more of a burden because, in the total absence of anything like carbon copies, every letter sent out had first to be copied into the 'Book of Copy of Letters'. Such copying, of course, was mostly the job of the apprentices. Otwell once asked John to 'let Master Pratt take a copy' of a letter for him, because he had no time to do it himself. Whenever an urgent and important letter was written, it was not only copied into the letter-book, but a second copy was made on a separate sheet of paper and sent off by the next post. The idea was that, if the original went astray, the duplicate would probably arrive safely. It sometimes happened, however, that the copy got there first. 'These of yours, being copies, do chance to come to my hands before the originals', wrote Richard once.

The receipt and dispatch of letters was part of the daily routine of the counting-house. Most of the correspondence of Johnson & Company was channelled through Otwell, who arranged for its collection and dispatch in London. The journey between Northamptonshire and the City was eighty miles and more, and took anything from two days to a week to accomplish, depending on the weather and the state of the roads. Fortunately for the brothers, the way to London lay over the old paved Roman roads running through Huntingdon and Ware, St. Albans and Royston. They were infinitely preferable to the rough tracks of the remoter country districts, but even so they must have been almost unbearable at times, with the dust rising in clouds under the horses' hooves in summer, a sea of mud and pot-holes in spring and autumn, and ice-bound in the depths of winter. During the winter months, many country houses in the Midlands and north were literally cut off from civilization for weeks at a time, and woe betide them if there was not sufficient meat and drink for men and animals in the storehouses and barns. 'I was at Sibbertoft,' wrote Christopher Breten to John one icy January day, 'supposing to have met you there the same night ye lay at Northampton, when I suppose you had as evil a journey as ever ye had.'

Many of their letters were carried by friends, or by their servants and apprentices when they could spare them, but for the regular journeys between London and the country they relied on the services of the professional carriers, the men who were an integral part of English country life until late in Victoria's reign, linking village with village, and town with town, like the willing Barkis in *David Copperfield*. Almost every town and village had its carrier in the Johnsons' England, and only rarely were there difficulties and wayside loss. The carters travelled up to London with John's wool and fells, and made the return journey loaded with letters and parcels of every description. We read of the Goodman Atkins, the poor poulter of Glapthorn, who carried everything imaginable — letters and comfits, wine, cloth, petticoats for Sabine, and cages of live quails. There were the carriers of Towcester and Newington and Oxford; there was Cocking, the 'gentle Mr. Carrier' of Newport Pagnell, hard by Tickford House, and his rival, 'Gentleman Wedd', who 'cometh always in haste, and departeth again even so'. There were the brothers Witt of Deene and Fotheringhay, and Ralph Capit at Melton Mowbray; there was the carrier of Flower village, and Birkett the cattle drover. All were good, honest men, the exception being a man named Evank. He was so well known to the Johnsons and their friends that if by any chance a messenger 'played Evank' on them, they knew at once what was meant. A superior being, he made a great favour and burden of carrying their letters at all. 'Your books and writings shall be sent you by this bearer, Sir Evank,' wrote Otwell once, 'if his mastership will take pains to carry them well, for at the writing hereof I was uncertain of his pleasure!'

Sending letters was a fairly simple matter, but money was always a problem, and was entrusted for the most part to their own servants. The sheer weight of the money alone was burdensome, whether it was a small amount sent in a glove, 120 angels dispatched to John in 'a small round leather bag, sealed and directed upon unto you', or the £60 sterling, £20 of it in solid gold, carried most unwillingly by Anthony Cave's servant, George Grant. 'You think it not much to write, I pray you send this or that sum of money to such a man in the country, Yea, or to yourself', wrote Otwell, rather annoyed by John's calm demands for more money when it was difficult to persuade people to carry it. He suggested that his brother should ask the local chapmen and merchants to deposit their money at Glapthorn Manor, instead of carrying it all the way to London, and that he would then repay them at Lombard Street. This was an interesting suggestion, with its hint of deposit banking, but John did not take it up. He probably felt the responsibility of other people's money was too great in an age when abram men and freshwater mariners, priggers of prances, bawdy baskets and walking morts haunted the highways and byways. Lady Stafford's tenant was robbed of forty pounds one Candlemas Eve outside Ware, and Thomas Smith deliberately delayed sending money down to Polebrook parsonage in the winter of 1543, because there was 'robbing by the ways now at the coming home of the soldiers'.

Communications with the Continent were far better than those between London and the country, for the twenty miles of sea between Dover and Calais were no real barrier except in wartime and rough weather. London, in fact, was far closer in time to Calais and Antwerp than she was to Carlisle or Penzance in the sixteenth century. Otwell's reference to 'th'overslipping of the tide at twice by Sandell, my great grout-head', shows that ships sailed from the Thames at every high water. If the vessels sailing direct round the Foreland of Kent were not used, there were frequent post services available, travelling by boat to Gravesend, and then along the Pilgrim's Way through Sittingbourne and Canterbury to Dover, and thence by the short sea route to Calais. Two days was the average time it took for a letter to travel between London and Calais, as the endorsements on John's letters reveal. The Dover post was originally begun as a royal service, carrying the King's mail, but merchants used it as much as the officers of the crown. Richard once sent a letter 'by the King's post in the night, when the merchants which had lain here four days for passage refused to go'. Besides the King's post, other competitive services were in operation. The Merchant Adventurers had a licence to carry letters out of England, and the Strangers' Post, established by the Flemings, had been running since 1514. The Johnsons probably used both these services. 'Payez le post', or 'payez le port' is a frequent instruction in the letters.

There were, of course, regular posts travelling between Antwerp, Calais and London, and the names of some of them are mentioned in the letters: Andrew Betterem, Christian the post, François the carrier of Mark, Jan de Laghers, the waggoner of Bruges, and Marcus the post. At Antwerp, as in London, the merchants knew the times of arrival of the regular services, and they used to go and pick up their letters at the post office. Sometimes also the post would wait for them to finish writing their letters before he set off. Letters from Antwerp took about a week to get to England. From Bordeaux they took rather longer. Otwell's brother-in-law, Bartholomew Warner, has left a vivid picture of how he worked all through the night to finish his correspondence, so that he could send it by the next wine ship: 'having sit up all this night, now in the morning my shop windows will scant be kept open, wherefore I will make an end'. Weary from lack of sleep, he gave the letter to the captain of the ship on October 22nd, but not until November 10th was it in John's hands. There were also regular services to Spain. 'Sir,' wrote Blase Saunders in the autumn of 1551, 'the ordinary post from Antwerp to Spain passeth now through England, and maketh London in his way.' And if the post had been missed in the City, it was still possible to catch him at Le Havre by sending a fast messenger through France. Letters from Seville took about six weeks to arrive, and from Venice and further east, the time was longer still; one letter, written from the city of St. Mark on 30th November, and sent overland through France and Flanders, did not arrive at Antwerp until late in the following April. But in almost every case, where there had been no deliberate 'juggling' with the mails on the part of governments, and when the weather did not delay them, letters arrived safely, and it was seldom indeed that the Johnsons complained. All over England and on the Continent, untold numbers of families and firms were exchanging hundreds of thousands of letters every year, nearly all of them arriving safely at their destinations, and bringing not only pleasure and comfort, but also all the necessary information and intelligence about men, money and affairs without which no business could possibly have survived. When all the natural disadvantages are considered, the frequency and regularity of the postal services stands out as one of the most wonderful features of the Tudor age.

CHAPTER 9

ADVENTURES IN TRADE

To be a merchant in the 1540s took both courage and skill, for never before had there been such obstacles to the pursuit of peaceful and prosperous trade. In the past, things had been otherwise. Henry VII had devoted his life to restoring his country's fortunes and prestige by the fostering of commerce. The Intercursus Magnus was negotiated with Flanders, and the Spanish Alliance was carried through; bounties were given for building merchant ships; the Navigation Acts were passed, and the cause of exploration furthered by the royal support given to the voyages of John Cabot and the Bristol men. Set beside his father, Henry VIII appears like the prodigal son, spending the prudent savings of a lifetime on masques and revels, music and architecture, jewels and every extravagant pleasure . . . and on war. Above all, Henry's money went on war. The role that he wished to assume was that of arbiter of Europe's destinies, and so the money rolled out on soldiers and armaments, on fortresses and ships of the line, until in the end he was pledged in millions of pounds sterling to the foreign bankers, the Fugger, Cavalcanti and Deodati of Antwerp. The first French war was followed by a second, and then in 1543 came the third French war of his reign, pregnant with consequences for England's future. These terrible years saw the birth of the English navy, and with it her huge privateering fleet. It was an era of piracy and privateering on a colossal scale, a never-ending guerrilla war in which merchant vessels of every nation became the prey of those who were strong and swift enough to capture them. Thousands of merchants on both sides of the Channel were ruined — the respectable, law-abiding members of the merchant class who desired neither to become involved in war, nor to make their fortunes out of plundered goods.

By the strange workings of fate, John and Otwell were to be directly involved in the incident that led to the outbreak of the war with France. Like most other merchants, they had already experienced trouble at sea. During the autumn of 1542, when there was war between the Empire and France, they had laden with herring for Boulogne the *Anna of Leigh* and the *James of Dover*, which had set sail only to be attacked by 'ships of war of the Sluys in Flanders' (so the entry in John's journal runs), boarded by Flemish soldiers, and the cargo seized. Immediately the news came through, John sent his apprentice hot-foot to England to seek the help of Anthony Cave. But even with powerful friends at Court it was months before the case was heard in Flanders, and over a year before he and his partners recovered even part of their losses.

News of a second loss followed hard on the heels of the first. During the late 'thirties, John and Otwell had joined with Anthony Cave, and a friend of theirs named Adam Waring, to buy the *George Bonaventure of Calais*. Under her master, Thomas Bassingbourne, she made many voyages to the wine ports of La Rochelle and Bordeaux, and did them loyal service. But, perhaps growing weary of the continual expenses that fell to the lot of a ship-owner — the cables and ropes and anchors that had to be bought, the brand-new cabin that had to be built amidships — John sold out his share. Soon afterwards, Anthony Cave and Adam Waring did the same, so that in the late autumn of 1542 the *George Bonaventure of Calais* belonged to Otwell alone. She lay in Calais harbour with a dozen other hoys and crayers, taking on board a cargo of herring for Newhaven (Havre) in Normandy, whither Otwell had already gone to arrange for its sale with his French factor. John was in charge of the lading and, with the loss of his own herring weighing on his mind, he was probably feeling anything but cheerful as the heavy barrels were rolled up the gang-planks and swung into the hold. When all was ready, the *George Bonaventure* set sail with a number of other ships, and John presently returned home to England, to spend Christmas with Sabine.

It was just as well that he did not know that the famous Scottish sea captain, John à Barton, was on the high seas with the *Lion* and the *Willoughby*. One of these ships had sailed into Newhaven early in December, 'a very merchant-like vessel', reads the report of an English spy. She remained in port for about ten days, discharging her cargo of salthides and salmon, an innocent merchantman to all eyes, except those of the curious spy. When she put out to sea again, he observed that she had eight guns at the ready, and that the complement of her crew was strangely large for so peaceful a vessel. On board were seventy men, among whom were twenty Frenchmen from Dieppe, 'speaking good Scottish . . . and disguising themselves accordingly in their garments. Utterly given to do Englishmen displeasure more promptly and violently than the Scots themselves . . . for divers of them were banished men and evil-disposed fellows'. They lurked at the harbour mouth, as motley a crew as ever wore the kilt, waiting for the Calais fleet to sail in.

Otwell, still in Newhaven (Havre), knew nothing of all this. He was busy making arrangements with his French factor to unlade and sell the *George Bonaventure's* herring when it arrived, and he then went on to lade another vessel, the *Michael of Calais*, which belonged to three Calais men he knew — the mariner John Palmer, the packet-owner William Spender, and the privateer John Malyn. The arrangements were finally settled, though not without friction, and shortly afterwards Otwell sailed safely back to Calais. John was still enjoying the Christmas merriment and feasting when a letter arrived from Thomas Holland, his apprentice, telling him of the fate that had overtaken the Calais ships.

Jesus anno 1543, the 9th in January,
at Calais.

Worshipful Sir, my duty remembered, desiring God for the continuance of your health, etc. It may please you to be advertised that a Scottish ship, which keepeth about Newhaven (Havre) and those parts, hath taken seven English ships, whereof five of them are of this town which were laden with herring to Newhaven: that is, Henry Vernham, George Weryott, one Goghe, John Orleans, and Edward Parsons, who was laden by Mr. Otwell; and the two other, one of them was an English hoy and th'other an English crayer. Edward Parsons he is thought shall not be proved good prize, forasmuch as the said Scot took him not by chase upon the sea, but aboarded him with both lying at an anchor in Newhaven Road, within two stones' cast of the Haven (as the mariners do say), which Scot and prizes aforesaid are entered into Dieppe. Whereas the Captain of Dieppe aforesaid hath caused all the said prizes to be stayed, and no partition or vendition to be made of them until such time as the French

King's pleasure therein be known; to which Captain, and to the Vice-Admiral of France (thorough the suit of Mr. Otwell and other) my Lord Deputy hath addressed his favourable letters, which are sent by Thomas Lychelad to John Bryskin, to be delivered by him to the foresaid Captain and Admiral, whereof I pray God send them good news. The masters of the ships, which are taken with their company, have abandoned all, and paid every one for his ransom 20s. sterling, and are returned hither, some of them.

It is reported for truth that the greatest part of men that are in the Scottish ship are Frenchmen of Dieppe, Honfleur, Harfleur, Fescamp and Newhaven. There is also two other Scottish barks upon the sea, whereof one of them hath sithence taken two English crayers laden toward Newhaven.

Mr. Otwell hath news for truth that his *George Bonaventure* arrived at Newhaven on Sunday last, thanks be to God, and came hard by one of the said Scottish ships, who suffered him to pass without offering him any wrong.

Your book which Hall hath to rule shall be sent you this week, with God's grace. Your trunk Mr. Otwell intends to stay here, except you send him contrary word. Other news be here none: yet Hollanders are yet none here, but they are looked for daily. Mr. Otwell hath bought a piece of Hazebrouck cloth containing 40½ sticks, which shall be sent you as soon as may be: it must cost 8d Fl. a stick. Thus I beseech the Holy Trinity have you in his merciful keeping.

By your apprentice,
Thomas Holland.

Unfortunately, Thomas Holland was wrong, for neither the *George Bonaventure* nor the *Michael of Calais* had escaped (nor another ship that John had laded in the fleet) and, curiously enough, the blame for the *Michael's* capture was laid at Otwell's door. Two years afterwards an enraged John Palmer related to the Admiralty judges how he had been manhandled on the wharf by Spender, and constrained by force to wait for Otwell's cargo, instead of sailing across the Channel to buy timber at Winchelsea, as he had originally planned. The French factor, who was responsible for the lading, did nothing about it for days, and when at last he bestirred himself, it was too late. The Scottish ships were lying in wait just beyond the harbour mouth. When the Calais fleet sailed in, they cut out two ships in the rear, captured them, and carried them off to Dieppe. Then they returned, anchoring just outside, as before, and it was gradually borne in on the masters of the English ships that they were virtually prisoners, bottled up in a French port. A few daring sea captains sailed out under cover of darkness, but the others decided to remain.

Since France and England were at peace, the incident was a great affront to good feeling. Otwell and the other owners sent off their protests to the French authorities, and soon the English Government itself was intervening on their behalf, trying to put pressure on the French to secure the release of the ships. William Paget, the able Secretary of State, was sent over to try to get some satisfaction from the French King, but Francis pretended to be completely ignorant of the whole affair. Ships of every country, he said, except those of the Emperor, were free to come and go as they pleased; if, however, his subjects were indeed guilty of any crime, he would see that they were punished. Realizing that nothing was to be got out of Francis, Paget next visited Cardinal de Tournon, and told him with perfect frankness that the loss of the crayers was the fault of France, for allowing the Scottish privateers to 'lie thus in the mouth of their havens'. After protesting long and hard, he finally received 'two cold letters' to forward to the authorities at Newhaven (Havre). Relations between France and England, after this rebuff, grew rapidly worse. French merchants in England were arrested, and the French Government promptly retaliated by arresting the English in France. Soon the situation became impossible, for the captured ships were still lying idle at Newhaven, and no representations would make the French release their hold. War was regarded as inevitable, and in the month of June hostilities were declared. Otwell, at Court, learned of the ultimatum that the Council had delivered to the French Ambassador, and in a postscript to his letter to John, he wrote: 'Raeff Hill is come home out of France privily, as I understand, and I fear that that shall cause poor Bassingbourne and other Englishmen to fare the worse there. I can have none answer from my master what I shall do with our Frenchmen at Calais.' Long before war was actually declared, Otwell had somehow come into possession of two French hostages, who were still in Calais jail months afterwards. John made the following entry in his journal for October 11th, 1543.

> Otwell Johnson, my brother, oweth for Accounts
> kept in Calais; and is for the sum of 38s mere
> sterling paid unto John Sutton's wife, the keeper
> of the prison in Calais, for two Frenchmen's
> boards which kept here for Thomas Bassing-
> bourne, who is prisoner in France —   £1 18s od

Otwell's fears about the possible ill-treatment of the English sailors were fortunately not realized. None of them seem to have suffered any hardships; rather the reverse, if John Palmer is to be believed, for he said that they were 'treated as friends by the French, just as if by their well-wishers and faithful friends, and of good faith in all things'. They had, however, to pay for their enforced stay at Newhaven, and Palmer claimed not only his back wages and those of the crew from Spender and Malyn, but the money they had spent on bread and meat, fish and vegetables, the candles they had burned in the ship's cabin, and the cost of the running repairs. What the eventual outcome was, it is impossible to say, for the vital Admiralty records of the case have long since disappeared. The fate of Thomas Bassingbourne is also a mystery, for except for a letter of 1545, when Otwell asked his brother to 'go into your counting-house at Mistress Baynham's' and fetch a bill due to 'poor Bassingbourne and me', there is no further word of the captain of the ill-fated *George Bonaventure*.

The whole course of the war with France is reflected in the letters that passed between John and Otwell during these years. They tell of the rumours about the King himself sailing to Calais, of the impressment of ships and mariners into the navy, so much so that the merchants could not even send their casks of beer over-seas; there were odd exciting incidents in the City, such as the time the Scottish spy confessed to trying to set Whitehall Palace on fire. Through their connection with Sir John Gage, the John-sons found that they, too, had a part to play, albeit a minor one. The Comptroller was responsible for organizing the transport overseas of all the 'King's army and carriages for His Majesty's battle', and there were tents and pavilions to be provided, javelins and staves and demi-lances, mares and wagons, most of the equip-ment coming from the Low Countries, and some of it ordered through John and Otwell. Anthony Cave was also busy with commissions for the great man, buying a magnificent beaver-lined cloak for him to wear, and trying to hire drummers and fifers to play the troops in. The musicians, temperamental as ever, apparently left much to be desired, for in one of his letters Anthony Cave wrote: 'The drum that we hired here was here this week, and fain he would have borrowed money of me, and I think he be a very drunkard. I pray God send us honesty of them!'

On land, the outstanding event of the war was the siege of Boulogne, a venture as dear to the hearts of the patriotic English merchants as it was to the King himself. 'I trust to ride with you to Boulogne pour passer le temps', we find Henry Southwick writing to John, 'car je ne doubte pas que le Roy notre ne lievera sa siège devant qu'elle soit Anglaise'. There was much hard and bitter fighting around Montreuil and Boulogne itself, and many engagements in which some of the army's most needed men were slain, and others wounded. Otwell, writing to his brother in August 1544, told of one such incident.

Thomas Flecton's letter containeth nothing but news, but we be here daily informed of later than therein is mentioned — which are not always so pleasant as our delight is to hear. To wit, by the relation of our drapers that come last from Calais, I hear that Bourgayte, the Surveyor of Calais, was slain before Boulogne on Wednesday or Thursday last with a small piece of ordnance; John Wenlocke stricken through the thigh with another; one Thomas Hunte, an excellent workman of iron guns, dwelling at Tower Hill, also slain; and one of our chief pioneers taken and carried into the town of Boulogne, another slain, and the third rescued from taking; and all these things done on Wednesday and Thursday aforesaid. Before Montreuil, my Lord Warden himself (as the saying is), shot through the thigh with a gun; and daily, by hot skirmish and issuing out of the town of Frenchmen, shrewd bickerings are betwixt our men and them, with loss of men on both sides; and of late Sir Thomas Ponynges' banner forcibly or by stealth was carried into the town of Montreuil by Frenchmen, and there set up in despite to look on, as we hear, trusting to have better news shortly.

After a prolonged siege, Boulogne fell in September 1544, but despite the Englishmen's joy that the Frenchmen's 'old acquaintance' had 'of late waxed wondrous strange to them', the good news was swiftly offset by bad. The Emperor, who until now had been Henry's ally in the war, decided to make a separate peace with Francis I, leaving England to fight on alone. 'It troubleth me and other poor men', wrote Cave in October, 'to hear th'Emperor and his subjects in peace, and the King's Majesty and his still at extremest war.' There was good reason for anxiety. On the face of it, England was no match for the immensely superior resources of France in men, money and materials, despite her victory at Boulogne. Yet there were already signs of the unexpected turn that events were to take. Soon after the Peace of Crespi was signed, Otwell wrote to John as follows:

> At the seas (the saying is) our English ships of war have sped well, but their conflict was against naked men: viz. laden French ships with wine and woad are taken to the number of twenty sail and above, saith some men, other say but a dozen sail. A thing for truth there is in it, but the just certainty I cannot write now. The next week, when I have tasted some of the wines, I will send you word that it is so.

With Crespi, the great burst of privateering activity began. From that time onwards, England literally became a pirates' lair. Rallying to the national emergency and, it must be admitted, filled with the hope of gain, every anchorage on the coast became a nest of privateering ships; Scarborough, Hull, Yarmouth, Lynn, Dover, Rye, Winchelsea, Southampton, Poole, the West of England ports and the Welsh havens are but a few of the centres. Half the seaport towns of the realm lived by their privateering voyages, and had well-organized contacts throughout the countryside for disposing of the booty, with hideouts in Ireland, the Scillies, the Channel Islands, and even France itself, when things became too hot for them. Armed with letters of marque to enable them legally to recoup their losses, real or invented, the merchant privateer came to fight the Frenchman, and stayed to plunder the ships of the Emperor — doubly disliked by the Protestant seaports as being Catholic and the cause of Crespi. Within three months after the treaty was signed, English piracy had reached such proportions that the Emperor was driven to declare the great restraint of trade at Antwerp. A letter that Henry Southwick wrote to John shows how the Flemings felt, and how well Calais was doing out of its privateering voyages; Hasby and his company were only small fry compared with the famous William Thompson and Cornelius of Calais.

Your letter was delivered to Adrian of Dunkirk, with whom I spake as I came hither, and he said that he hath written you answer thereof, to wit, that you shall have locatur there (by means of the prizes which be of late taken off the Flemings) better cheap than at Dunkirk. And so I reckon you shall, but I told him that all was for the King, and that there was no locatur amongst the same. But he will not be persuaded.

I offered him to give him part of the money to provide you there, but he would not hear of that side: he is too crafty to be circumvented. I can say no more, but you must provide for yourself there; or if you cannot, then I reckon I can provide for you here in this town, by means of three or four ships which Hasby and his company hath taken. Write me what way you will take, and I will follow your advice.

The attitude of Adrian van Weede is understandable, for the Flemings had suffered outrage on outrage. Their ships had been captured at sea, the cargoes transferred into pirate vessels, the merchants' marks removed and destroyed, and the wares sold by impudent seamen at a good price, while their own suits in the High Court of Admiralty were deliberately spun out by the Judges, whose sympathies were mostly on the pirates' side. The arrest of trade in the Low Countries, where Paget was now endeavouring to negotiate a release, was hardly undeserved, although the merchants naturally wanted it raised as soon as possible.

All men's expectation of good news out of Flanders (wrote Otwell) dependeth upon Mr. Paget's answer. Before his departing hence, or (at least) even about the same time, writing come from some of our Englishmen there that our ships and mariners might depart homeward at their pleasure, but neither merchants nor goods were released, nor be not as yet that I can hear of. Some merchants are gotten from thence by stealth, but all have left their goods behind them. Divers also have adventured to go thither since the restraint, for to set some order for their debts, belike, which have had liberty to return home again without trouble. This is a strange kind of restraint in mine opinion, and to last so long, after the King's Majesty hath so gently used th'Emperor's subjects here that could complain of any loss, for to the uttermost denier they have been recompensed of all their loss, not escaping so much as a ship tankard. Well, all men's hope is yet good, and the worst shall shortly be known.

Despite all Paget's efforts, however, the arrest lasted for months, and while Englishmen were free to journey to the marts and back, they began to find difficulties put in their way. It was forbidden to export wines and food from Flanders, and some of the merchants who had bought wool at the Staple refused to pay their bills until the restraint was lifted. 'I pray God they play the honest men with us', wrote Henry Southwick grimly. 'Now they must be handled with fair words, but I trust the day will come that I may call them javelles, as they be indeed.'

Meanwhile, the war with France continued. All through the spring of 1545 there were rumours of impending French naval operations, and the privateers brought back news of activity in the French ports, and of their encounters with the black galleys in the Narrow Seas. In April that year, John went over to Calais, in company with the Commissioners for the Diet of Bourbourg. It was by pure good luck that they missed being captured at sea.

This day, I thank God, I arrived here in safety, in company with the Commissioners that be come over for the Diet. The French galleys have roomth in the sea, for upon Thursday last, the weather being calm, they came bragging into Dover Road, being in number but four, and they rowed up and down, not far from the King's ships, who shot at them very much, but the galleys not at them, seeking advantage as it seemed; howbeit, afterwards the gale amended, and then the galleys fled. But they were overtaken, and one of them with forty men brought to Dover, where I saw her; another driven aground between Boulogne and Étaples, where English horsemen received them as they came a-land, and slew them, and afterward brought the galley to Boulogne. The two other escaped away, so that we think to hear no more of them this year.

But the rumours did not die down, and soon there came news of 'a great navy of ships . . . that not long since is arrived in Bretagne from Marseilles, thirty great ships and twenty galleys, God send them small power and worse fortune'. It was all part of the preparations for the invasion of England that summer, which was to take place under the command of d'Annebaut and Strozzi. The invasion fleet set sail in July, and for a while their success seemed likely, for they managed to land on the Isle of Wight, and the encounter with English ships in the Solent gave no great proof of decisive English supremacy at sea. Fortunately for England, plague and typhus broke out in the French galleys, and decimated the crews. During a second attempt in August, the French ships never got within striking distance of the English coast. The result was a stalemate, with the balance slightly in England's favour. In the autumn, peace negotiations began, and were brought to a successful conclusion in the spring of 1546.

English privateers did not lay up their ships when the Peace of Ardres was signed. On the contrary, they had not the least desire to become respectable citizens, and the prospect of trading quietly from one dull little port to the next, haggling over weevily flour and malodorous salthides, had no appeal for the bearded seadogs whose lives had been spent fighting battles at sea. They desired adventure, and when Thomas Seymour, the Protector's brother, became Lord High Admiral of England, they got it in full measure. This handsome man, now married to Queen Catherine Parr, became the leader of a nation-wide piracy campaign. He bought the Scilly Isles and turned them into a pirate hideout where Piers the Rover, Thompson of Calais, Little Dick of Yarmouth, and all the other gentlemen of the high seas could find sanctuary. There they used to unlade their captured bales of silk and spices; take their ease in the castle on the hill, and overhaul their ships before putting out to sea again. It was piracy on a giant, organized scale, operated for the Lord Admiral's personal benefit, and under his personal protection. What cut he got, what rake-off on the spoils, only he knew. Strangely enough, no one objected to this sideline until Seymour's ambition got the better of him in another direction. He cast his eye on the young Elizabeth. He would have married her if he could, and therein lay the cause of his downfall. As the year 1548 drew to a close, his brother and colleagues of the Council caught him fast in a mesh of his own making and, on a cold January morning in 1549, Seymour died on Tower Hill. And yet his work was done, for by then the English had learned that they were the masters of the sea, and a match for all comers. One solitary incident recorded by Richard Johnson shows how the little *Falcon*, with perhaps forty men on board, fought and captured single-handed a great French galley, with 160 armed men on board, and 140 wretched slaves. And at the moment when Seymour met his end, Otwell was writing that 'robbery on the seas by our nation increaseth still, and hourly complaints thereof are brought to the Council'. The French and Imperial Ambassadors in England were clamouring for the condign punishment of the pirates, for the redress of pillaged and plundered ships and goods. As the situation grew ever more tense, Otwell again wrote of the restraint in Flanders.

> . . . the general restraint or rather arrest at Antwerp of all our English merchants' bodies and goods, which is also chanced this last week, beginning upon occasion of a stay made by certain our English ships in the Narrow of forty or fifty hoys and other ships bound with herring into France, which indeed were shortly released again. But those news go not so soon to the Flemings' ears as other did, and so our men and goods aforesaid remain still under arrest, with threatenings (as we hear) that they will be recompensed of all the robberies that they have suffered at rovers' hands this two years past, which they put forth to be little less than £100,000 (I say) one hundred thousand pounds Flemish, as the talk goeth.

Notwithstanding war, piracy, and arrests in the Low Countries, the Staple trade continued without serious interruption, although not at its former level. Fifty years before, when the Celys wrote their letters, the Staple had been at the zenith of its pride and prosperity: the ancient trading company possessed a monopoly of the finest wool Europe had to offer; they were assured of their position as an instrument of royal finance, and as a potential economic weapon against the might of Flanders. But by the time that John had begun to trade, the situation was radically different. Cloth was now the leading English industry, and home-grown wool was fed to English looms in such quantities that only a narrow margin was left for the staplers and the export trade. During the fourteenth century, more than 30,000 sacks of raw wool had been exported every year against about 5000 cloths: now the cloth exports were mounting year by year, reaching a peak of 132,767 cloths in 1550, while only about 3000 sacks of wool were shipped annually to the Staple. As supplies of English wool became ever shorter on the Continent, while at the same time English kerseys and broadcloths flooded the Antwerp market, the Dutch and Flemish weavers turned to the New Draperies, the novelty woollen cloths which, though inferior in quality, still sold well, and which could be woven from the Spanish merino wool. It was under the pressure of this double competition that the staplers now traded to Calais. They themselves were 'few in number'. The Company that once boasted four hundred members was reduced to less than two hundred, and the lofts and woolhouses in Calais were many of them lying empty for lack of wool to store in them. Forced to compound with Henry VIII for the dues they were unable to pay, the staplers lost large sums of money, and even the Staple Inn, their magnificent hall in Calais, was made over to the King. This, it is true, was supposed to have been returned to them in 1545, as soon as the Lord Deputy could find another lodging, but it was several years before the promise was fulfilled. 'Although it hath pleased the King's Majesty to give us the Staple Inn again,' complained Henry Southwick in 1545, 'we have yet had no general letter thereof, so that no man here knoweth what we may do therein.'

The staplers may have been few in number, compared with their membership in the past, but it is doubtful if their cry of poverty was individually true. The impression left by the Johnson Letters is rather that of a small and exclusive monopoly, dominated by an inner ring of wealthy London merchants, whose word was law in the City as well as in the Company itself—men like Sir Michael Dormer and Sir William Chester, Thomas Leigh, Sir Andrew Judde, the prudent Sir Thomas Offley, Sir Ralph Warren, Stephen Kyrton and David Woodrof. From such as these were the Mayors and Lieutenants of the Staple chosen. 'Our masters' at Westminster had the ordering of the shippings, the casting vote in the ordinances, and they manœuvred everything to the advantage of their friends in a way that caused intense bitterness. 'Mr. Constable ne veut pas entendre raison sinon que pour ses amis', wrote John. 'Well, everything is ended as men be friended.' It was this inner ring, incidentally, who backed the remarkable wool voyages to Venice in 1544 and 1545. Launched by a syndicate of 'rich brethren' as a private trading venture, from which the ordinary merchants of the Company were excluded, the voyages were successful enough, but they added nothing to the popularity of 'our masters'. John himself believed that their sole aim was to have the trade to themselves, and 'like a canker to eat out other', and certainly they frequently managed to ship more than their fair share.

Company regulations permitted staplers to ship only a certain fixed quantity of wool and fells each year. John himself, as a married freeman, was allowed a maximum of thirty-five sarplers a year; his two widowed friends, Mrs. Baynham and Mrs. Fayrey, were allowed thirty sarplers each; while Anthony Cave, as an ex-Constable of the Staple, was allowed forty sarplers a year. Every spring and autumn there was great activity among the merchants shipping to Calais. For weeks before the wool fleet was due to sail, there was an endless procession of carts rumbling and jolting their way towards the woolhouses in the City. When they arrived at their destination, the holding ropes were cut and the vast, unwieldy sarplers were shoved and pushed, pulled and dragged into the woolhouses. There the canvas was split open and the wool spread out on to the floor, piled into great fluffy heaps for regrading and packing. At times there was hardly room to move in the Lime Street warehouse.

> There is no room in the woolhouse to pack one pocket nother of end nor clift (wrote Otwell). It is paystered with sarplers already, and yet there is two load more to come, as I understand. There is scantly room for the scales, and but a strait way to the clift pile to fetch wool unto them, for sarplers stand in both th'ends of the house, for there was no more wool piled up since your departing than was before, nor cannot yet, if any should be packed in pockets.

It was the London winders and packers, such as Alexander Haynes and Mr. Maundsell, who had the unenviable task of setting the country-wound wool to rights. Two of John's packers, Pinner and Thomas Farrandal, once included 'such baggage' in the sarplers that Ambrose Saunders thought them 'worthy to answer therefore in the pillory', and the Masters of the Woolwinders Company themselves took action against them. One of

Otwell's letters shows what Mr. Haynes found when he looked over the wool sent up from Flower.

Mr. Haynes hath packed to rights your four sarplers of wool that come from Flower into 12 pockets and a blot, besides certain rests; of the which it hath not been possible for him to find but 2½ of A. Cotswold, 3 middle Cotswold, and 7 A. Berks, and yet he hath used the thing with very much circumspection to your profit, so as he could do no more to stand with his honesty and yours. What shall follow of the rest that is to come from Flower, I nor he can judge, but I doubt rather worse than better: for your packer in the country of these that we have received had marked three of them for Cotswold and but one Berks, and yet you perceive what they come unto.

When the staplers bought their wool, it was sometimes sold direct to clothiers in London and the country. But by far the biggest proportion of that bought by Anthony Cave and John Johnson was destined for Calais. Fragments of John's shipping journals that have survived detail every stage of the journey and the expenses involved. When the wool and fells were taken out of the woolhouse, after being re-sorted and packed, the apprentices used to follow the carts on foot to Southwark, to see that nothing was lost or stolen on the way. (During the years when the plague was bad, Anthony Cave never allowed his apprentices to do this, because of the risk of infection.) On reaching the Wool Quay, the sarplers of wool and fells were gauged and weighed, and the imposition paid, and then they were laden on board ship. The consignments were always split up and parcelled out among several vessels as a safety measure, and when at last the lading was complete, the ships sailed downstream to Gravesend, waiting for the royal convoy which was to escort them to Calais.

With the advent of war, Staple shipping no longer had first priority and the wool fleet was often delayed. 'The shipping is appointed or (at least) denominated to begin the morrow after Midlent Sunday', wrote Otwell, early in March 1544. 'Howbeit yesterday, at the receipt of your letter of the 26th in the last, Mr. Anthony Cave and Mr. Smith showed me that they suppose it will not be then, by reason of lack of ships meet for the purpose, and mariners, which are put daily so much unto the King's business that it is very much doubted that your said shipping of force shall be deferred longer.' And it was the same story in the years that followed. On one occasion John and two other merchants of the Staple were forced to ride down to Greenwich Palace to make a personal and urgent plea for the royal convoy.

But despite all the difficulties, and the continual menace of the French galleys in the Channel, damage and loss were the exception rather than the rule. Occasionally, after a rough crossing, some of the ships would arrive in leak, and once Richard reported the loss of some of their fells by combustion; but usually the fleet got to Calais in perfect safety. There, it was the task of the apprentices to supervise the unlading of the wool and fells, which were then carried into the town's woolhouses to await inspection by the foreign buyers. The sales themselves, when John and Anthony Cave were not in Calais, were handled for them by their friend and attorney Henry Southwick, or by Richard Johnson and Ambrose Saunders, both of whom also held powers of attorney, enabling them to arrange the conditions of sale and the terms of payment. In 1547, after John's attack of ague, Henry Southwick was permanently replaced by Richard Johnson, now a full-fledged merchant of the Staple. 'Ye shall not now need to stand for a fifer,' wrote John encouragingly, 'but may set yourself in the second or third place, as ye think good.'

Every year a great number of foreign merchants came to Calais for the wool sales. There were the town representatives from Haarlem and Leyden (the two centres of the New Draperies), Walloon merchants from Bruges and Lille, and Italians from Antwerp. Relations between the staplers and their customers were usually good, and John had many foreign friends, chief among them being Daniel van Heed, Bartram Haghe and Victor Meawe of Bruges. But the inflation of the 'forties brought trouble in its wake. Forced to pay more for their wool and fells in England, the staplers passed the higher prices on to their foreign buyers, to the gradual and insidious destruction of friendly feeling. During 1545, an attempt was made to remedy the grievances of both the English and the Low Countries merchants at the Diet of Bourbourg, and John, clearly an eloquent and persuasive speaker, was chosen as one of the Staple delegates.

It may please you to understand (he wrote to Anthony

Cave) that since my coming hither from Antwerp, I have written you at large of all things . . . Since which time I have been letted to write you any further, forasmuch as it pleased Mr. Lieutenant and the Company in anywise to appoint me (all excuses set apart on my behalf) to ride to Bourbourg with John Perch, to answer such articles as was laid against the Company, and to fortify certain our complaints before the commissioners there, where we tarried ever since Monday until this day. Howbeit, we be returned with honesty, for the complaints against us be proved of no value, for the which the King's Majesty's Commissioners hath given commendations unto thole Company, and hath promised us friendship, especially my Lord of Westminster, whom we have found very gentle, and our friend. I omit th'articles and answer unto my coming into England, for it were too long to make you rehearsal of them.

The results achieved by the Diet were inconclusive, and prices continued to rise during the years that followed. March wool, for example (the fine quality wool from the Welsh borders), was selling at £41 a sarpler in 1544, but had reached £48 a sarpler in the spring of 1546. The best variety of Cotswold wool rose from £32 in 1543 to £39 in 1547, and fells showed the same upward trend. Summer Londons sold for 18½ nobles a hundred in February 1545, but had risen to 20 nobles a hundred in 1546. The attempts of the Hollanders to bring these prices down met with stiff resistance. 'The prices of fells exceed all reason (as ye know),' wrote John to Richard in 1547, 'and it is against all reason that a man shall be compelled to sell better cheap than he can buy again. What if we bought better cheap than we can now do? Shall we therefore give the profit that should come to us for disbursing our money to the Hollanders? I see no honest reason for it.'

For a time the staplers held the whip hand, but gradually the Hollanders began to take a stiffer line. In the summer of 1548 the Commercial Convention of 1522, based on the Intercursus Magnus (the great Anglo-Flemish treaty of 1496), was due to expire, and the Flemish buyers seized their opportunity. When Richard arrived in Calais that spring, he and the other staplers were astonished to find that none of the leading Hollanders had arrived.

The reason, however, was soon revealed. Jacop Stevinzon of Haarlem and Dirike Franzon Goile of Leyden had gone on a special mission to England, petitioning the Council for a return to the prices set nearly fifty years before. The Imperial Ambassador pressed their case, and the Council, apparently unwilling or unable to offend the Emperor, gave in. The irate staplers were informed that, while they might come to whatever agreement they chose with the Hollanders, 'th'Intercourse cannot be altered, though thole Staple should decay'.

Furious at the way they had been tricked, the Staple was in an uproar for some days. Then they realized that, if they refused to sell, the Hollanders would have to come to terms with them. The prices of fifty years before were in fact disregarded, since to every bargain made, the Hollanders added a 'reward', as Richard's letter shows.

... To enlarge their evil pretences with simple policy, I pray you accept these few words. Their going over from hence was (as they reckoned) very close. At their being at London they desired friendship at the Company's hands, which was that (doing as other men would do) they might have all the low sorts of wools (which immediately was granted, and letters written hither in their favour). Then wrought they their feats, and did obtain the ratifying of th' Intercourse, which done, they made a glorious return, and as ye do understand by my former, made us somewhat afraid, and do that which some of us do repent, for some sold Fine Cotswold for £42, and March for £37.

Well, they then communed with us, and found us thus determined, and so were answered that the goods were ours, and we could not live to sell them after the old price: wherefore, like as when we bought good cheap, we abated of the price set, so now, buying dear, they should above that price give us as we would agree, for we declared unto them that rather than sell as they would have us to do, we would keep our wools, and forced not. But they then went to all other strangers, and ... them that they would complain if they bought at ... prices of the Intercourse. But that stayed us not, forasmuch as we were advertised that th'Emperor's Ambassador in England had declared to the King's Majesty's

Council that he thought it to be reasonable that we should enhance our prices in time of dearth, as we had abated in the contrary.

Then for a refuge the botte knaves went to the Mayor's Deputy, and required a protest under the town seal to declare that we had refused to sell them wool under the old prices. The same was refused them, wherefore their shot anchor being spent, they fell to requiring of friendship as they did at London, and so upon submission favour hath been showed them by 10s in a sarpler. And at the prices which I have sold they have bought eighty sarplers, whereas if they had not played the jaques, they might have had a hundred sarplers more; and on my faith, if they had not bargained with me when they did, I had saved for you and me £6 which is given to louts.

Selling prices, far from dropping, merely continued their upward trend, and that autumn Fine Cotswold wool was changing hands at the unheard-of price of £47 a sarpler, while Summer London fells were at 28 nobles a hundred. So high did the prices rise that the Hollanders now began to hold off in good earnest, and to turn increasingly to Spanish wool. It would seem that not until after the devaluation of 1551 did the Walloon clothiers come back to the Staple. In that year, John told his master that Daniel van Heed had written 'that their drapery of Spanish wool at Bruges hath marred all, and they intend when their cloths be sold to begin again with us'. That the trade of the Low Countries was essential to England, neither John nor Anthony Cave doubted for a moment. 'I agree to your opinion', John wrote, 'that we shall never profit by the Staple again until we find means to get Bruges and other places to occupy with us again, but they that should go about it pass not.' It was ironical that when the Staple did finally return to Bruges, in 1563, after the fall of Calais, their trade was shrunk beyond repair.

All things considered, the good relations existing between the English and Low Countries merchants, both Protestant and Catholic, are rather remarkable. One has the feeling that merchants such as the Johnsons and their friends, of whatever nationality, would have been perfectly happy to talk and trade together for the rest of their lives, had not the usual machinations of kings, popes and politicians made this impossible. Throughout these years John and Otwell had regular business relations with Flemish merchants and almost always these were pleasant. Cloth was one of Johnson & Company's chosen lines of trade, particularly the New Draperies, woven in the towns of Haarlem and Leyden. The famous bayes and says, mockadoes and frizadoes, though inferior in quality to the English kerseys and broadcloths, were far more varied in texture and subtle in colour, and there was always a market for them in England. In the summer of 1543 John and Otwell were buying cloths 'of Haarlem making' from the town factor at Antwerp and soon frizadoes became a regular part of their trade. In May of 1545, when Dutch cloths were selling so well that they were 'bespoken ere they be made', Otwell recommended John to bargain for 'a case or two of Haarlem and also Leyden frizadoes', if 'very excellent' ones could be obtained. His hopes of selling them at a good profit were realized and by November they were 'all dispatched away, lacking a remnant or two', and there were only one or two pieces of Holland linen cloth left unsold out of the great bale that John had shipped over.

So successful were their linen sales that John decided to engage in a trading partnership the following year with Jacop Stevinzon, a leading Haarlem merchant, by which each man paid his share of the linen which Stevinzon would provide, and would share equally in 'gains and losses'. Besides this, Dirike Franzon of Leyden agreed to sell John a dozen bolts of cloth, to which half a dozen frizadoes were added later. By a misunderstanding, however, these cloths were sent to Calais before they arrived at their destination, London, and the extra expense reduced their hopes of profit. Otwell was almost despondent.

From Calais yesterday is arrived Richard Harwood's ship, who hath brought the twelve Leyden cloths in two cases that Robert Andrew's letter doth make mention of, the same being sent thither directly from Antwerp by Peter Symons, and in your absence directed to Robert Mattrys my gossip, whom I have allowed for freight and charges of the same thither, and have paid here the like again, and the King's custom also, which is 2s of a piece, so that these frizadoes stand us in double charges, and therefore we shall be the less gainers by them. I have received them but this day a-land, and for that

cause have not yet showed them to any person, but I trust
not to keep them long. The Haarlems cost at Antwerp clear
aboard the ship, £23 1s 2d Fl., and the custom, freight, and
other charges here amount to 17s sterling or thereabout, so
that they stand us in above £14 Fl. apiece, which is full 16
groats a yard, and the monies account but at 25s; and yet
Thomas Lok and other men serve Mr. White th'Alderman
for 5s 6d sterling the yard of Haarlems, and for 5s the
Leydens, which is a very slender reckoning in my judgment,
and scantly worth a man's venture. Well, if I can dispatch
ours for 17 groats and 15½ they shall away, and then you may
advise yourself whether you will meddle with mo or not.
Your linen cloth will not yet away neither.

Contrary to expectations, the frizadoes sold well, and John
ordered a fresh consignment from abroad. The linen, however,
was on their hands for months. Otwell reduced the price by a
penny an ell, and 'yet', he wrote, 'no man will approach, neither by
sorts, nor pole over head'. Accustomed to take the rough with the
smooth, their failure did not discourage them, for it was almost
impossible to predict what the demand would be at any period
of the year. Linen remained one of their staple lines of trade,
and they dealt in later years not only with Jacop Stevinzon, but
with the Dutchmen Willem Rukehaver and Joos Gaalles as well,
importing large quantities from Flanders.

One of the most amusing passages in the Johnson Letters
concerns the son of a Flemish friend, young Victor Meawe of
Bruges. The father died after a brief illness in 1545, and soon
afterwards young Victor came over to London on a visit, but,
instead of behaving in the decent and sober fashion prescribed for
sensible merchants, Victor, released from parental authority for
the first time in his life, proceeded to paint the town red. John
went to see him and talked to him very earnestly indeed, but
without much success, as he told Henry Southwick.

Young Victor Meawe I have spoken with, and I thought it
had been as he declared me, that with the consent of his
friends, he had taken upon him a voyage unto Spain; but
perceiving by your letter the contrary, I have communed
with him my fantasy so far that he hath consented to return
with me to Calais at my next coming. The young man is

given to riot and women: as I perceive, he hath evil counsel, and I fear me he will not thrive. As for money, I owe him none, therefore he told you a teasing, and am glad that ye have some assurance of that he hath of yours, for in good faith I like not his conditions.

His words of wisdom had indeed fallen on deaf ears. Victor merely waited until John had ridden into the country and was well out of sight and earshot. Then he went back to the bottle and his lady friends on the Southwark side. For two wonderful, delirious months he had the time of his life and, when John came up to London again in December, he found that Victor was dead broke.

Young Victor Meawe is here in the City, who I promise you doth very well present himself the prodigal child, for whereas at my last being here he was full gallant and pleasance, now he is in extreme need, in such sort that he hath nothing to help himself. The story of his life is too long to recite by writing, and therefore omit I it until we may talk thereof. The said Victor Meawe doth return home to Bruges very shortly, as I do perceive, as well by his own report as otherwise, and therefore have I not arrested him, thinking that not to be the best way, because I perceive that very poverty shall constrain him to go home. He hath promised me by his false faith he will come by you at Calais, and that or he depart thence, though his abode should be there a year, ye shall be paid that he oweth you.

But the failure with wild young Victor was merely incidental (one sighs for the hair-raising tales that John omitted from his letter), and did nothing to interrupt John's own confidence in his Flemish friends. It was indeed about this time that John and Otwell entered into a series of partnership ventures with a Flemish firm. One of their acquaintances in Calais, Henry Garbrand, had married a foreign girl, with whom he was now living in Flanders. He had joined an old-established trading firm in Lille, whose partners (beside himself) were John and Hugh de Lobell, and Michel Mulier, the Antwerp representative. During the winter of 1544 and the spring of 1545, when English privateers were so signally avenging the Peace of Crespi, Garbrand's firm had suffered the loss of four of their ships, which were captured at sea and taken into Plymouth harbour. While he was in England, suing for the return of the ships, Henry Garbrand called on Otwell Johnson in Lime Street, asking him to act as his agent for the sale and distribution of the Plymouth wine, when it was released. This Otwell gladly promised to do and, in return, Garbrand did him a great favour. Before the war with France, Johnson & Company had dealt largely in wines, importing red and white wine, claret and auserose from France. The advent of war had ruined their trade, for the import of all French wares was forbidden without the 'King's especial licence', which only the richest merchants could afford. Others had mostly to rely on captured cargoes. Henry Garbrand was a way out of the difficulty. France and Flanders were at peace and, as a member of a Flemish firm, married to a Flemish girl, he could travel at will through France and buy all the wines he pleased, as he did in the autumn of 1545.

In the spring of 1546, the Peace of Ardres was signed between England and France. It was not really peace, in the true sense of the word, for during the years that followed there was continual fighting around Boulogne, skirmishing round Calais, galleys in the Channel, and such 'muttering of war with France' that Otwell echoed Job's sentiments about the life of man being a continual warfare. But any peace that gave liberty to trade brought new life to the merchants, many of whom had lost everything during the war years. 'I must begin the world anew again,' wrote John's brother-in-law, Robert Lake, 'trusting with the help of the living God to recover some of my losses which I have lost these wars.' Almost immediately, French ships began to arrive in the Thames, laden with wine and canvas, and John was writing to his French friends, hoping that they would be able to trade together soon, as they had done in the past. During the summer of 1546, John and Otwell journeyed to Rouen and Paris, visiting their acquaintances there and planning new trading ventures. Every year after that, wines were imported for Johnson & Company from France. Some of it came from the big dealers at La Rochelle, like Chalmot, but the biggest proportion was bought for them by Henry Garbrand at Bordeaux. Otwell in turn acted as agent for Garbrand's company in London, receiving and selling their cargoes of wine and rosin, woad and prunes.

Curiously enough, it was the Haarlem merchant Jacop Stevinzon who was indirectly responsible for Johnson & Company entering on a fresh series of trading ventures with the Flemish firm, centred on King's Lynn. The pleasant seaport with the great square of Tuesday Market, the ancient Guildhall and church of St. Nicholas, the lovely Custom House along the quay, and the charming red-brick houses with their gabled roofs, still bespeak the influence of Holland and the sea. Then as now, Norfolk was the granary of England, and the wide and lonely acres of the Marshland yielded thousands of bushels of grain a year. Long, slender keels, weighed down to the water's edge with sacks of corn and barley, were wont to glide slowly along the waterways from Yaxley and Cambridge and Peterborough, until they reached the outfall of the River Ouse at Lynn. It was grain that the Johnsons chose to deal in, and at a time when those who exported it were regarded askance, as taking the very bread out of the mouths of the poor and hungry. Yaxley itself, where the keels were laded, was once the scene of a pretty disturbance against the rich buyers. During the scarcity of 1529, one Thomas Alward of Lynn was lading his keel with peas, and a poor man, louring at him, asked where he was going to send them. 'Hast thou anything to do with it?' said Alward. 'You men of Lynn did carry our peas into Scotland the last year,' was the retort, 'and pined us for hunger here.' The argument developed into a brawl, and the brawl into the case of The People of Yaxley v. Thomas Alward.[107] Despite the fact that grain export was frequently forbidden during these years of bad harvests, except by licence-holders, while the justices were also empowered to control prices and the activities of the middleman, the grain trade continued, because for those who could manage it there was always a way.

Lynn was a particularly convenient trading centre for Johnson & Company. Edmund Solme, Maria's cousin, lived there. A merchant like themselves, he was always willing to help in the receiving and dispatch of cargoes, and in selling their wares. In return, John used to order wares for him in Flanders. The Johnsons were also acquainted with many other merchants at Lynn, together with Mr. Pace the customs officer, whose friendship would ensure that their dues were no heavier than need be. Lynn was within fairly easy reach of Glapthorn Manor, along the waterways of the River Nene, so that it was no hardship for John's

factotum, Richard Preston, to travel back and forth between the
two places. Much of Preston's time was spent in buying grain in
the country districts, and seeing to its shipment abroad, as he did
for the first cargo of barley and malt laden in the *Nicholas of Lynn*,
to be followed shortly afterwards by a second crayer.

The Haarlem merchant's cargoes arrived safely. The market
for malt was good that year in Flanders, and in a little while
Henry Garbrand wrote and told Otwell that he could dispose of
as much as 10,000 quarters if he had it. He asked John and
Otwell to arrange for an export licence, buy the grain in Norfolk,
and ship it over to Sluys, the most convenient port for Lille
where his firm's headquarters lay, 'trusting in Almighty Jesu it
shall bring us to profit and more acquaintance'. Fortunately the
restraint on the export of grain had just been lifted and Otwell
felt free to go ahead. He sent John enough money to buy and
earnest a thousand quarters of malt, an amount which he thought
was ample, not only because he suspected that Garbrand had
made 'one cipher too much' in his letter, but for fear of 'a restraint
coming upon hand, which indeed I somewhat fear, because the
bruit of war with France again increaseth much daily, or (at least)
many shrewd likelihoods thereof appear'.

On the Flemish side, Henry Garbrand hired the *George of
Rosindale*, laded her with iron, pitch, soap, rosin and hops, and
dispatched her to Lynn to take a return cargo of grain on board.
As well as the *George*, four other ships were also making ready in
the Norfolk port, lading some six hundred quarters of grain at first.
Richard Preston worked hard to get the ships away as soon as
possible but, as so often happened in those days, the vessels were
delayed far beyond their time. It was the end of June before they
arrived in Flanders, only to find that the price had fallen, and
'scantly the third penny profit' could be expected from the sales.
Eventually Garbrand's firm decided to warehouse the grain and
wait until the price rose again. They were a wealthy firm and a
few months' delay meant little to them one way or another. To
the Johnsons such a move might well have proved disastrous. They
lived always, as it were, from hand to mouth, planning their next
trading ventures on the profits of the last; if the delicate balance of
money coming in and going out were upset, they had no capital
reserves to fall back on. The immediate result of this particular
crisis was that Robert Andrew had no money to clear their bills at

Antwerp, and the only remedy that John could devise was to ask the Flemish firm to advance them the large sum that was required to pay their debts. He breathed not a word to Otwell of what he had done and, when at last his brother learned about it, he was exceedingly wroth. Since Henry Garbrand had already lent them a hundred pounds, and promised to double it if need be, Otwell thought John's request an unpardonable imposition.

Both he and they do think it much marvel (and also may justly take it for an excessive boldness) that they should be charged with payments of so large sums in such haste, considering the quantity of the grain already come unto their hands, or bought to be sent them, not to pass 2500 quarters in thole, and they having furnished you with wares to the value of one hundred marks sterling, and having good in my hands almost as much more, which all I have sent you and paid out for you here, besides that which they must disburse also presently for freight of the grain, thole amounting to a great sum of money.

Wherefore truly I am at a great stay with myself how to answer or excuse this matter with our honesties to Garbrand's company (as for himself, he is wholly ours, I daresay, to his power), which be men of much consideration and good discretion . . . I shall with the gentlest writing I can devise, entreat them to patience, and promise the like friendship to them from us, in some things hereafter to be used betwixt us, God to friend. And thus (brother) you may perceive how this case standeth but wildly. . . .

Eventually matters were smoothed over. Otwell was hopeful of settling their payments satisfactorily when the other grain ships had been laded and sent off in July. 'Tout est arrivé à bon port, Dieu en soit loué!' he exclaimed, when news came that they had docked safely. Then he learned that the grain was selling at 'small profit or none', and that a return on the sales was not expected until the end of September. Once again, Otwell was anxious about the overcharging of Robert Andrew, 'du préjudice de notre crédit, ce qu'est quasi advenu. But I will gently again write unto our said friends not to leave us at the worst, but rather to charge us with the payment of one hundred pounds or two for usance, or double usance back again, et puis, Holla!' The big

264

Flemish firm willingly came to their aid, but so uncertain were Johnson & Company's money affairs, that Otwell refused to allow his brother to write for a fresh cargo of Flanders wares to be sent to Lynn. 'I perceive us to be already too much in their danger', he wrote, and from this opinion John could not budge him.

When at last the grain was sold in Flanders, all their money difficulties disentangled themselves, and by the time that Otwell was ready to meet Henry Garbrand at Calais in the autumn they were completely in the clear. At this meeting, important decisions were taken. Both firms decided to invest in more grain voyages, to be run for their mutual profit and advantage. From the Low Countries were sent cargoes of sweet wine, sack and Gascon wine, iron, pitch, tar, bales of canvas and paper, soap, Burgundian glass, salt, raisins and dyestuffs; and in return went cargoes of rich golden grain, to be sold for 'short days to sure men'. At last Johnson & Company's gains were proportioned to their expenditure and, for the time being, all was well.

CHAPTER 10

THE TRAGEDY OF 1551

THERE are some years in the lives of men and women which seem to bring with them extremes of joy or sorrow. So it was with 1551, a year that brought misfortune not only to the Johnsons, but to thousands of other families, and when every disaster save war seemed to engulf the nation. Sudden death could never for one moment be forgotten in the sixteenth century, for it struck home in so many terrible ways. But no one in the bright spring of 1551 could have foreseen the hideous disease that was so shortly to come upon them.

Even today, the origins of the Sweating Sickness are utterly unknown. The only certain thing is that in 1485, exactly one month after Henry Tudor's victorious army had defeated Richard III on Bosworth Field, 'a new kind of disease from which no former age had suffered' broke out in London. The historian Polydore Vergil combed through Galen and Pliny, but he could find no single instance of it in recorded history. Beside the sweat, however, even the dreaded plague paled into insignificance. 'This sickness cometh with a great sweating and stinking, with redness of the face and of all the body, and a continual thirst, with a great heat and headache because of the fumes and venoms.' It was a killer. One moment a man would be talking carelessly to his friends; a second later he would keel to the ground, and they would find that he was dead. Fifteen thousand people are said to have died in that first outbreak of the sweat, before it came to an end in October. For several years nothing more was heard of it; and then in 1508 it came again, so severely that prayers for the nation's safety were offered in St. Paul's Cathedral. No one was allowed to approach the Court from London, and the King amused himself by hunting in the royal forests, journeying from palace to palace, until it was considered safe for him to return.[108]

The third epidemic came nine years later, during the early summer of 1517, when it spread like wildfire through the towns and villages of England. In Oxford four hundred of the students died, and University life was brought to a standstill. In London the King's Italian Secretary, Ammonio, died of the disease; the Bishop of Winchester fell dangerously ill, and so did the Venetian Ambassador and his son. Rumours of the heavy death-rate reached the Continent and, rather than visit Wolsey at such a time, the Cardinal of Aragon and his retinue waited for weeks on the French side of the Channel. Wolsey himself was so alarmed that he undertook a pilgrimage to the shrine at Walsingham, remaining there until the end of September, when all was over. It was during this third outbreak that the first remedies were used, though whether they could have saved many lives must be doubtful. The physicians of the day recommended that all the windows of the sickroom should be tightly closed, and a fire lit to keep the room warm. The bedclothes were to be tucked up high, and the patient's arms crossed on his breast so that not even the smallest breath of air should reach his armpits. No cold water was to be drunk, but only a crust of bread soaked in ale, whole mace, and sugar. Above all, the patient had to be kept wide awake until the sweat had run its course, for it had been observed that those who slept sank into a fatal coma.

For the whole of the next decade the sweat was quiescent and not a single case was reported. But in 1528 it broke out again to the consternation of every man and woman in the country. Not least alarmed was Henry VIII. He was at this time passionately in love with Anne Boleyn and, when he learned that one of her waiting-women was sick, he sent his 'sweet heart' down to her father's house in Kent, to be out of the infection. He was desperately anxious for her safety, writing her frequent love-letters, sending his personal physician to attend her, and trying to comfort her with the words: 'Few women have this disease, and moreover, none of our Court have died.' Both Anne and her father did in fact fall ill of the sweat, although not seriously. It is interesting to speculate how far England's history depended on the recovery she made. If Anne had died then, she would have been spared her tragic fate; there would have been no Royal Divorce, no break with Rome, and none of the glories of Elizabeth's reign.

London suffered very heavily during this outbreak. By the end of June forty thousand people had been attacked by the disease, and thousands more in the country. The law courts adjourned their sittings, the assizes were stopped. Cardinal Wolsey fled to

Hampton Court, where he shut himself away from everyone, admitting only a few attendants to wait on him and help to while away the hours. The French Ambassador slyly suggested that anyone who wanted to speak to the Cardinal would have to shout through a trumpet. Nevertheless, the gay and witty Frenchman could find nothing amusing about the course of the sweat in the City. He saw men and women 'as thick as flies rushing from the streets or shops to take the sweat wherever they felt ill', and remarked: 'One has a little pain in the head and heart; suddenly a sweat begins, and a physician is useless, for whether you wrap yourself up much or little, in four hours, sometimes in two or three, you are despatched without languishing as in those troublesome fevers.'[109]

The disease gradually burned itself out in England, only to break out abroad. Throughout 1529 the Continent was ravaged by the Sudor Anglicanus, the English sweat. In Hamburg alone, a thousand people are reported to have died in a single week; then it broke out in Bremen and Danzig, and so on into Lithuania, Poland and Russia, killing thousands as it went. It spread down the Rhine into Switzerland and Austria, and even while the soldiers of the Emperor were defending Vienna against the Turkish janissaries, the sweat was decimating their ranks. Vienna marked the southernmost point of the sweat, and slowly Europe began to recover. For more than twenty years the world was free of it and life went on at the normal sixteenth-century tempo. As the years succeeded one another, people began to forget about the mysterious epidemic of the 'twenties; it became no more than a nightmare recollection.

And then, in 1551, it broke out again. On March 22nd, while the country was in the grip of a desperate financial crisis, a young man fell sick and died of the sweat at Shrewsbury. It spread rapidly through the town, and the terrified merchants and craftsmen fled with their families to the villages round about, carrying the disease with them. From Shrewsbury the sweat travelled to Ludlow and then to Presteign, Westchester, Coventry and Oxford. Towards the end of June it reached Loughborough, only a hundred miles from London, and the dutiful parish clerk wrote in his register that the 'Sweat called New Acquaintance, alias Stop, Knave, and know thy Master', had begun.

It was now only a matter of time before it reached London, and in the hot July weather the first cases were reported. Soon Otwell wrote and told John that it had broken out in his own parish, Saints Peter and Bartholomew, the heart of the business sector of the City, where all the well-to-do merchants lived. Twenty houses, reported Otwell, were stricken 'with sweat and sudden death, Yea, and that of the youngest and likeliest men and women to live, not leaving young children to escape, if they be not well looked to'. Indeed, it was a strange peculiarity of the sweat that it attacked the healthy and well-fed far more than the poor, who had perhaps managed to acquire a certain immunity to the disease. The little house in Lombard Street waited anxiously, like every other house in London, to see whether by some miracle they would be spared. It was perhaps some curious premonition that led Otwell to set all his business affairs in perfect order during those troubled days, and to write on his letters: 'The Lord liveth', as if to comfort and reassure the worried John. For Otwell, that kind, cheerful, sensible young man, was destined to be one of the victims of the horrible disease. The only consolation was that he did not suffer long. On July 8th he folded and sealed his last letter to John as carefully as was his wont, and at three o'clock on the morning of the 10th he died of the sweat. His brother-in-law, Bartholomew Warner, broke the sad news to John.

With so sorrowful a heart did I never write as now I do unto you, good Mr. Johnson, to signify unto you the departure out of this life of your loving brother and mine, Otwell Johnson, this day in the morning about three of the clock, of the sweating sickness, which here reigneth wonderfully, God be merciful unto us. And hearing of the death of Harry Bostock, and many other of his very familiar acquaintance yesternight, coming from the Street at seven of the clock, he went to his bed; and suddenly was in so extreme pain that within four or five hours we could get no word of him, and so continued in pain till three o'clock. This bearer Walter Paget I send expressly to you, to th'intent you may take order in his reckonings in time, for in you was all his trust for his poor sorrowful wife and children. At the beginning of his sickness he began to have uttered something to me therein, but I, being sent for to my wife (who in like wise lay in great pains, but I trust now past danger), he would needs I should go to her, and so I heard no more ofthose things. Wherefore, good Mr. Johnson, take some good order therein. And thus in heaviness I make an end, committing you to the preservation of th'Almighty, unto whom I beseech you pray for us, and we shall pray for you. From London, the 10th of July, 1551.

Yours,
Bartholomew Warner.

Your brother Ambrose hath had it, and so hath Mr. Blase Saunders; and your sister Marget departed.

No words are needed to describe the unutterable grief of his family. The true sweetness of Otwell's disposition, his kindness, courage and strength of mind, and the loyalty he bore his friends, gained him the affection of even chance acquaintance and the love of all who knew him well. Maria mourned him for ten long years before she married again. As for John, the death of Otwell was a crushing blow, an irreparable loss from which he was never to recover. When the news reached him, he was staying at Bruges with Sabine, and they at once set out for Calais, intending to make their way home. At Calais more sad news awaited them. The household at Glapthorn Manor was in a state of panic; the servants were terrified out of their wits by the strange disease, and did nothing they were bid. Richard Preston wrote to tell them that his wife was 'sad and sick for loss of Sabine, my daughter. God has take her, and very many is dead in this country'. Ambrose Saunders had nearly died from a second attack of the sweat; Lady Cromwell was sick at Laund; Lord Cromwell had died, and with him Sir Thomas Speke, the two sons of the Duchess of Suffolk, and the famous soldier Sir John Wallop, in whose service Bartholomew Warner had been for many years. There was, however, no question of John and Sabine being able to return home, for they found Calais prostrate with the sweating sickness, to which after a few days they too succumbed. John's letter to Robert Andrew ('God deliver us and be merciful unto us,' he wrote, 'for we have had a terrible time') reveals what had happened.

A copy of a letter sent
unto Robert Andrew to
Antwerp, per Michael Hill.

Jesus anno 1551, the 24th in July,
at Calais.

Since my departing from you, in manner ever since it hath
been (beloved friend) the lamentablest time that ever I abode,
for what with the knowledge at Bruges of the death of my
brother Otwell at London, and of many other honest men of
friends and acquaintance; and since with the terrible days that
Saturday and Sunday last was, at which time suddenly
Henry Southwick, George Parsons, Erasmus Cope, Thomas
Umpton and other of our Company departed this life, which
terribleness hath in manner ever since continued, by the sickness of a great many more here in this town, amongst which
my wife and myself hath had our parts: these things, I say,
hath caused me to forget business and in manner all the
world, and therefore have I not written unto you, trusting ye
will take it in no ill part, for in good faith I promise you I had
no joy of anything. And therefore is there unsent unto you a
£100 Fl. that I have had ready ever since I came hither from
Antwerp, but now with the first messenger that I may convey it
safely, I will send it you, God to friend. In the meantime, and
until God send my brother home, that I may know how he
hath left everything with you, I pray you conceive no unkind-
ness in anything.

The Lord's Visitation, I understand, hath been at Antwerp, and hath taken my countryman Tempest and other.
I beseech God to preserve you all, as I hope he will. If God
send it you, with good keeping I hope ye shall do well. There
is to be observed three things: that is, the sweat being begun,
no air to be suffered to come into the bed, but yet not to be
kept over hot; to drink as little as may be, but if need be, to
have beer or ale sodden with a crust of bread, whole maces
and sugar, and thereof to take at one time, warm, more than
two spoonfuls; and the third and principal thing is to be kept
from sleep so long as sleep is desired in the twenty-four hours,
and not to spare beard nor thing else to keep away sleep, for
he that sleepeth, dieth, as it hath here appeared. God keep you

from it, and that there be not such a battle amongst your beards as hath been with mine and other here, for many of us have lost almost all our beard, and some have none left.

God hath altered my brother's purpose and mine for Bordeaux voyage. Howbeit, if Bartholomew Warner will take it upon him — as I think he will — I advise to do somewhat, but not so much as if my brother had lived. But in that which shall be done, if ye please to write me that ye will have part, I will do no less than I said to you at Antwerp, nor no otherwise than for myself. So knoweth God, who keep you. In haste, as appeareth.

Your friend to his power,
John Johnson.

Herein is a bill of exchange payable le 28 of this month, containing £32 5s 10d Fl., by Benedict Capriano. I pray you, put it to my account.

Mercifully the outbreak on the Continent was less severe than it had been in 1529, though it was bad enough. In England it was over by the end of July. The bells, Bartholomew Warner reported, had stopped their melancholy tolling, and when on July 23rd he went to consult the mortality bills at Clerks' Hall, he found that only six people had died in the City the previous day; one of the sweat, one of the plague, and the rest of ague and other illnesses. Business, of course, was at a standstill. Hundreds had abandoned London altogether and taken refuge in the countryside, the shops had put up their shutters, and when autumn came there was still, in John's words, 'no doings of anything'. The Imperial Ambassador estimated that fifty thousand people died that year from the sweat in England, five thousand of them in the City of London alone, and while his report was probably exaggerated, it is evident from the letters that hardly a family escaped. At all events, the epidemic was horrifying enough for the Spaniards to bar their ports to English ships that autumn, for fear the disease might ravage Spain. But with the coming of winter the fears of Europe subsided, for the sweat vanished as swiftly as it had come and to this day has never returned. No one could foresee at the time that the disease had run its course, and the learned Dr. Caius published a work on the sweating sickness which sold like wildfire. Why it ceased is as great a mystery as the reason for its beginning. Various conjectures have been made: polluted water supplies, lack of proper sanitation, the crowded, vermin-infested houses. The extraordinary fact remains, however, that the sweat never came again, although living conditions can hardly be said to have improved so very much for the next three hundred years, and the plague was rampant until the middle of the seventeenth century. The only remotely similar disease that has ever occurred is the Picardy sweat, a mild sickness that broke out in northern France during the early years of the eighteenth century — strangely enough, in the very district where once, long ago, Henry VII had recruited mercenaries for the invasion of England in 1485. It is just possible that there may be some connection here, though none has so far been proved.

It was weeks before John began to recover from his own illness and the shock of his brother's death, and before he could rouse himself to attend to business. The loss of Otwell was more than a personal blow. It meant that Johnson & Company was bereft of the one partner who could least be spared, and there his loss must be felt every hour of every day. The relationship between John and Otwell was in some ways a strange one, for while John presented to the world the appearance of a successful businessman — the picture of a wealthy merchant, with a pretty wife and young family, an estate in the country, and a bevy of rich and influential relations — it was Otwell who was really the more able of the two. For all his clear brain, his ability to marshal facts and argue cases, John was not really a practical man of affairs. His chosen friends were intellectual divines, not merchants, and of late years he had grown ever more attached to a life of idyllic leisure in the country, far from Lombard Street and the little counting-house where Otwell worked long hours and hard, making money for both of them. Sitting in the parlour with Sabine and his friends, strolling through the sunny meadows of the farm, buying cattle and sheep, fishing in the streams, John was cut off from the realities of business, and much of what he had once known of bills and brokers and rates of exchange had slipped almost insensibly from his mind. Otwell and Robert Andrew had handled his affairs, disguising their real control by the deference they paid to the opinion of the nominal head of the family; but now, suddenly, John was called on to take sole charge, and to direct the activities of the unwilling Richard and the inexperienced Ambrose Saunders, both of whom were looking to him for guidance.

The immediate problem, as John realized, was to find someone to take Otwell's place in London and, after much thought, he decided to ask Bartholomew Warner. A capable man, Warner had been trained as a draper in his youth, and now, apart from the sinecure he held at Calais, where he was Collector of Customs for Newenham Bridge, he was free to do as he wished in life, for his master, Sir John Wallop, had perished, like so many others, of the sweat. At first, however, Warner was not altogether decided.

> Whereas you require me to send you word whether I will begin where my brother left, I know not well what to answer therein, both for that as before I am out of ure in merchandise, and also I would not begin in a broken reckoning. Till you and I speak I will do in the things as well as I can, and then I will govern myself by your good counsel, for as yet I am clear of all business, and have gotten my master his quietus est, and else have nothing to do.

But, when eventually they met, John was able to persuade him to return to a merchant's career. Bartholomew Warner became the new partner in the firm, and the association was symbolized in the name by which they now became known, 'John Johnson, Bartholomew Warner & Company'.

It would be difficult to imagine a worse time for the partners to organize their trading ventures, for 1551 is notorious not only as the year of the sweat, but also for the greatest financial chaos, on a national scale, that England had ever known. It literally brought ruin to thousands, and was to the sixteenth century what the South Sea Bubble and the Wall Street crash were to generations yet unborn. Henry VIII died leaving colossal debts. He had engaged in expensive wars and diplomacy, and when he had exhausted the millions that his father had accumulated with such loving care, he was forced to borrow gigantic sums at high rates of interest from the banking-houses at Antwerp. It was Thomas Wriothesley, that unamiable man, who had suggested debasement of the coinage as a partial solution of the royal problem, and who had been rewarded with a peerage as a result. Henry used debasement only to a limited extent, but now that the Antwerp bankers were pressing for payment, the Protector's government — among them Wriothesley, newly created Earl of Southampton — resorted to it on a hitherto unknown scale. From 1549 onwards a stream of worthless coinage was pouring out of the English mints.

Inevitably the cost of living at home began to soar upwards, while the rates of exchange began that inexorable glissade downhill which was to end in a quotation of 12s. 6d. Fl. to the pound sterling. As Richard informed his brother in a letter from Antwerp, 'Englishmen's credits are nothing esteemed', and yet somehow the merchants' bills for goods had to be paid, and in the kind of money that the foreign merchants would accept. The axiom of Sir Thomas Gresham, that 'bad money drives out good', was already in operation, for gold was flowing out of England in a one-way torrent. Throughout 1550 and the ominous spring of 1551, Otwell Johnson had been bargaining for hundreds of pounds' worth of gold sovereigns to export to Calais and thence to Antwerp to pay their debts, but as the weeks went by, gold became increasingly difficult to obtain. 'Daily it scanteth and increaseth in price above measure', Otwell wrote, until at last it was so 'wonderful scant to come by' that there was 'no more gold to be had at any reasonable price', and they were reduced to the desperate expedient of selling their bills before they fell due. But it is to be feared that some part of their trouble was due to Richard. Never very efficient, Richard was in a complete muddle over the book-keeping, the wine-buying, the wool sales and the bills of exchange, and, as far as the gold was concerned, Otwell simply did not know what had happened to it.

At London, the 6th in May, 1551.

Having at large (brother) written unto you in both my former sent as well per Nicholas Berry, as on Monday last to Tickford or Chicheley per George Grant, of all things then occurrent, this may be the briefer, most chiefly letting you to wit that since my said last, I have received a letter from our friend Robert Andrew of the 29th of this last, wherein he writeth as followeth:

'I have received both yours of the 19th of this present (meaning yours and mine), and as the same attaineth to one effect, so I require you that this may suffice for my answer. As I esteem not my travail in your business, so far as it may be kept within the limits of my power, and also my service to minister no displeasure, neither find I myself anything offended with you, though I have just cause to think your brother Richard with me. But above all it grieveth me that it is not my fortune to render your account with as little trouble as to other men, and that you should be no better advertised in your own affairs, than that you cannot directly judge the same to be either true or false: the perfect knowledge whereof I shall much desire, as you may think me in the meantime not to remain quiet, for albeit it pleaseth you thankfully to accept my provision and order therein, yet it little contenteth me to see it hang in such doubtful balance. Sithen I received from your brother Richard £100 in single ducats, he hath neither sent me gold nor paper, albeit I have paid your bill of £83 6s 8d Fl. to Jeffrey Walkden, and shall shortly want more money, both for the refurniture thereof, and also for the payment of Mr. Whethill, desiring your provision and order for the same, th'exchange being now at 15s 3d usance, etc.

Hitherto extend Robert Andrew's words, which please me not at all, and therefore have I written to my brother Richard of them yesternight per George Perrott. Howbeit, I fear he will have no respect thereunto, for since the 16th of the last there is not come one jot of a letter from him to us. It is high time therefore that one of us were with him at Calais, to see whereunto he applieth the gold that is sent him from hence, or else we shall bring our things to utter confusion. . . .

Your loving brother,
Otwell Johnson.

Immediately he received this letter, John set out for Calais, and as soon as he arrived he wrote to Robert Andrew, apologizing for Richard's mishandling of their affairs and promising that things would be very different in future. But, as John was beginning to realize, they were in a very sticky situation. The wool and fell sales were everywhere at an impossibly low ebb, while their Gascon wines had arrived so late from Bordeaux that they missed their markets. Moreover, the cargoes of Spanish wine, ordered by Otwell the previous autumn, had proved an immense disappointment. 'Our sacks do rise the most ungraciously that ever I see any wine in all my life, both for naughtiness and emptiness,' he had written, 'so as I fear we shall be losers of a third penny of our principal.' Johnson & Company had no large capital reserves to fall back on, like some of the big business houses; their creditors were clamouring for payment and, with business so bad, they had no money to pay their debts or buy new wares. In June, Otwell wrote that he was 'utterly at my wits' end to how make any provision for wares or money against the vintage, either for Spain or Bourdeaux, and I am sure I am not alone in that case'.

To add to the confusion were the rumours of immediate devaluation which went spinning and twisting through Lombard Street during those anxious weeks. Everything, however, was thrown completely into the background by the sudden abolition of the exchange on June 12th.

First (wrote Otwell to his brother) concerning gold and the course of th'exchange, know that this day at our noon Street time was published th'enclosed proclamation for the stay, or rather abolishing of the said exchange, rechange, etc., whereby most merchants are brought into a wonderful perplexity of their trade, and very few or none can understand the ground of the Council's meaning therein, saving that some construe a money matter toward to grant a licence to some of our great cobs, who shall eat most of our forward youth clean up, as it is doubted of most part of all merchants, as hereafter more shall be perceived.

Not long after this preliminary move, the threatened devaluation of the coinage took place. The shilling was called down first to ninepence, and then to sixpence, and the fourpenny groat to threepence, and then twopence by a 'wonderful sudden alteration' which caused many merchants to exclaim, like Anthony Cave: 'I shall lose a good portion by it, and many other do much lament their losses.' It was no wonder that 'few men's wits or none can assuredly comprehend, or rather compass, the well doing of their things'. Soon the situation became almost farcical, for no one knew from one day to the next what was going to happen. Creditors were imploring their debtors not to pay their bills, debtors were threatening to pay them on the nail, and so uncertain was the future monetary position that John and Otwell were able to borrow hundreds of pounds practically free of interest.

The Government, having created a panic, did little to restore confidence and allay anxiety. As a sop to public opinion, they announced that a new gold coinage would be minted, and the fineness of the silver coinage improved — measures that Cave had always advocated as the only possible remedy for the situation. Few people, however, were surprised when it was reported that the new coinage was 'not very plentiful abroad, and scarcely so perfect as they had hoped'. It was indeed a red herring to distract attention from the dissensions in the Council. For months past Warwick and his supporters had been barracking the Protector and, in the *coup d'état* of 1551, they managed to seize power. Somerset, Lord Grey, Sir Thomas Palmer and many others were consigned to the Tower. 'What the matter is, God knoweth,' wrote John to his master on October 17th, 'but exceeding sudden it is to all the ears.' A few days later, he gave to Anthony Cave the official explanation which had been offered to the merchants.

The number in the Tower increaseth, but the Lord Paget is not there as it was said. The Council have given the Lord Mayor to understand the causes to be as followeth: that the Duke of Somerset hath practised to get the Tower of London, where he would have brought the King, and then have ruled the King's realm as pleased him; also that he would have had the Isle of Wight, where he would have fortified; also that he practised to get the Great Seal, that nothing should pass, proclamation nor other, but such as he pleased; and fourthly he would have made an insurrection, and been in the coffers of rich men of London. This is opened in all our halls here in London and to the whole commons. I beseech God be merciful to us, and send an agreement, and that our noble King may be preserved.

That any explanation at all was felt necessary is remarkable, and is a recognition of the power of the merchant class. Even so, it was really a superfluous courtesy, for the sixteenth-century man in the street had no right either to hold or express a viewpoint in national affairs, which were regarded as 'princes' matter'. John made no comment on the *coup d'état*, gave no opinion on the plausible story arranged for his benefit, and said nothing which could be construed as sympathy for the Protector, a man to whom he had personal cause to feel grateful. Sensible and intelligent as he and his fellow-merchants were, they had perforce to hold their tongues while a group of megalomaniacs fought out their private struggle for power. Only in laconic phrases here and there do they reveal their acute interest in the tragedy that was being enacted before their eyes, reporting the sinister news of the arrival of the Calais hangman, 'it is thought by some they shall not come to arraignment', and 'le bruit ici est des pardons'. The end, which they were powerless to avert, was really a foregone conclusion. Acquitted of treason — he had planned none — Somerset was convicted under the newly passed Act of Unlawful Assemblies. In January 1552 he died by the headsman's axe on Tower Hill. Warwick's triumph was complete, and England was plunged still further into the morass of corruption and maladministration which marked these troubled years.

In such uncertain times as these, Anthony Cave felt that the only course to follow was to bide quietly and await the return of a 'more stable world'. John at first agreed with him. 'God hath altered my brother's purpose and mine for Bordeaux voyage', he had written to Robert Andrew. 'Howbeit, if Bartholomew Warner will take it upon him — as I think he will — I advise to do somewhat, but not so much as if my brother had lived.' Circumstances, however, were to change John's resolve to limit his trading ventures and be content with modest profits. In August 1551 war broke out between France and the Empire, and the war at sea soon reached such proportions that it was obvious that few Flemish vessels would ever reach Bordeaux, much less return safely through the network of privateers in the Channel, while French ships would almost certainly be barred from Imperial ports. It seemed to John that here was an unrivalled opportunity for neutral English ships, and that wine cargoes would be able to command a high price. And since he had observed that 'few in these days profit by wares but such as trade in wares continually', he decided to plunge more deeply into trading ventures than ever before, particularly in Gascon wine, which Bartholomew Warner would travel to Bordeaux to buy.

For shipping, the partners turned first to Lynn. In the middle of August, John asked his friend Solme to hire 'some handsome ballinger of 50 or 60 ton for Bordeaux', to set sail as soon as possible, the master to be 'such a fellow as will be diligent, and not tarry after company when God sendeth fair wind and weather, for the tarrying for company most times hindreth the merchant, Yea, and the owner of the ship loseth by it also'. Eventually the *Mary Fortune of Lynn* was hired, with her master Anthony Williamson, and the charter-party was drawn up between John and the owner, Ralph Taylor. At the same time, other vessels were hired in London: the *Mary Gallant of St. Osyth's*, the *Mary Katherine of London*, and the little *John of Gillingham*. When John insured them through his Italian friend, Peter Champanty, he tried to take out additional insurance on two ships as yet unnamed, but this Champanty could not do. 'He hath made assurance both to this City and also to Lynn for 5 on the hundred,' wrote the young apprentice, 'which is well, saith he, as the world goeth, considering the wars. He dispatched the same upon Monday, and he saith he hath saved you 20s in the hundred; that it would have been more if it were to do this day. But for th'unknown ships, men will not meddle.' The underwriters indeed could hardly be blamed for giving the unknown vessels a wide berth. They suspected, and quite rightly, that John was going to take a chance and freight French ships, in which case they would lose heavily if these were captured by Flemings on the high seas. In his letter of instruction to Bartholomew Warner, John had written: 'If any Bretons be laden, use secretness, and let me have speedy word for assurance. And suffer no man to meddle but yourself, I pray you, with those kind of people — ye wot what I mean.'

By the end of September, Bartholomew Warner had reached Bordeaux and was comfortably installed in his host's house, waiting for the fine wines to come down from the vineyards of the high country. It was early for vintage wines, and 'as yet', he wrote, 'the best mouthed may be deceived'. It soon became apparent that other English merchants had had the same idea as John. Bordeaux was thronged with 'such a sort of merchants as I think came not out of England many a day, which also is a cause that the wines will be dear still'. At last the wine came in. Bartholomew Warner made his selection, and began to lade the waiting vessels. The *Mary Gallant* weighed anchor first, with two French ships, the *Trinity* and *Radegonde of Olonne*. The *John of Gillingham* got away soon afterwards, with twenty-seven tons of claret in her hold. The bungs of the great casks were all marked with John's and Bartholomew's merchants' marks, and one cask was specially labelled, 'T, which is a note of the soil' — evidence of the choice vineyard where the wine had been made. Among the casks that the *Mary Katherine* carried were three tierce of extra good wine for the insurance broker, Peter Champanty, with his initials 'P.C.' carved on the bung. One of the ships, the *Mary Fortune of Lynn*, laded over forty-two tons; and, besides that, Warner managed to freight another ten tons in her sister ship, the *Greater Mary Fortune of Lynn*. 'I trust there are laden as good wines as any man shall have,' he wrote to John, 'and indeed, very dear.' So dear, in fact, that Warner was wondering whether the Government would impose a maximum selling price. 'If there be, men shall be undone by it.'

The long voyage home was always a matter of anxious waiting until the ships reached port, and that autumn many English vessels were lost or captured while returning from Bordeaux. Anthony Cave, who had put a hundred crowns into the common stock of the Gascon venture, was constantly worrying John for news. Early in November, John was able to send him the good tidings that 'sundry ships of Lynn were in the Downs from Bordeaux, and am put in comfort Ralph Taylor that I freighted to be one. I hope by this they be at Lynn in safety, for the wind hath been fair'. But alas for their hopes. A fortnight later, the *Mary Fortune* and her greater consort limped into port, and it became known that the partners had sustained heavy losses. Ralph Taylor's ship had been 'almost cast away and for spoiled', losing her 'mainmast and all her upper-decking'. The pirates who captured her had spared no effort to make her unworkable, and they had plundered the greater part of her cargo, all that their own vessel would hold. As for the wine that they left on board the *Mary Fortune*, 'the leakage was very much. There was so little in some of the cask that, if we had known the truth, might have been left for the freight which now is past'.

Fortunately, the other vessels arrived safely at Dover and, although many other English ships had lost their cargoes, and the wine its colour in the wintry seas, John's was 'excellent good and fair cask' when Richard Sandell opened it. The wines were re-laded into other vessels and sent by way of the Foreland into the Thames, where the casks were unshipped again and cellared against the Christmas sales. For a time the wine sold well and the partners made a good profit on it. But suddenly, as they had feared, the Government imposed a maximum selling price, and refused to alter their decision, despite the outcry from the merchants. Bartholomew managed somehow to get hold of an advance copy of the proclamation, which he sent to John, writing later that 'even to the hour that it was proclaimed I was doing, and if it had tarried till today, I had sold a ton or two more than I have. Patience!'

Although the Bordeaux voyages were only partly successful, John still cherished great hopes of his Spanish ventures. Convinced that there was 'grand apparence de profite sur vins d'Espaigne cette année', and that they would be 'readier and better cheap' in London than at Antwerp or Zealand, because of the wars, John had committed himself to large purchases of sack and bastard wines at Jerez and Cadiz. He had arranged that the agents of Henry Garbrand's firm in Spain should buy seventy tons of each kind of wine, promising that the money should be paid to Michel Mulier at Antwerp three months after the lading, with 2 per cent commission on top of the purchase price. It was at first decided that Michel should freight ships in the Low Countries, but, since the Spanish vessels were refusing to leave port 'till they shall be strong and conducted with men of war', while the Breton vessels were rocking idly at anchor in the Zealand harbours because 'l'Empereur a defendu que nulle navire sorte hors du pays de par d'ici', there was no alternative but to make a last-minute search for shipping in England.

September was really far too late to begin freighting ships for Spain. The time to give advice was in June, and the ships should have been on their way during July, or August at the very latest, so as to be in time for lading the wine in September or October. After a frantic search, John finally managed to hire the *Phoenix* and the *John Evangelist of Lynn.* This, however, was only accomplished by dint of much persuasion, and by a solemn promise that the master should have not only the customary ten or fifteen tons of cargo space for wine, but also three or four tons for Malaga fruit, 'raisins ou figues, car aussi j'ai lui a promis pour tant mieux charger le dit navire là, ou une botte de sack ne pourra entrer'. The ships were assured in England, like the Bordeaux ventures, 'car il est ici toujours meilleur marché 2 ou 3 pour-cent qu'en Espaigne qu' en Anvers'.

Detailed instructions were sent to the Spanish agents, with constant reminders to buy only the very finest wines, even if they were dearer (John had not forgotten the fiasco of the previous year). Above all the charter-parties were to be made out in the English language, in case of capture by French or Flemish privateers at sea. Time and again, John wrote anxious letters to Michel Mulier and Henry Garbrand, begging and imploring them to leave nothing undone that might contribute to the success of the Spanish voyage. 'I would not endure the shame for £100 to be known that I should send ships into Spain and not to be laden.'

Early in November, the first ships were seen coming up the misty Thames. One great hulk, laden with a cargo of fruit and sherry, beat all the rest. It belonged to John's wealthy brother-in-law, Blase Saunders. The wind and the weather were fair and, as the autumn days wore on, more and more vessels began to arrive. Only there was no news of John's two ships. He did not even know whether they had got as far as Spain, let alone any news of their lading. And when John heard that English ships were forbidden to cross the bar at Cadiz, 'à cause de la mortalité qui était ici de la sueur', fear struck at his heart. 'Plaît-à Dieu que le Seigneur Arnoult de Suierpont et Jehan de Myllebroucque ont fait la partie!' he wrote to Michel, 'Pour car je doubte que les navires que j'ai frettés et envoiés en Espaigne ne seront aussi reçus en Espaigne.' At last, John took to haunting the wharves, asking the bearded captains if they had heard anything, but 'ils m'ont dit que non'. There was 'no tidings of other of our ships'. Then, early in December, John learnt what had happened. French ships of war had attacked the *Phoenix* and *John Evangelist*, and had plundered all their equipment — anchors, cables, sails, ordnance and victuals. They had even robbed the sailors of their clothes. The two ships had managed to crawl into Falmouth harbour, and from there, by slow degrees, they made their way along the coast to Lynn. Edmund Solme watched them stagger home.

As concerning the two ships ye freighted into Spain, surely, as I perceive, ye are disappointed of them. The *Phoenix*, my brother's ship, was beat down to the water with weather, having nothing standing but her foremast and sail, being in great jeopardy. The other, as I can learn, was robbed of victuals, sails, money and clothes, after such a sort, if it be true that they report, as I have not heard the like, and the men in fear of their lives.

Fortunately, John was partly covered by insurance. However, there still remained the problem of the wine in Spain: 280 buts of the finest and most expensive Xeres wine, lying in a cool dark cellar in Seville. There was scarcely a hope of getting it away before it turned sour and musty, although, as Michel never ceased reminding them, it had to be paid for on the nail. At last, one of the Spanish agents managed to freight a ship named the *Mary Katherine* with ten buts of wine, sending advice in a long letter 'written in Flemish, whereof I understand almost nothing', said Bartholomew Warner, asking John to translate it for him.

Bartholomew was then trying desperately to get ships, hesitating between the huge and famous *Matthew Gonson* (where the leakage was tremendous, since the casks were stored four deep in the hold), and the smaller *Bark Aucher*. Eventually, however, he decided in favour of the *John Evangelist* and the *Trinity of London*, which were sailing 'in conserva' with the *Great Bark Aucher*. Still they had not sufficient cargo space to bring back all their wine, and John finally asked the agents to dispose of the surplus in Spain if they possibly could. The voyage from Spain, if the ships managed to arrive safely, was bound to be dangerous, for, as he told Michel: 'quasi toutes les navires qui sont venues cette année d'Espaigne ont été dépouillés des Français', and he was naturally worried about the possibility of further losses. But, either way, the unfortunate partners stood to lose a vast sum of money, for if the wine came home in safety it would be old stuff, soured by months in storage, and if it was sold in Spain, it had long since lost the first markets.

The outcome of the southern voyages was exactly what Anthony Cave had prophesied. In letter after letter he had warned John to be prepared for trouble, and had often emphasized the old saw: 'He that doth not perils foresee, in perils falleth.' He told John time and again that it was no small compass of things he had entered into, and quoted the 'wise and old saying' that Otwell himself had used long years before. 'Qui trop embrasse, mal attraint! For God's sake, look as well to th'end as to the beginning!' These outspoken criticisms, with all their implied lack of confidence, wounded John deeply, coming as they did from the man who had taught him everything he knew, and to whom he bore great affection. John replied patiently to all Cave's letters, only asking him to 'bear me your goodwill as ye have done in all my doings, and to my power I will be yours as I have been'. But at last he was moved to put into words what is surely the perfect expression of a merchant's faith, the doctrine of the Calling.

For your good counsel, which I know proceedeth of earnest goodwill, I do most heartily thank you, wishing it had pleased God so to have provided for me that I might with less embracing of business have passed my times in the world. But God having appointed me to be a merchant (and such one as cannot live only to myself or for myself) I am compelled to enter into much business, and to take money and much things in hand. He that hath hitherto holpen me, I mistrust not, will provide that th'end shall be as good as it hath pleased him to suffer me to begin. I am not entered altogether of my own seeking, but occasioned by others' beginnings, which, if it please God, I may live to see th'end. If not, his Will be done, for I make no other reckoning, supposing not to displease God to be occupied while I am here in that which is my calling, and in an uncertain place to make sure account of nothing but that God's Will shall be, for further than he hath of me determined to follow, my little doings or great doings can neither help or further.

But while his letters to Anthony Cave breathe the spirit of patience and resignation, John in fact was nearly worried out of his life. All his small capital was tied up in the voyages, sales everywhere were at a standstill, he owed hundreds of pounds and, worse than anything else, one of his bills had just been publicly protested on the Antwerp Bourse. Such a thing had never happened during the whole of his career as a merchant, and he at once rounded on Richard and Ambrose, who were supposed to be looking after affairs abroad, but who had not written to him for weeks. Richard, of course, as John might have guessed, was not in Antwerp at all; he had ridden south to Rouen to extricate his handsome Flemish servant from the clutches of the French authorities. And when Ambrose at last arrived in Antwerp, after getting their herring ships away from Dunkirk, he found everything in a state of chaos. Richard's sudden departure was 'so much and evil spoken of', that he hardly knew what to do. Worse still, he found that he himself was the object of suspicion and dark looks. 'I am here as prisoner . . .' he wrote to John, 'with a heavy heart and a light purse', a kind of hostage for the payment of

Johnson & Company's debts. The public protestation of John's bill had had the effect of a vote of No Confidence and Ambrose found himself slighted and cold-shouldered everywhere he went. One morning, in the crowded Bourse, the famous Sir William Chester took hold of him and said that, while he had plenty of money free to lend them, he would not on any account do so. ' "We are suspected men," he said, "not like . . . to continue." Thus much and more he said, in great society, meaning good faith.'

Ambrose found his position difficult enough to bear, and it was not made any easier by John. From the distance of Glapthorn Manor, John was perhaps not fully able to appreciate the gravity of their situation, and he began to put all the blame on Ambrose. The tone of John's letters, 'chiding without a cause', irritated the young man beyond endurance. 'I would I could answer your letters before I receive them', he wrote, protesting that he would 'as willingly as ye sit up nights, rather than things should be unanswered'. For a long time John refused to believe this, and he dealt the unfortunate Ambrose so many 'taunts' that his brother-in-law said he was weary of opening the letters from England. Once, writing 'at three of the clock this morning, before mine eyesight was comen down', he swore that 'if this grief continue, I had rather be a shepherd than a merchant, and so saith Michel, who is weary of his travail, both for his own business and yours'.

Their difficulties were indeed overwhelming. The Emperor at this time was engaged in tightening up the economic war against France. A half per cent levy (illegal so far as the English were concerned) had been imposed on all goods, and safe conducts were now declared essential for 'marchandise de France en Flanders, et de Flanders en France'. This had an immediate bearing on the affairs of Johnson & Company. Richard had bought several shiploads of Orleans wine when he was at Rouen, and had sent most of it to Middleburg in Zealand, where it was promptly arrested as contraband French goods. The resulting lawsuits dragged on for months, with no remedy, as Ambrose said, but patience. Ambrose rode all the way to Brussels in the hope of getting the wine returned, but to no avail. The Imperial Council made him kick his heels for ten days while they made up their minds, and then they sent him 'to the place from whence I came, which is Zealand, and there to end the matter by order of the law'.

Needless to say, when spring came, the cargoes were still under arrest, and there seemed little prospect of getting them back before the wine turned to vinegar.

Most of Johnson & Company's herring that year met with a similar fate. They had bought a great deal of herring at Dunkirk, some of it in partnership with a firm of French merchants who, however, defaulted when it came to paying their two-thirds share of the money. 'Knaves will be knaves', wrote Ambrose ruefully, and later: 'Make them merchants, make them Frenchmen!' Ambrose just managed to get two of the ships away, but the effort left him so short of cash that he could not afford to buy a safe-conduct for the third ship. As he explained to John, safe-conducts were not cheap. They cost '8 pour-cent before a man do ship any-thing, and our wares that we shall bring shall be priced certainly. All the mischiefs that they can devise, they go about to accomplish, to our great hindrance'.

Despite the threatening situation in the Low Countries, John still believed that 'Master Herring' offered them their best chance of profit now that the southern voyages had failed, and he in-structed Ambrose to buy nearly a thousand pounds' worth on credit. Ambrose, nearer to the realities of life, did as he was bid with acute misgivings. Indeed, no clearer indication of the firm's financial position can be found than the demand made by the big herring dealers, the Rondinelli. They insisted that Robert Andrew and Michel Mulier countersign the bills, before a single barrel changed hands. Even so, the partners were in a cleft stick. Three ships were now lading herring in Zealand, but none of them could leave port 'till the Emperor's droits be paid, which draw to near £100'. The want of money had 'brought all out of square'.

It was about this time, after Christmas, that Richard put in a belated appearance at Antwerp again, weeks after he had pro-mised to come. By dint of pinching and scraping, he and Ambrose managed to raise the money for two safe-conducts, and the latter went to Brussels to get them sealed. He paid for both of them, and then, to his horror, the Officer of the Seal kept one back, refusing to give it up, despite Ambrose's prayers and entreaties. The only possible reason was the protest that Ambrose once had signed, in an effort to recover from the Receiver-General 'all such sums as they received of me more than th'Intercourse did specify, which I was counselled unto by my Lord Ambassador; and now, being refused the seal, I know not what to do'. There was not much he could do, except write to the Advocate of the English Nation in Flanders, and he quit the subject with the prophetic remark: 'This miserable restraint of liberty will undo this country surely.' By the following spring, only one ship had got away, and her cargo proved a bitter disappointment to them. When the barrels were opened by the searchers at St. Ives, the herring was found to be 'so shamefully handled', and 'so falsely packed', that the profit was next to nothing.

Misfortune trailed in the wake of all John's ventures during this disastrous year, whether it was herring that was involved, or raisins, or Rouen cloth, or the attempted purchase of captured cargoes of molasses and sugar. Almost the only voyage that was a complete success was the mixed cargo of Flanders wares that John brought over for his friend Edmund Solme, and on which he received a commission of twelve per cent. So well did this cargo sell at Lynn, that John began to think about importing wares on his own account. Eventually he agreed with Solme and Anthony Cave to bring over a cargo of iron, pitch and tar, white sugar, salmon, hops and Ghent cloth, and instructions were according given in Flanders. Ambrose, however, was unimpressed. 'I perceive ye will send a ship hither to lade for Lynn', he remarked. 'If credit serve not better than money present, she shall be very light laden.' They hired the *Greater Mary Fortune of Lynn*, at considerable expense. The owner, Thomas Dyson, demanded not only two tons of cargo space for his own use, but also 'a great freight, viz. £32', for the short journey between Norfolk and the Low Countries. So long did the ship take over her outward voyage, that they began to despair of ever seeing her and, when at last she did reach Antwerp, she ran smack into one of the most violent storms of the century. Richard sent John a vivid description of the terrible tempest of January 12th, 1552.

The Mary Fortune of Lynn is not yet laden, but provision is made for her lading, and so soon as she is rigged, shall be laden, by God's grace. It hath not chanced evil that she is yet to lade, for the great storms which have been here of late have put her in great jeopardy of wrack, lying at the quay, but thanks be to God she hath escaped the danger of sinking, which twenty-three hoys and crayers lying at the wharfs here have sustained. Upon Wednesday last was here the most terrible storm that ever I heard or saw. The water, overflowing most streets in this town, hath brought down near twenty houses standing on the royes; the wind hath blown down chimneys, pinnacles, and gable ends, and some houses down to the ground; the thunder hath burnt one part of Barrow, the water hath drowned another, with all the madder ground, and also hath overflown Romerswale Barke and other grounds thereby. Into Flanders the sea is also broken, and is 14 fathom deep in the breach, and 10 fathom in divers parts of the land. Zealand hath escaped at this time (God be praised therefore).

While the mariners lay aloft, repairing the ship's tackle, Richard and Michel got the cargo together and watched it being stowed away in the hold. But even though she was soon in good enough shape to sail, the *Mary Fortune* was not yet destined to get away. Because of the half per cent imposition, the Governor of the Merchant Adventurers at Antwerp had asked all the English merchants in the Low Countries to delay lading their vessels, by way of protest. As patriotic Englishmen, they had of course no choice but to agree — 'such commandment being given, Yea, and letters written over from the Council for the same, what could be done by obedient subjects but obey?' Thomas Dyson, however, let out a howl of protest, complaining that his ship had been delayed ten days longer than the time laid down in the charter-party, and swearing that he would get compensation. 'It is the crabbedest little wretch that ever was born!' exclaimed Richard. 'Ye may do with him as ye think good, for I am sure he will not let to make exclamation at Lynn as well as he did here.' The prophecy was correct. Thomas Dyson made all the trouble he could, forwarding John a certificate 'saying that Mr. Richard Johnson has evil used him, and that he will stop so much wares in the ship to he be agreed for his harms. Mr. Johnson', complained Preston, 'writes nothing but that he is a wrangling fellow, and will send him a salve for his sore legs!'

It was left to John to try and convince the furious captain that 'reason is meet to rule us both', that no good ever came from violent quarrels, and that impartial mediators were best qualified to settle the affair. Richard had his own troubles to take care of.

Johnson & Company's account was now at an afterdeal, and Richard simply did not know where to find the money to pay their debts. He begged John not to charge him with any more payments, for he could scarcely manage even to raise money on the few bills of exchange which they possessed.

After my most hearty commendations (beloved brother), my last was sent hence the 10 of this month by one Anthony Crede, one which came this way from Venice. My trust is that the same is come unto your hands. I have little matter to write unto you more than I therein wrote, but that ye shall herewith receive the estate which I found our business in at my coming hither, whereby ye shall perceive that we yet are and like shortly to be at a great afterdeal of our account here. By the sight thereof, my hope is ye will conceive some speedy provision necessary for the furniture thereof here (or at the leastway, for part of it) from London. For undoubtedly there is no reckoning to be made of any money to be had, either by interest or for any of those bills which be here due of day to come, for in the sale of Daniel van den Heede's bill, I have been so troubled as I never was the like, being forced (besides the payment of unreasonable interest) to be Art van Dale's man to gather in his debts, about the which having trudged these four days past, yet have I £130 to receive of my bill containing £280; and remedy is there none but so to do, or else to go without money, for the foul carl would not tell me one penny out of his house. Other bills he will buy none, and money is so scant here in other men's hands that I can perceive no shift to be made with our bills, but that we shall be forced to tarry our days, in the meantime not knowing how to clear our instant payments, but trust honestly to content all men (as they have hitherto been, God be praised) by one mean or other.

Poor Richard, trudging hopelessly round Antwerp in the icy January weather, his cloak pulled tight about his face, could see no way of paying what they owed. And then he heard of a fantastic bargain. A rich merchant of Venice, Philip Prini by name, offered him a rare jewel worth £1000, together with £1700 in ready money, in return for forty-eight sarplers of Fine

Cotswold wool. Knowing nothing of diamonds and pearls, Richard nevertheless leapt eagerly at the offer, and persuaded Robert Andrew, Michel Mulier, and Gheret de Villar to give their bond as surety. Richard himself made no attempt to buy the wool. This he left to John, apparently assuming that his brother could do it by a wave of his hand. 'This being performed, it will undoubtedly much augment our credit', he wrote. A few days later he saddled his horse, tightened the stirrup-leathers, and rode quietly out of Antwerp bound for his beloved France. He told no one that he was leaving. He simply vanished, and Ambrose returned from Brussels to find his lodging empty, and the counting-house thick with dust. The only tangible evidence that Richard had ever been there was a four-line note on the table, 'Our business is in this stay'. It is possible that personal reasons were at the back of his disappearance. Richard's temper was none too certain at the best of times, and he was now in one of his rages. Through no fault of his own, Richard was no businessman. For weeks past, although they said nothing to his face, Ambrose and Robert Andrew, Michel Mulier and Henry Garbrand, had all been making complaints about him in their letters to John, and John in turn had been nagging him to do what he did not want to do, and had no intention of doing — to write frequent, fully documented accounts of all their business, to handle money scrupulously and wisely, to keep his books in meticulous order, to behave on all occasions like a worthy merchant. John once told Richard that he always answered those things he did not like with silence, and now, it seems, Richard was determined to show them just what he could do. As John guessed, this was the real story behind Richard's disappearance. He hinted as much to Ambrose, who, however, could hardly credit it. But then Ambrose did not really know Richard very well.

Nicoloche hath divers times demanded £4 of me for brokage which you owe him, he saith. If you will that I shall pay him, write me. My cousin Johnson promised payment before his departure, and even so did he to Oste Mahiew for a small sum for my master's account for the bettering of wool; but he is gone, and left no word for remembrance thereof. Such small matters not cared for will nothing augment a man his good name, and even so have I written him this day, as I have of a great sort of lacks which I have of understanding of his doings here, which I am sure will make him angry, even as he wrote you before that he was. But that anger I pass not much of, having never burthened him but with matters of truth, as God only knoweth, etc., who defend us from this secret enmity, which is most ungodly and unnatural. He would never write me, or break unto me his mind after any such sort that he seemed to be angry, much less should he do you to understand his anger. . . .

If Richard had indeed desired revenge, he had it now. In his little note he had put their debts at £448 17s. 8d. It turned out to be far more than that, as Ambrose discovered when he had time to sort out the papers piled in confusion on the shelves and in the boxes. When he came to analyse their assets and liabilities, he found that they owed more than a thousand pounds in Antwerp alone, without the slightest hope of paying half of it back, if that. It seemed to Ambrose that, the more money that came into their hands, the more they were in debt. Richard had carelessly promised to pay everyone — four pounds here to Nicoloche, more there to Oste Mahiew — and Ambrose found that in addition he was being dunned five or six times a day by Rondinelli's men, lean, hawk-eyed Italians 'that will not have one day escaped after their money is due'. Everything was going to rack and ruin, 'and yet must I dwell here for nothing', Ambrose cried, 'and may not think the thing grievous'. The strain of the long, weary, frustrating winter was telling on him, the incessant struggle and the continual failure to make ends meet. His nerves were at the breaking-point.

Brother, you have divers times written unto me that lack of use to be in this care and trouble was only th'occasion of my grief, but now I shall desire you most heartily to take in good part my writing, assuring you even as truly as the Lord liveth, I will rather dig the ground continually for a poor living than to be in this disquieture; and suppose truly that you were never in this case, but that evermore you had some shift to make or order given you to use th'exchange which I have not, nother from you or my cousin Richard, or appearance of care to clear the same debts. . . .

Only eight months had passed since Otwell's death, but their affairs were in chaos. Ruin now literally stared them in the face, as venture after venture failed. For one year longer the unhappy partners struggled on, sinking ever deeper into debt and despair, unable to borrow money, buy goods, or even sell what they had, and in the month of March 1553 the end finally came.

CHAPTER II

THE BANKRUPTCY

A T the end of the last, red-bound volume of the letters is a
worn, much-thumbed sheet of paper with the words, 'Mr.
Johnson his remembrance in all haste' scrawled across it.
A mysterious Mr. Boswell was to ride post-haste to London, to
intervene hurriedly with Mr. Throgmorton, with 'my lord his
master', with Mr. Ramsay, Mr. Portemas, and above all Sir
Edward Montagu, 'and declare the truth to them, and desire
them to be Mr. Johnson's good lord'. Reading that agonized,
crumpled piece of paper, we know that what they had dreaded for
so many months had now come to pass. The firm was bankrupt,
and John was desperately trying to persuade his influential friends
to help him. It was eventually through the good offices of Lord
Chief Justice Montagu that all John's 'writings and books' — his
great ledgers and account-books, his letters and letter-books —
were gathered together and sent up to the Privy Council early in
the month of April 1553. After the lords of the Council had considered them at a meeting, the mass of papers was forwarded
to the Lord Chancellor, then one of the statutory judges in all
bankruptcy cases, together with two other co-opted members of
the Council. All the documents were held in reserve for the great
lawsuits even then beginning in the High Court of Admiralty.

But, despite the appeals he made to his friends, there was little
they could or would do. Once Johnson & Company had been
declared 'bancquaroutta' there was no hope for them, any more
than there had been for the unhappy Watkins, for the Kentish
clothier Robert Pyx, for Mr. Garway, William Cooper, Mynheer
van Loo, and the Spaniards of the letters. The sixteenth century
was not a very pleasant age to live in, and those who were unfortunate in life received no mercy. John himself regarded what
had happened as 'the punishment of God justly laid upon me for
my sins, having deserved a great deal more, but that God of His
mercy punisheth me not according to my deservings' — a view
that was heartily endorsed by all around him. The eminent

statesman, Sir William Cecil, to whom John owed money, is on record as advocating 'that bankruptcy be made felony, and bankrupts' lands sold and divided among their creditors . . . Where a poor thief doth steal a sheep or pick a purse, they come away with hundreds and thousands at least, and undo a great many honest men'.[110]

The most tragic wounds were inflicted by the law itself, for in England creditors were permitted to imprison their debtors, and to swoop down and seize such of their property as they could get. English literature to the time of Dickens is filled with denunciations of the evil system which made it impossible for a man to repay what he owed, but it continued in force until well into the nineteenth century, with Newgate and the Marshalsea as two of the greatest monuments of tragedy in the land. In Tudor England, unless the Lord Chancellor was so impartial that all the writs of attachment were stayed, and (as in Watkins's case) the debtor's goods 'divided amongst all his creditors, pro rata of the credit', the lion's share went always to the rich. Henry Brinklow, John's acquaintance, had inveighed against the system years before, in *The Complaint of Roderick Mors*. 'Ye have a partial law in making of 'tachments, first come first served; so one or two shall be all paid, and the rest shall have nothing. And commonly even the rich shall have the foredeal thereof by this 'tachment, to the great damage and oppression of the poor. For lightly the rich have the first knowledge of such things. . . .'

This was to be John's fate for, although through the kindness of their landlord he and Sabine were allowed to stay on at Glapthorn Manor, all their possessions were seized and carried away: clothes, linen, furniture, hangings, all Sabine's trinkets, and things that she valued as much for their associations as their actual worth. Anything that they could realize money on, the creditors seized. It is true that vast sums of money were owing to the merchants from whom the partners had bought goods and borrowed money, and to their friends and relations as well. According to the records of the Admiralty Court in 1553, they owed some £8000 to twenty of their creditors alone. Four years later, the sum of £9000 was still owing to eighty men and women, who then gathered together and signed a petition to the Privy Council, declaring that fourteen of the richest and most rapacious of the creditors had got 'divers goods, wares and merchandises belonging

T   295

to the said Johnsons and Saunders, to the value of £3000 and more' into their own hands 'by attachments, condemnations and otherwise by covin', and that they had flatly refused to bring their spoils to 'equal division amongst all the rest'. Indeed, so swift and efficient were the successful fourteen in stripping John of all he owned, that before the month of March 1553 had fairly run its course, he was writing to Sir William Cecil.

> Truly, Sir, I have the possession of nothing in the world, nor have not fraudulently conveyed my goods into other men's hands as it is reported, nor done anything else to the defrauding of my creditors, yet in all places my goods be spoiled and attached, and of them that their days of payment be long to come; which considered, I beseech you be my good master, as I perceive by my friends that ye are, and then I hope there will be some good order taken that my goods may be distributed amongst my creditors, and not thus spoiled as they be.

But despite John's heartfelt plea for some good order to be taken in his affairs, the Principal Secretary's chief concern was apparently the recovery of £41 2s. od. that John had owed his father for wool. Being, as he said, 'dispossessed of all that ever I had', John did not know how he was to repay the money, until late in May he received secret information that the little *Trinity of London* was returning from Spain with a cargo of Seville oil on board. He wrote immediately to urge Cecil 'to enter an action upon the same before the ship do arrive, which may be an assurance unto you for the same. For if it be deferred until th'arrival of the ship, others (I doubt) will be before you, and then if every man shall enjoy that which they get of our goods by attachments, I know not how to satisfy your mastership'. Cecil needed no urging, and so quietly did he go to work that only two other creditors, Edward and Thomas Onley, got wind of the ship's arrival. Warrants for her arrest were issued, the cargo was unladed, and the oil sold off at £14 a ton. Thomas Onley received the money, paying Sir William Cecil his due share, so that the debt could be written off in his books.

The other creditors were now at work on the *Mary Flower of Brittlesea*, which had arrived in the Thames from Bordeaux with a cargo of '75 tons wines de haut pays, as white, clarets and reds'. William Knight, a leading London mercer, who claimed that

John owed him £1500, succeeded in getting his warrant in before anyone else, and managed to sell some of the wine. Eager at all costs to get his money back, Knight had never once questioned the actual ownership of the cargo. He had merely taken it for granted that the wine belonged to Johnson & Company. It was the more unexpected, therefore, when a Bordeaux merchant named Jenot de Gaist arrived out of the blue, asserting that the cargo of the *Mary Flower* was his, together with the wine in another ship, the *Christopher of Ipswich*. This second vessel had been consigned to Richard Johnson, and was now under arrest at Calais, claimed by Thomas Egerton, the Treasurer of the Mint, to whom John owed £1500.

The Privy Council decided that the Frenchman should be allowed to have the unsold wines on surety. When the case came up for trial, it was revealed that Jenot and his brother William de Gaist were merchants of great wealth. They owned extensive vineyards at 'Tortyfuma', eleven leagues from Bordeaux, and every year they made wine which was famous for its quality, and which attracted buyers from far and wide. De Gaist told the court that so many ships had been captured at sea, because of the war between France and the Empire, that during 1553 they had decided not to ship under their own names. He had accordingly gone to Bordeaux and contacted a young Englishman named James Elliot, who (without any authority) permitted him to use the name of Johnson & Company in the charter-parties and on the bills of lading. In order to confirm the Frenchman's story, the court summoned before it all the captains who were known to have been in Bordeaux at the time. Their evidence was entertaining as well as instructive. One after another, the sailors climbed into the witness-box and related how they 'brake their fast and made merry' on all the ships at Bordeaux in turn. But, after they had been heard, there was no room for doubt. The Judges decided that de Gaist was telling the truth and, despite William Knight's violent protests, they upheld the Privy Council's conditional award, and gave their verdict in the Frenchman's favour.

The third case in which Johnson & Company were involved was that of the *Salvator of Venice*. It proved to be one of the greatest lawsuits handled by the High Court of Admiralty during the whole of the sixteenth century. The story begins during the summer of 1552, when the war between France and the Empire was at its height. Michel Mulier wrote over to Bartholomew Warner early in August. He said that his firm wanted to send a cargo of wares to Spain, and asked Bartholomew if he could find a suitable ship in England, desiring also to borrow Johnson & Company's name for the voyage, so that there would be less danger of losing the cargo, if by any chance they encountered a French privateer at sea. Bartholomew duly made inquiries in Lombard Street, and learnt that the *Matthew Gonson* was making another voyage to the Mediterranean, and several Venetian ships as well. In his reply to Michel, he gave the Flemish firm permission to use their name, and promised to give all the help he could in lading their ship. Michel now set about getting the cargo together. It was a valuable one. The cargo list reveals that they shipped over sixty thousand ells of Oudenarde and Brabant linen, some grey, the rest white and brown; bolts of buckram and Naples fustian; fustian of Osebourg and Gyen, damask, black and grey; white fustian of Bruges; dozens of diaper table-cloths and napkins; great trusses of white thread; painted cloths and say for hangings; magnificent tapestries — the Story of Saul, the Story of Absalom and Tamar, the Story of Poetry; smaller tapestries with an overall design of leaves; cushions by the score; ninety-two dozen gross of pins; twenty dozen of extra large ribands; forty dozen of ribbons of Tournai; cases of delicate white lace, made in Brussels; dozens of small coffers, leather girdles and buff skins; sixty pounds of flax; pots, and porringers made of tin. When all was ready, the bales and barrels and boxes were laden on board an English hoy, bound for the Kentish coast.

The hoy was expected to arrive in the Downs shortly after Christmas, and Bartholomew rode down to Margate to watch her sail in. Unfortunately the little ship was delayed by contrary winds. The *Matthew Gonson* set sail for Spain some days before she arrived, and Bartholomew had perforce to search for another ship, finally choosing the *Salvator of Venice* as the most likely looking vessel. At last the hoy arrived, and trans-shipment of the cargo began without delay. This was never an easy feat and, although nearly all the goods were safely stowed away in the *Salvator*, several of the packs of cloth fell into the sea and got soaking wet before they could be hauled on board. At the time, no one worried much about it. The bills of lading were checked through against Michel's cargo list and certified as correct, and Bartholomew rode back to London to make the final arrangements with the patrone of the *Salvator*, Giovanni-Maria Zuccharini, who was lodging at a house in Seething Lane. After some bargaining, the sum of 140 ducats in Spanish gold was agreed on for freight money, and they were sitting down to sign the charter-party, when the patrone's eye happened to light on the list of damaged goods. Afraid of possible trouble with factors at Cadiz, Zuccharini refused point-blank to accept the cargo unless the damage was put right.

As the patrone was well within his rights, there was nothing to do but give in. However, Bartholomew was now far too anxious about his own firm's affairs to spend any more time on the *Salvator*, and he asked Michel to send someone over from Flanders. Eventually, Henry Garbrand arrived. He went straightaway to see his old friend the Flemish postmaster, Jacob van der Hoven, and with his help managed to hire two packers. The postmaster also lent him the services of his own Italian-speaking apprentice, and all four set off for Margate. They spent the night at an inn, and next morning rowed out to the Venetian ship, where the packers opened up the damaged bales. Twenty-seven pieces of cloth were found to be soaked through, and these were taken away to be dried. By four o'clock that afternoon, the work was done, and they all rode back to the City.

On his return, Henry Garbrand went to the postmaster's house, and it was then that he learned for the first time that Johnson & Company were bankrupt. He realized that it would now be far too risky to use John's name and merchant's mark, and so he asked van der Hoven if he would be willing to oblige. The good-natured postmaster agreed, and the charter-party and bills of lading were written out anew for the patrone and scrivener of the *Salvator* to sign. They were too late. Word had reached the creditors' ears, and throughout the month of April 1553 warrant after warrant showered down on the cargo of the Venetian ship. Anthony Cave claimed £1500, Thomas Cave sued for £700; Richard Cresswell wanted £1100. Aunt Saunders and the cousins at Harington entered their warrants too, as did Edmund Brudenell, the Onleys, William Knight, Sebastian Danckard, Hector del Hoven, Justinian Schorer et Frères of Augsburg, John Spencer of Althorp, and many other merchants in

London and the country. Officials were sent down from the Admiralty Court to arrest the ship at Margate. Zuccharini was paid his freight money and told that he could sail. The cargo was taken off and shipped to London, to be stacked in the Custom House until the case came up for trial.

Henry Garbrand now sent in a petition to the Privy Council, explaining how his company had 'bought and provided at Antwerp with their own money and credit certain wares and merchandise which they purposed to have laden for Spain in the ship called Matthew', and which, 'to avoid the danger of enemies', were eventually shipped 'under the name of one John Johnson of London', and put on board the *Salvator* to be sent to Cadiz. By ill fortune, John, who was 'in good estimation' at the time of the lading, had since gone bankrupt, and 'divers of his creditors of their greedy and insatiable mind', had seized the goods, 'pretending that they should belong to Johnson, whereas in very deed it is not so, but belong only to the said Mulier and his company, with other merchants of Flanders'. If the goods were retained or 'long deferred from them', he continued, 'it should be the utter undoing of them and all theirs', and he implored the Council 'not to suffer their goods to pay other men's debts', but to hand the cargo back to them on surety until the trial was over.

William Knight, one of the principal witnesses, was not convinced. He insisted that the cargo was the property of Johnson & Company and of no one else, and that it was not until the news of the bankruptcy that Henry Garbrand took any interest in the goods. Then, said Knight, he went down to the Venetian ship, opened certain packs that were marked with John's mark, altered them, and put others on the canvas. Other merchants supported this view. Richard Stockbridge, later prominent in the Guinea trade, told how he and others had seen the cargo carried from the waterside to a house in Mincing Lane; how, when the great packs were opened, they found pieces of canvas, marked with a merchant's mark, sewn on to the linen, 'and because the same pieces of canvas and marks seemed suspicious', they, in the presence of the Judges and Registrar of the High Court of Admiralty:

> ... did rip off and take away the same pieces of canvas ...
> and on th'other side of the said piece of canvas, being
> inwards ... they found within side of the same canvas the

very proper, usual and accustomed mark and note of the forenamed John Johnson . . . being there very deceitfully and colourably after that sort set and made, for every man seeing the same would have judged no less but a great and wonderful craft and guile therein contained and hid.

Nevertheless, all the merchants giving evidence, including the creditors, admitted that it was the general practice to ship goods in other men's names, especially in wartime, and to borrow their marks as well. They did so, as one Frenchman said, to 'preserve and save' their wares. The fact that an Englishman shipping from Antwerp had to swear on the Holy Evangelist of God that he was the true owner according to the mark on his goods, to the officers both of the English and Imperial Customs Houses, and that he was heavily penalized if he perjured himself, meant little. As the Johnson Letters reveal, defrauding the customs was one of the principal pastimes of Tudor merchants. Henry Garbrand, of course, had merely sewn another mark over John's easily recognizable trefoil, in an effort to elude the creditors, just as he had used van der Hoven's name on the bill of lading.

The creditors, afraid that they were going to lose the case, now proceeded to invoke international co-operation. In the autumn of 1553, the Mayor of Calais, the Mayor and Constables of the Staple, and the Burgomasters of Bruges and Antwerp, all received official letters from Queen Mary, inviting them to hold courts and examine further witnesses in the case, particularly Michel Mulier. Special interpreters in German and Latin were provided, and articles, evidence, depositions and interrogatories were sent out from England to brief the lawyers thoroughly. And by special request of the High Court of Admiralty, the books and registers of the municipal archives were combed for evidence. The result was the complete vindication of Michel Mulier & Company.

Among the documents sent over to England were eight letters written in French, seven of them from Bartholomew Warner to Michel, and one from John himself to Arnold de Suierpont at Cadiz. To identify the handwriting, the High Court of Admiralty summoned various witnesses. Richard Sandell, once Otwell's young apprentice, and now a full-fledged member of the Drapers' Company, stood up in the witness-box and testified to his personal knowledge of the writers, saying that 'by the space of two years and an half together he was in house' with them, and during 'all that time continually was well acquainted and knew their hands and writing, for sundry time this examinant saw them write, and hath perused and seen their writing divers times, both in the French and English tongues'. John's brother-in-law, John Gery, also appeared, and declared (as well he might) that he knew their handwriting very well, for he had been reading it daily for the past six years. All the letters before the court related to the lading of the goods in the *Salvator*, but in none of them was there the slightest indication that they actually belonged to Johnson & Company.

The evidence of the letters was supported by that of John's own ledgers, for the Lord Chancellor had appointed a committee of merchants to examine them. The famous Sir Andrew Judde testified in court that he had 'perused the books of account of the said John Johnson, Richard Johnson, Ambrose Saunders and Bartholomew Warner', and, although he had seen Michel Mulier's name, and reckoning between them, there was nothing that concerned the cargo of the *Salvator of Venice*. William Garrard, the great Levant merchant, also stated that he did 'thoroughly view, search and read the books of debit and credit' belonging to the company, but that he could find no trace of the goods in the cargo list, and giving, for the benefit of the court, an explanation of mercantile practice in the keeping of accounts.

This point was seized on by the suspicious Knight, who declared it to be his opinion that:

> ... sundry merchantmen, meaning truly the course and trade of merchandises, do observe and keep books of account in manner and form as in the said 'positions is deduced. But other false bankrupts and broken merchants, as the said John Johnson and his company, are meaning falsehood and untruth with their creditors as they have done, and do use other false ways and means by private books and other for their own memory that never cometh to their creditors' sight, nor to any other person, to the defrauding of their creditors; in which private book they do use to enter such goods of theirs as they would should not come to the creditors' knowledge after they are broken....

It would, of course, have been perfectly possible for John to have kept a double set of books, and many a sharp merchant must have done so. But John was not that kind of man; if he had been, he would have yielded to the pressure of his creditors long since, and claimed the cargo of the *Salvator* as his own, in order to clear part of his debts. John was a serious-minded, honest man — too honest, some people would say, for his own good in the business world — and he scorned such double dealing. Several of his friends testified that he denied ownership of the goods. The post-master, for example, related how he walked along to the Lombard Street house and asked John straight out if the goods were really his, and John had said, No, he only lent his name to help Michel. Perhaps the most vivid story of those last awful days comes from the lips of John Gery, written down verbatim by the Clerk of the Admiralty Court. Soon after the news had come that Johnson & Company was 'escaped and broken', John Gery had gone along to Alderman William Garrard's house in the Stocks. Ambrose and his brother Laurence Saunders were there as well, and,

. . . the said John Johnson communing and talking with the said Parson Saunders as they came forth of the garden, stand-ing in the court or yard going into Mr. Garrard's parlour, said . . . that the goods articulated which were laden in the Venetian ship named to be his goods, were not appertaining unto him, but to the said Michel Mulier, Henry Garbrand and their company, saying further and protesting before God, holding up his hands, that the same goods nor yet any pennyworth thereof were his, but the goods and wares of the said Mulier and his associates. And to die therefore he would never otherwise confess, for rather and he should so do as he then declared — to favour or claim those goods which were none of his — he would suffer himself to be torn with wild horses, confessing still the said goods articulated to belong unto the 'bovesaid Mulier and his company, who for safe-guard of the same their goods from enemies and for none other cause, had borrowed and taken his name as he then said, declaring that he himself could commit no greater theft in this world to claim and take away those goods . . . Where-withal the said Parson Saunders spake unto the said Johnson, desiring him for goods not to burden and charge his con-science with the said goods, knowing the same to be none of his.

With the evidence as clear as it was, and the Imperial Ambassador urging Mulier's case in the Queen's ear, the outcome was never really in doubt. In July 1554 the Admiralty Judges gave their verdict in favour of Michel Mulier & Company. The cargo was handed over to them, to be shipped at last to Spain, and the Clerk entered the final decree among the vellum records and scarlet seals of the High Court of Admiralty. The case of the *Salvator of Venice* was over at last.

But the end of the case brought no improvement in the fortunes of the unhappy partners. Rather did it mean a change for the worse. In April 1554 they had been granted one year of grace, so that they might move freely about the country without fear of imprisonment for debt. When the time expired, they were as vulnerable as they had ever been. Only six days after the time-limit was up, John was again summoned before the Admiralty Court for non-payment of a large sum of money which he owed 'Ambling' Dunne. Shortly afterwards, he was 'committed to close prison in the Fleet', in company with his brother Richard and Ambrose Saunders. It is probable that during the next two years they were in and out of jail as often as Mr. Micawber, consigned if they were lucky to Tower Chambers, but more likely to the horrors of Bolton's Wards. John did occasionally manage to scrape a little money together, but as soon as he managed to pay something on account to one creditor, the next would have him put in prison again. Eventually the majority of the creditors realized that John had been squeezed dry, and they petitioned the Lord Chancellor for a full investigation into the conduct of the fourteen creditors who were said to have seized everything for themselves.

In the summer of 1557, the authorities at last made up their minds to set some good order in the affairs of Johnson & Company. A committee of merchants and aldermen was set up, empowered to receive everything of which John, Richard and Ambrose had not been lawfully dispossessed on March 20th, 1553, to summon disobedient creditors, and to issue subpoenas against them. In the words of their letter to Sir William Cecil, the committee's aim and object was 'to make a final end for ever between all the said creditors and the said debtors'. With this aim in view, they stopped all the actions pending against the firm in the lawcourts, and forbade any new actions to be prosecuted against them. The

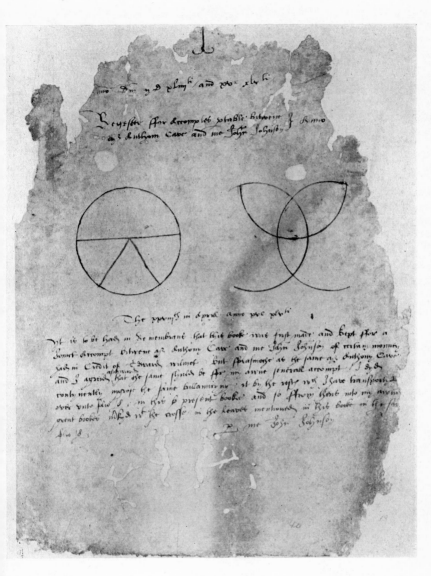

JOHN JOHNSON'S ACCOUNT-BOOK

names of the fourteen rapacious creditors were never once mentioned. Sir William Cecil is the only one we know, and as he had not the faintest intention of parting with the money if he could help it, he told the Committee that it had been 'recovered bona fide, and without any pretence of covin', and 'no order can require the same to be restored'. Four years had passed since the little *Trinity of London* had crept into the Thames with her cargo of Seville oil on board, but Cecil's phenomenal brain had forgotten no single detail of the transaction.

The partners were now, at last, released from prison, and came out to try somehow to make a living in the harsh world. Ambrose was the most fortunate of the three. He had never been considered as guilty as the others, and his family settled him on a comfortable estate near Sibbertoft. There he was able to live the country life he loved, with his 'well-beloved wife' Mary, his children and his friends. The fate of Richard, on the other hand, is an enigma. It is possible that he returned to Margaret at Calais and lived there until its fall. But from now on he disappears without a trace. Poor John was the hardest hit of them all. After six years of appalling strain that were enough to break any man, he came out of prison to find that everything he owned was gone, and that he had Sabine and the children to support, with no money to do it on. During these nightmare years, Sabine had been allowed to stay on at the manor house. In March 1555 John's name was included in the rental with a note that the rent paid was £4 for the demesne lands — exactly half the usual sum due for Glapthorn Manor. It is clear that they had relinquished the valuable enclosed pastures. The closes they rented from Lord Cromwell had also to be given up, and the office of bailiff passed to another man, John Cooke by name, who was soon to build a fine new manor house on the estate. John's name was still included among the tenants of the manor in April 1557; after that, the woods and fields he loved knew him no more.

No longer a merchant or a country gentleman, John's task now was to find some form of employment at which he could earn his living. It was impossible even to think of returning to his profession, for no one would trust a penniless bankrupt, and without capital he could not trade. At the time of the bankruptcy John had realized this, and had implored his 'very good master', Sir William Cecil, to help him:

... most humbly beseeching you to continue your goodness towards me, not doubting but the rather by the same to be relieved, and to have an end of my misery, which I desire most earnestly to have an end of, though I begin the world again with never a farthing; for I have a steadfast hope in the living Lord (whose is the earth, and the fullness thereof), that he will provide all things needful for me, my wife and children, being nevertheless willing to be occupied as a member of the commonwealth with my travail in that I can in anywise do, and although wanting ability in the trade of merchandise (wherein from my childhood I have been brought up), yet in something else whereunto it shall please God to call me. ...

It was fortunate that John had influential friends to whom he could apply, for otherwise he and Sabine must have sunk into dire poverty, from which they could never have recovered. From Anthony Cave, no help could be expected. Infuriated at the loss of that vast sum of money, £1500, Anthony Cave turned against the man whom he had once been happy to love and regard as a son. For what John had done, no forgiveness was possible, and when Cave died in 1558, it was as though he had never been. In all the great long will, folio after folio, detailing his lands and possessions, plate and jewels, there is no mention of John's or Sabine's name, although all the other relatives are remembered with affectionate gifts. There were others, however, who did not cast John off. The sixteenth century was, generally speaking, an age in which the remotest family claims were acknowledged and allowed. Some of his kinsfolk felt bound to help him, for the sake of Sabine and the family, if not for his own.

It may have been through Sir William Cecil that John obtained his first post with Lord Paget, the French Ambassador of Henry's reign. With his knowledge of letterwriting and accounts, John was well fitted to act as an accounts secretary, and this is probably what he did. It was while he was in Paget's service, at all events, that he first became obsessed with the idea of making his fortune through projects in trade. Projects and patents were the theme-song of the Elizabethan age, fertile in ideas as it was in poetry and action. There were projects for glass-working, the coal trade, copper-mining, dyeing, projects for the Persian trade, for Virginia, for gold in Newfoundland, for the discovery of El Dorado. The

Government itself called for projects and weighed them in the balance, and, since the fortunate few prospered by them, anything and everything of the get-rich-quick variety was in vogue. For John it was a vision and a dream, a fantastic castle in the clouds from which, happily, he was never to awaken. For while his religion enabled him to bear poverty with fortitude, it was his projects for trade that gave him eternal hope.

The first project on which John worked was that of increasing the customs duty on cloth. It was a reform long overdue, and one which the staplers had advocated for years past, for they paid far heavier taxes on their raw wool than the Adventurers paid on cloth. The project was accepted by the Government, and actually put into operation, despite the indignation of the Merchant Adventurers. In return for his efforts, John hoped that the grateful Crown would reward him with at least a small pension, but he never received so much as a thank you for his pains. This is what he wrote in 1580.

> By the raising of the custom from 14d paid by th'Englishmen to 6s 8d, Her Highness hath gained, since she came to the crown, five hundred thousand pounds more than any of Her Majesty's progenitors ever had, and th'English merchants have had thereby the whole trade, more to their gain than ever they have had by any of their own devices, though I, the first deviser thereof, being a poor man, had never anything for my study and pains therein, and . . . the merchants for their parts for my doings, instead of some goodwill, bear me evil will and hatred for the same. . . .

For the time being, however, it was enough for John that he had gained the approval of the Government, even though the merchants themselves were 'unthankful, disliking much of the deviser and author thereof'. Almost at once, he began to evolve another plan; nothing less than that the Queen should take over the Staple. The fall of Calais in 1558 had meant the virtual end of the Staple's greatness. Nevertheless, the staplers managed to re-establish their headquarters in Bruges and, soon after Elizabeth I came to the throne, they petitioned her for a new charter. The Government seized the opportunity to make a thorough inquiry into the state of the wool trade, and a Committee was appointed to consider the future of the Staple. There was at this time no lack of opposition to the staplers' trade. The Clothiers and Adventurers, two of the most powerful mercantile influences in the country, had long condemned the export of wool as a wilful waste of raw material so badly needed at home. Had the Staple been entirely abolished, they would have been the last to object. Another idea that was current was that of establishing home staples in English ports, and Cecil himself was apparently considering this in 1559. Side by side with this plan was John's proposal that the Queen should take over the Staple and buy up wool in England, selling it again to the staplers, who would in turn dispose of it to the foreign buyers. To support his case, John worked out a vast mass of reckonings and analyses of the state of the wool trade in the reigns of Henry VIII and Edward VI, based on his own experience. All were forwarded to Sir William Cecil, with a note that the project was not conceived 'against the merchants of the Staple, for I have all my life been brought up in that trade, and therefore intend not to be against them, but rather wish to do them good'.

John had not fully considered the effect of his proposals on his former friends. They, as might be expected, showed themselves hotly resentful and, although Cecil kept John's identity secret for a while, they ceaselessly attacked the unknown informer who was hoping 'to be the Queen's merchant' and 'more gainer than Her Highness'. Moreover, they sent in angry papers completely refuting the figures and statistics that John had produced. Soon — indeed, it could hardly be otherwise — their suspicions fell on John himself. 'It hath been said to me by one of the Staple,' he wrote to Cecil, 'that there is marvellous instructions given against them, and the matter is such as it must needs be one of the Company, which also your honour confessed. But I hope still of your honour's defence, and I trust I shall receive no hurt for my goodwill to the Prince.' A little later, the truth came out. 'I beseech your honour, let not my handwriting be seen. I am suspected already, but I force not for it, so your honour be my buckler.'

Alas, this was not what Cecil was prepared to do. And, even if he had defended him, the staplers would never have forgiven John for betraying the innermost secrets of their trade. All John's work this time was for nothing; and moreover, soon after the staplers received their coveted charter in April 1561, he lost his job. In sheer desperation, he wrote to Lord Robert Dudley, begging him to take him into his service, and submitting a discourse on abuses in the customs of wool and fells. But Dudley had nothing to offer him and, for the second time in his life, John had to apply to his relatives for assistance.

Strangely enough, it was at about this time that Maria, with whom they shared the Lombard Street house, decided that she would marry again. Maria had never lacked offers — what Tudor widow ever did? — and barely six months after Otwell's death she received a proposal of marriage from one of the Goodwyns of Winchingdon, a 'very great man' in Buckinghamshire, whose wealth was proverbial, and who desired nothing more than to marry John's pretty sister-in-law. 'If God so will that she do match with him,' wrote Robert Saunders, the go-between, 'both herself, her children, and friends might have great cause to give God thanks therefore.' Maria could not have been blamed if she had married him for money alone, and for the excellent establishment that would have been hers for the rest of her life. But she had married Otwell for love, and she loved him still. She was content to live quietly in the City with her children, and steadfastly refused all the offers that came her way. There was one man, however, Matthew Colclough, whom she had known from the early days of her marriage. He was a draper like Otwell, probably a pleasant, even-tempered man with whom she knew she could be happy, and who would be good to her children. In 1561 she married him, and left the Lombard Street house for ever.

John's relatives did not fail him at his hour of need. His statesman-cousin, Walter Haddon, the Master of the Requests, now came forward, using his influence with Sir Christopher Hatton and the Bishop of Rochester to obtain for him the presentation of a living at West Wickham in Kent, so that 'having the same, he might by the farm thereof get him a dwelling house, and something towards his living and great charge of children'. At Christmas 1561, John went to see the Bishop, and between them they agreed to present the living to William Fane, the Bishop's chaplain, thinking in that way John would have the 'most reasonable lease for his help', and indeed, Fane agreed to let him have the parsonage and farm for £8 a year.

Looked at dispassionately, the whole affair was a put-up job.

It is doubtful whether the Bishop would have been so willing to foist a bad bargain on his chaplain, had Fane not been a staunch Roman Catholic. And, although Fane at first agreed to let John have the parsonage, he soon changed his mind, and obstinately refused to co-operate. Neither threats nor entreaties would make him consent to perform the offices of the Reformed Church while a layman, however needy, received the fruits of the benefice, all the hay, wheat and malt, timber and milk. It was the Parson of Cotterstock all over again, only with an accession of bitter violence. After months of persuasion, argument and interminable meetings, the Bishop grew suddenly weary of it all and clapped his stubborn chaplain in jail. In the meantime, although they had no lease, John, Sabine and the children all went down to live in West Wickham, and made themselves at home there. The villagers, apparently, were not very pleased to see them, particularly when the collector nailed up an Interdict on the church door, because the subsidy and tenth had not been paid. Parson Fane was a man of resource. When he emerged from prison, he obtained an eviction order against John from some sympathetic justice, and led a procession through the village against the intruders. The bailiff hammered loudly on the parsonage door, and they were all vastly disappointed when Charity popped her head out of an upstairs window, and said that her parents were away from home. Since the order was in their possession, however, they felt they had to evict somebody, and so the children were solemnly set to play in the garden, and the door was locked until John and Sabine came home. Not until 1567, after years of quarrelling, did Fane eventually give in, and agree to abide by the decision of independent arbitrators. After that, John and Sabine were at last able to live peacefully in their Kentish parsonage. Their income now was a reasonable one. The benefice was worth at least £40 a year, they had a large garden, farmland and cattle, and their rich relations put small but lucrative incomes in their way, such as wardships and the like.

Many men in John's situation, after so many stormy years, would have been content to have found a haven at last, to enjoy moderate comfort without fear of imprisonment for debt, to walk and ride freely amid the beautiful countryside. But not so John. It was a tragedy that he should grow restless when he was most secure, and that he should throw everything away to seek his fortune in London once more. The reason was simple enough. A great project — the great project of his life — had taken hold of him, and he was unable to resist that all-compelling impulse. During those years of country life, perhaps while on a brief visit to Maria in town, John had bought for himself a copy of Guiccardini's *Antwerp*, the best-seller of the age. John drank in that marvellous account of people he once had known, and places he had visited, and out of that work of 'Ludovick Guiccardini, Florentine, exquisitely searching out the original of the great traffic to the said town', came the grand design.

Guiccardini revealed Antwerp in all her glory, the glowing, legendary city of the sixteenth century, the jewel in the crown of Spain and the Indies, the wonder of all the civilized world. It was the residence of millionaire bankers, merchants, shipowners and industrialists, and the resort of all the nations and all the trade of Europe. In her ateliers, gorgeous tapestries were woven, fit to deck the halls of kings; here the delicate Antwerp glass was engraved, while Antwerp's famous jewellers set the green, square-cut emeralds from Peru, and the cabochon rubies and sapphires of the East. Hither came the bales of satins and damasks and velvets of Italy; and the strange drugs, perfumes and spices of Arabia. Here were the fiery furnaces where armourers and gun-founders hammered out the molten sinews of new wars; here were vast cellars stored with wine, warehouses piled high with timber and heaped with grain. Antwerp was a vast and beautiful city but, until Guiccardini made his survey, none of those who stood amazed at her prosperity had troubled to analyse the source of all her wealth. Guiccardini was the first to realize that, far more than her geographical situation, Antwerp's meteoric rise to fame and fortune lay in the freedom of her trade — freedom from the crippling tolls and customs that burdened other cities, freedom to hold each year the four greatest marts in all the world.

Once in town again, settled in a small house not far from the Palace of Westminster, John immediately set to work on the project. Soon, he found a collaborator in Christopher Goodwyn, a young and well-to-do Ipswich merchant. Together they planned to create in England a mart town which was to possess all the liberties and virtues that had made Antwerp supreme. The idea itself was not a new one. Throughout the chaotic middle years of the century it had made a fitful, fleeting appearance, always to be abandoned before it was begun. The Privy Council had considered it during the wars between France and the Empire, and the brilliant young Edward VI had recorded their discussion in his diary. Men as far apart as William Cholmeley and Sir Thomas Smith both thought that 'if the trade could be removed from Antwerp and settled in England, it would be the fairest diamond in the Queen's crown'.[111] The troubled 'fifties were followed by the ever-darkening 'sixties, with Granvelle at the helm in the Netherlands, religious persecution at a hitherto unknown pitch, and in 1563 the Spanish embargo, with its resulting arrest of trade. The culminating point of the great cold war was reached in 1568, when Elizabeth confiscated the Spanish treasure ships. It was against this background, as John said, that his *Antwerp in England* was born.

This great damage sustained by the people of all degrees of this realm, and the experience of great losses, and undoings of divers honest merchants of this realm, by arrests and other troubles which happened many times when the English nation kept their marts and trade to Antwerp and into the Low Countries: moved me to call to remembrance mine experience in those things, and also that I had heard it much desired (and some attempts had been given) that the Merchant Adventurers should keep their marts and staple of cloth in England, and no more in those dangerous places, subject to so many great losses and hindrances of the whole state of this realm; and that in the time of Cardinal Wolsey's government, marts were begun to be kept at Calais, and divers times that I can remember, there hath been great desire to put the same in practice, but there was always some hindrances and doubts made.

Upon these occasions I was moved (as methought in conscience) to invent some means that the enormities and inconveniences before rehearsed might be avoided whereby the state of this realm was and is annoyed: for the occasion of the time ministered occasion unto me so to do, because I have dealt in the world, and namely, that I have known (as a doer in merchandise) Antwerp and the Low Countries at least forty-seven years now past. . . .

And besides the safeguard of the English merchants and

their goods (without whose trade and safe occupyings this realm nor commonweal cannot long flourish), Her Majesty shall have all the Princes her neighbours to this realm, so much in her danger, as they shall by no means be able to execute their enmity upon this realm, which their enmities and hatred they have secretly conspired against us, and we shall be sure so to find it, if they can find opportunity for their purposes. And it can no otherwise be, so long as God's glorious Gospel is received in this realm, and that they are joined with the Pope and clergy, who pronounce us for heretics and the worst people of the world, and therefore no faith, promise, or anything that may be for our good, to be fulfilled and kept with us (Yea) if they can so dissemble with us to work our destructions, they think they shall do unto their God the Pope, highest service. . . .

The project was in many ways remarkable. It was brilliant in its conception and lucid in all its details. In an age when many men still fondly dwelt on the interdependence of Anglo-Flemish trade, John and Christopher looked forward with perfect coolness to the disintegration of the Low Countries, and regarded the hopes of peace as a disappearing miasma. But their limitations were apparent in their choice of Ipswich as the mart town. No doubt Christopher wanted to benefit his native city, while John, thinking in typical sixteenth-century terms, was trying to encourage the provincial ports; in his heart, he had always disapproved of London, the Great Wen. But London was now the capital city of realm, the seat of government and the nation's trade. One day London would become the golden city that Antwerp once had been, but this was something that neither John nor Christopher, steeped in Tudor tradition, was able to see.

On Christmas Eve 1571 the completed plan was sent to Cecil, now Lord Burghley, who was sufficiently impressed to show it to his colleagues of the Council. John later said that, when the project first appeared, there was 'some liking thereof, for the time was such as moved a great many of wise men to wish that the same might take effect'. However, when the plan was shown to some of the leading merchants of London, their reactions were so hostile that no further move was made. After six months of silence, during which he heard nothing, John wrote to Cecil, asking what had become of his book. The project, it seems, had now been completely shelved, for the hiatus in trade with the Low Countries was balanced by the increasingly friendly relations with France, which made it possible for Sir Thomas Smith to negotiate treaties for the removal of the wool staple and cloth mart to a French port, and clauses to this effect were actually included in the Treaty of Blois. But then Catherine performed her most celebrated volte-face, and the alliance was dissolved as the Massacre of St. Bartholomew took place. In England, the mart project was once more revived, so that, John said, there grew 'an universal speech thereof, and the copy of the book before-named for the device of the marts to be in England came into many hands, and of a great many (after good consideration), was very well liked of Englishmen and strangers, and wished to take effect, and by a godly wise gentleman, zealous to do good to his native country, very much furthered to some in authority'.

The reopening of trade with the Low Countries put an end to John's hopes for the time being. He did not entirely despair of success, however, and that winter he managed to interest the Earl of Leicester in the project. While English merchants were still trading to Antwerp there were too many objections to be overborne. Another chance seemed to come in 1576, after the terrible sack of Antwerp by Alva's soldiery, and John himself wrote an *Addition to the Book of Marts*, urging that the project be adopted, since Antwerp was 'without any manner of hope that ever the same shall be restored again to be a place for any great traffic of merchants'. But all to no avail. And then, in 1578, it was revived again, at a time when the hostility of the Hansa League was making it impossible for the Merchant Adventurers to carry on their trade in Hamburg, and to combat the free-trading inter-lopers who cut in on their profits in England. During the autumn of that year, *Antwerp in England* was brought before the Council, and the excited John forwarded paper after paper in its support, recommending, amending, commending, detailing magistrates and offices and orders, customs and profits in a terrific, feverish burst of activity. It was Peter Osborne, Cecil's right-hand man, who was commanded to interview the authors, and he promised faithfully to write about the plan 'without glory or curiosity . . . upon some new conference with Johnson and his fellow, whom I will seek out'. Osborne saw them and talked with them, and has left us a vivid picture of how John's whole bearing was transformed when hope came once more.

I have by conference with Johnson and Goodwyn (he wrote to Lord Burghley) set down in articles the whole plat of their erection of a mart town at Ipswich. I have since, according to your pleasure for the mart, added all the reasons I could pick out of them, and have set down besides all they would or could have said for the matter. Against the mart I have made such simple reasons and objections as I thought meet or might be gathered.

There is no middle to be had between them. All must go after Antwerp fashion for freedom and small toll, and as experience is found there already, or else there can be no free mart here; and so do the devisers make their ground, and be able to defend and maintain their plat. Surely great charges, th'opportunity of the time, much travail, and as great liberties as be at Antwerp, may draw on a resemblance at Ipswich with Antwerp, but that it will continue, being encountered hereafter, I see not, our defects and differences from Antwerp being so great and so many.

On Tuesday next I mind to send Johnson to your lordship to Court, who, at my first sending for him, came to me lame and sickly, since by our conferences is well cheered up and well sprighted, hoping the mart will go forward and be some relief to his state, th'amendment whereof hath long depended upon the same, so as your lordship is now to use him as it shall seem good. . . .

Alas for John's hopes. After Osborne had seen them, he listed all the objections he could think of, not least of which was the fear of immediate invasion by the Holy League. He also made the shrewd observation that if the foreign merchants came to settle at Ipswich with their wives, children and servants, English craftsmanship might benefit, but 'our English people will not bear their vice, freedom, enriching, pride, slight and fair speeches, nor yet will endure to be made able to live by them'. And so, he concluded, 'I fear the device will never be executed'. As for the merchants of London, to whom the project was again submitted, they gave it an even colder reception than before. They remarked, somewhat sourly, on the God-given geographical situation of the

Low Countries, and declared that its prosperity had been founded by impositions on wine, so that 'the beauty of Antwerp hath been maintained by drunkenness'. If the mart was established at Ipswich, they would certainly be free of Alva, but they would also be free from any gain, and, confined to English ports, would have to look out on the world like prisoners. Adventure-loving, passionately interested in voyages of discovery, they loathed the very idea of being pent up at home, and declared roundly that the plan would spell nothing but ruin for the 'whole state of the wealthiest island in Christendom'.

So far as Antwerp in England was concerned, this was the end. That most typical of Tudor projects, embodying all the faults and all the virtues of sixteenth-century thinking, had failed, for there were those who realized that it belonged to the past, rather than the future. But, during these anxious years, John had never allowed himself to be discouraged, nor his hopes to rest entirely in one single plan. He was the author of innumerable pamphlets, devising remedies for abuses in the Assize of Wood and Fuel, trying to persuade the Government to create a special office for the survey of export licences, and reporting on disorders in the buying and selling of wool by the broggers. He carried out investigations for Sir Francis Walsingham into the conduct of the wool licensees; he worked out a colossal plan for the reform of the customs under a Surveyor-General; and he devised a special plan for the provincial ports, in the course of which he tilted so heavily at Parliament as to make it almost certain that *Antwerp in England* was discussed and rejected there. One of his most remarkable ideas was the plan for establishing a Strangers' Staple in England, involving a great development of the cloth trade at Norwich, Canterbury and Southampton, where the refugees from Alva's persecution had settled. How John actually supported himself during this period it is difficult to say: small offices and sinecures would probably have brought him in a little money. We know, however, from a letter to Lord Burghley, that John found himself at a low ebb after the rejection of the mart project.

My most humble request unto your honour is that it may please your honour to receive me into your service, wherein your lordship shall find me faithful and true during my life. And if it shall please your honour to use me in accounts, or such things as I have been practised in, I trust by God's help so to behave myself, as your honour will like well of. Your honour's long knowing of me, and favourable countenance (specially since the device abovesaid exhibited unto your honour), hath boldened me to make this suit unto your honour myself, without suit of my Lord Chief Baron or other my friends: hoping your honour will accept my goodwill, and to prove if experience now in my old years (though discontinued and without help this twenty years past) may in anywise be meet for your honour's service, which I most earnestly desire, and pray unto God that it may be to his honour and your lordship's contentment.

This time Lord Burghley did indeed do something material for him, which ensured that John would have a comfortable income for the rest of his days. He used his influence with the merchants of the Staple, and John became the official clerk to the Company. The duties were not burdensome: he was to take charge of all the records and ordinances, and enter such complaints as were made. The salary was generous: forty pounds a year. And to ensure that he should have some assistance, John's youngest son, Edward, was given the position of under-clerk, at a salary of forty marks a year. Moreover, Sir Francis Walsingham now came to John's aid, and the older man was proud to wear that ardent Protestant's livery in token of his patronage.

John was growing old now. We know from his letters to Burghley and Walsingham that he suffered from gout, and that his eyes sometimes troubled him. Once, when Walsingham asked to see him, he said he was 'ill provided to travel, wanting both good feet and other necessaries for one that should go from home'. His life was quiet, but he was always hard at work upon his projects and pamphlets. Occasionally he went to Court, where he had the entrée, meeting and talking with his patrons and kinsmen, recalling the days of his youth, and doubtless disapproving heartily of the wild gallants of the new reign. It does seem as if, despite the disappointments and vexations that attended his projects, John's last years were comparatively tranquil and content, for he had a secure income at last, he was completely absorbed in his writing and, more than anything else, his children were a source of pride and joy. Edward was doing well in the Staple

Company; Faith, we know, married a gentleman by the name of William Wood; and Evangelist, the 'young master' of the old days, took up his father's profession. He was apprenticed in the Drapers' Company, and became a successful merchant. In 1582, Evangelist married. His bride was a girl named Alice Spencer, and in the course of time several children were born to them — Evangelist, named for his father; a second son, called Peter; then a daughter, named Sabine after her grandmother; and finally, Emanuel.

In their children and grandchildren, John and Sabine found delight and pleasure, hope for the future, and some measure of consolation for the years of unhappiness. They seemed to live again in the younger generation, only it was a better and brighter reflection. Here would be no waste of talents, no bankruptcy, no ruined lives, but instead a family of prosperous, moneyed men, calmly and skilfully navigating their course through life, symbolic of the new age that had dawned when Elizabeth I took the reins of government into her thin, capable hands. In the course of a long life, John had witnessed great events, and had seen many strange and terrible things. Born in the first light of the Renaissance, he had lived through the colossal revolution of Henry's reign, survived the corruption and disasters of Edward VI, watched helpless while Mary imperilled the Protestant faith, and rejoiced to see his country rise like a Phoenix from the ashes, to triumph over the Armada. Throughout these years, as his letters reveal, John was constant in his support of the twin pillars of England's security — the Prince (as he always called the Queen) and the Protestant religion. His faith in his country's future was not misplaced, for the Englishmen who served Gloriana were of a magnificent kind. They were men who dared everything, adventuring, trading and plundering where they pleased. They were men to whom the uttermost ends of the earth were familiar, who dreamed of El Dorado and Cathay, whose leaders were Drake and Hawkins, Raleigh and Grenville, whose poets were Shakespeare and Sidney, Marlowe and Spenser — a galaxy of immortal genius in whom all the promise of England was at last fulfilled.

REFERENCES

[1] Considerations delivered to the Parliament, 1559, Tawney and Power, *Tudor Economic Documents*, Vols. I, VII (1).
[2] John Brinsley, *Ludus Literarius*.
[3] Sir Thomas Elyot, *The Boke named the Gouernour*.
[4] Michael Drayton, *Endimion and Phoebe*.
[5] Richard Hakluyt, *Principal Navigations*.
[6] Thomas Heywood, *A Curtaine Lecture*.
[7] L. F. Salzman, *England in Tudor Times*.
[8] Sir Thomas Wyatt, *Poems*.
[9] Alexander Niccholes, *A Discourse of Marriage and Wiving*.
[10] Michael Drayton, *Poems*.
[11] J. Earle, *Micro-Cosmographie*.
[12] William Shakespeare, *Twelfth Night*.
[13] Van Meteren, *Nederlandtsche Historie*.
[14] Gervase Markham, *The English Hus-wif*.
[15] *A Relation of the Island of England*, *c.1500*, ed. by Charlotte A. Sneyd.
[16] Robert Greene, *Morando*.
[17] Starkey, *England Temp. Henry VIII* (E.E.T.S.).
[18] J. Earle, *Micro-Cosmographie*.
[19] Sir Thomas Wyatt, *Poems*.
[20] Andrew Boorde, *Dyetary of Helth*.
[21] Gervase Markham, op. cit.
[22] A. Fitzherbert, *Boke of Husbandry*.
[23] Edward Gosynhill, *The Praise of All Women, called Mulierum Pean*.
[24] John Lyly, *Euphues and His England*.
[25] A. Fitzherbert, op. cit.
[26] Margaret Jourdain, *English Interior Decoration, 1500-1830*.
[27] Inventory of Sir John Cope's house at Canons Ashby (Exchequer Inventories).
[28] Perrin, *Description of . . . England and Scotland*.
[29] W. Harrison, *Description of England*.
[30] J. Lees-Milne, *Tudor Renaissance*.
[31] Thomas Tusser, *Five Hundred Pointes of Good Husbandrie*.
[32] William Shakespeare, *The Taming of the Shrew*.
[33] Ibid.
[34] Ibid.
[35] Thomas Tusser, op. cit.
[36] L. F. Salzman, op. cit.
[37] Thomas Tusser, op. cit.
[38] Sylvia Thrupp, *The Merchant Class of Mediaeval London, 1300-1500*.
[39] Professor B. Putnam, *Northamptonshire Wage Assessments, 1560*, Ec. H.R.I.
[40] Thorold Rogers, *History of Agriculture & Prices*, IV, p. 121, Proclamation of the Rutland Justices, 1563.
[41] W. Harrison, op. cit.
[42] Professor B. Putnam, op. cit.
[43] Thomas Churchyard, *A Fayned Fancye betweene the Spider and the Gowte*.
[44] Philip Stubbes, *The Anatomie of Abuses*.
[45] W. Harrison, op. cit.
[46] William Shakespeare, *Venus and Adonis*.
[47] Thomas Tusser, op. cit.
[48] F. J. Fisher, *The Development of the London Food Market*, Ec. H.R., 5.
[49] Thomas Tusser, op. cit.
[50] Andrew Boorde, op. cit.
[51] Perrin, op. cit.

REFERENCES

[52] *A Relation of the Island of England, c. 1500,* op. cit.

[53] E. Barrington-Haynes, *Glass.*

[54] W. Harrison, op. cit.

[55] J. Nevinson, *Catalogue of English Domestic Embroidery of the 16th and 17th Centuries* (Victoria and Albert Museum).

[56] James Laver, *Costume of the Western World, Early Tudor, 1485-1558.*

[57] William Shakespeare, *Henry IV,* Part I.

[58] Sir Christopher Garnish to Henry VIII, December 28th, 1515. *Letters and Papers of the Reign of Henry VIII,* Vol. II, I, 1350.

[59] *Anything for a Quiet Life,* quoted by M. Channing Linthicum, *Costume in the Drama.*

[60] *Satiro-mastix,* quoted by M. Channing Linthicum, op. cit.

[61] Ibid.

[62] Ben Jonson, *Poetaster.*

[63] Philip Stubbes, op. cit.

[64] Ibid.

[65] Sir Hugh Plat, *Delights for Ladies.*

[66] Thomas Tusser, op. cit.

[67] Sir Hugh Plat, op. cit.

[68] John Leland, *Itinerary.*

[69] Camden, *Britannia.*

[70] Thomas Tusser, op. cit.

[71] Fitzherbert, op. cit.

[72] William Shakespeare, *As You Like It.*

[73] J. Stephens, *Essayes and Characters.*

[74] Michael Drayton, *Poems.*

[75] Thomas Tusser, op. cit.

[76] Michael Drayton, op. cit.

[77] William Shakespeare, *The Winter's Tale.*

[78] Thomas Tusser, op. cit.

[79] Fitzherbert, op. cit.

[80] Thomas Tusser, op. cit.

[81] Ibid.

[82] Ibid.

[83] Fitzherbert, op. cit.

[84] Thomas Tusser, op. cit.

[85] Tawney and Power, *Tudor Economic Documents,* Vol. I, VII (3) and Professor B. Putnam, op. cit.

[86] Tawney and Power, op. cit.

[87] Thomas Tusser, op. cit.

[88] Thorold Rogers, *Six Centuries of Work & Wages.*

[89] Considerations delivered to the Parliament, 1559, Tawney and Power, op. cit., Vol. I, VII, 1 (6).

[90] *Ovid's Metamorphosis,* trans. by Arthur Golding.

[91] Thomas Tusser, op. cit.

[92] John Ruskin, *Cornhill Magazine,* March 1860.

[93] John Stow, *Survey of London.*

[94] Ibid.

[95] A. H. Johnson, *History of the Drapers Company,* Vol. II.

[96] *Brief Survey of the Growthe of Usury in England, 1673,* quoted by R. H. Tawney, Introduction to Th. Wilson's *A Discourse upon Usury.*

[97] *A Relation of the Island of England,* op. cit.

[98] Richard Clough to Sir Thomas Gresham, December 31st, 1561 (Tawney and Power, op. cit., Vol. II, V (7).

[99] Ludovico Guiccardini, *Description of the Trade of Antwerp, 1560* (Tawney and Power, op. cit., Vol. III, II (6).).

[100] See pp. 129-30 above.

[101] John Stow, op. cit.

[102] Richard Hakluyt, op. cit.

[103] C. A. Hager, Buchhalter (? 1660), quoted by B. S. Yamey, *Scientific Book-keeping & the Rise of Capitalism* (Econ. Hist. Rev., 2nd Ser., Vol. I, 1949).

REFERENCES

[104] J. Mair, *Book-keeping Methodiz'd*, quoted by B. S. Yamey, op. cit.
[105] Hakluyt, op. cit.
[106] Ibid.
[107] Tawney and Power, op. cit., Vol. I, III (3).
[108] C. Creighton, *History of Epidemics*.
[109] Ibid.
[110] Considerations delivered to the Parliament, 1559. Tawney and Power, op. cit., Vol. I, VII (1).
[111] William Cholmeley, *Request and Sute of a True-Harted Englishman*, and Sir Thomas Smith, Ambassador in Paris, to Cecil, *Cal. S.P. Foreign, 1564-65*, p. 172.

INDEX

INDEX

INDEX

Giorgione, 114
Gisze, George, 209
Glapthorn, 71, 82-3, 88, 98, 101, 107-10, 112-14, 121, 127, 129-31, 138, 140, 145, 148, 152, 169, 171, 173, 178-81, 186-8, 190, 193, 195-6, 200-2, 221-2, 235
Glapthorn, Church of St. Leonard, 195, 200
Glapthorn, Fields — Bodger's Close, Clark's Close, Caies Stybbing, Lord's Close, Willow Row Close, 169; Great Close, 169, 187 Batesman's Close, 189
Glapthorn, Parson of, 195-9
Glapthorn Manor, 56, 71, 75, 77, 85-6, 92-3, 96, 100, 106, 109, 111, 115-17, 119-20, 127-9, 134, 138-9, 141, 143, 145, 151, 164-5, 169-70, 172, 174, 177, 180, 183, 185, 191, 198, 209, 219-20, 236, 262, 270, 286, 295, 305
Goddard, Mrs., 63
Goghe, 241
Goile, Dirike Franzon, 256, 258
Golding, Arthur, 191
Goodwyn family, of Winchingdon, 309
Goodwyn, Mary (see Mary Saunders)
Goodwyn, Christopher, of Ipswich, 311, 313-15
Grain trade, 183-4, 213, 262-5
Grant, George, 105, 136, 211, 230, 236, 275
Grant, Mrs., 211
Granvelle, Cardinal, 312
Gravesend, 41, 164, 237, 253
Great Master of the Household (Lord St. John), 46
Great Turk's Letter to the King of Poland, 45
Greene, Robert, 80, 135
Greenwich, 213
Greenwich Palace, 254
Gregory XIII, Pope, 313
Grenville, Sir Richard, 318
Gresham family, 223
Gresham, Sir Thomas, 34, 217, 229, 275
Grey, Lady Jane, 47, 63-4, 107
Grey, William Lord, 278
Griffin, Sir Edward, Solicitor General, 71, 198
Grocers' Company, 27
Guiccardini, Ludovico, 217, 311
Guinea Coast, 40, 300
Gye, Goodwife, 187
Gyen fustian, 298

Haarlem, 51, 254, 256, 258-9, 261
Haarlem, Molenmeester of, 51
Haarlem, frizadoes, 258-9
Haberdashers' School, 27
Haddon, James, 25, 47, 93
Haddon, Walter, Master of the Requests, 25, 210, 309
Haghe, Bartram, 254
Hakluyt, Richard, 40-2, 227, 229
Haldenby, 176
Hall, 242
Hamburg, 268, 314
Hampton Court, 34, 127, 213, 268
Hansa League, 314
Hans of Antwerp, 152-3
Hapsburgs, 43, 47
Harborough, 96, 128, 202
Harfleur, 242
Harington, Sir John, 63, 113, 118, 122
Harington, 299
Harrison, Richard, 71, 96-9, 102, 171-2, 177-8, 194
Harrison, William, 112, 126-7, 148, 191
Harwood, 258
Hasby & Company, 247
Hatfield, 37
Hatton family, 25, 109
Hatton, Sir Christopher, 309
Hawkins, John, 40
Hawkins, Sir John, 318
Havre, 238, 240-4

Haynes, Alexander, 252-3
Hazebrouck, 84, 242
van Heed, Daniel, 254, 257, 290
Helierd family, 23
Helierd, John, 163
Hengrave Hall, 34
Henry VII, King, 30, 239, 266, 273, 308
Henry VIII, King, 23, 25-6, 31, 33-50, 64, 80, 88-9, 133, 143, 152, 156, 162, 185, 195, 200, 239, 244-8, 251, 253, 255, 261, 267, 274, 306, 308, 318
Hereford, 27
Hereford, Walwyn's School, 27
Herring trade, 22, 26, 85, 213, 228, 240-1, 247, 285, 287-8
Heywood, John, 78
Higham Ferrers, 78
High Butler of England (see Mr. Elderton)
Hill, Mr. Alban, 75
Hill, Michael, 271
Hill, Raeff, 243
Hoby, Margaret, 149
Holbein, Hans, 33, 35, 54, 64, 81, 153-4, 161, 209-10
Holland, Thomas, 54, 133, 153-4, 156, 222, 227 241-2
Holland, 155, 262
Holland cloth, 258
Hollanders, 76, 242, 255-7
Holwell, 176
Holy League, 315
Honfleur, 242
Hore, Master, 41
Horseley, Bess, 121
Hose, Bartholomew, 103
Hose, Mrs., 103, 165
Hostage Wood, 92
Hothorpe, 103
Houghton, Thomas, 229
del Hoven, Hector, 299
van der Hoven, Jacob, 299, 301, 303
Howard, Thomas, Duke of Norfolk, 36, 46, 107
Howham, William, 120
Howham, daughter, 120
Hull, 246
Humphrey, Mr. 175
Hunte, Thomas, 245
Huntingdon, 235
Hythloday, Ralph, 25

Imperial Council of State (see Netherlands)
Indies, 28, 311
Ingarsby, 163
Inquisition, 53
Ipswich, 311, 313, 315-16
Ireland, 246
Ireland, Wild Irish lords, 39
Isle of Wight, 249
Israelites, 106
Istambul, 31
Italy, 144, 311
Italy, diplomat, 24-5, 61, 146, 215-16
Italy, merchants, 144, 217, 228, 254, 292

Jackson the Grocer, 216
Jacob, 101
Jane Seymour, Queen, 36, 64
Jankinson, 111, 190
Jankinson, Mrs., 187
Jansen, Willem, 22
Janus, 234
Jasper, 108, 130, 179, 186
Java Head, 31
Jennyns, John, 81
Jerez, 282, 284
Job, 261
Johnson family, 32, 34, 41, 44-5, 47, 51, 127, 137-8, 141-2, 144, 146, 153, 236-7, 262, 266

INDEX

Seville, oil, 296, 305
Sergeant, William, 108, 173-4, 180
de Sevigné, Madame, 156
Seymour, Edward, Duke of Somerset, Lord Protector, 49-52, 200-1, 249, 274, 278-9
Seymour, Thomas, Lord High Admiral of England, 50, 185, 193, 249, 250
Shakespeare, William, 27, 116, 156, 318
Sherwood Forest, 134
Shipe, William, 225
Ships:
   Anna of Leigh, 240; *Barbara*, 40; *Bark Aucher*, 284; *Christopher of Ipswich*, 297; *Falcon*, 250; *George Bonaventure of Calais*, 240-2, 244; *George of Rosindale* 263; *Great Bark Aucher*, 284; *Greater Mary Fortune of Lynn*, 281, 288-9; *James of Dover*, 240; *John Evangelist of London*, 284; *John Evangelist of Lynn*, 282-3; *John of Gillingham*, 280; *Lion*, 240; *Mary Flower of Brittlesea*, 296-7; *Mary Fortune of Lynn*, 280-1; *Mary Gallant of St. Osyth's*, 280; *Mary Katherine*, 284; *Mary Katherine of London*, 280-1; *Matthew Gonson*, 284, 298, 300; *Michael of Calais*, 241-2; *Minion*, 41; *Neder Yere of Antwerp*, 112; *Nicholas of Lynn*, 263; *Phoenix of Lynn*, 282-3; *Radegonde of Olonne*, 280; *Salvator of Venice*, 22, 297-300, 302-4; *Trinity*, 41; *Trinity of London*, 284, 296, 305; *Trinity of Olonne*, 280; *Willoughby*, 240; Breton ships, 280, 282; Calais ships, 240-2; Flemish ships, 284; French galleys, 248-50, 254; ships, 42, 261, 280, 283; Scottish ships, 240-3
Shire Hill, 92
Shor, William, 225
Shrewsbury, 268
Sibbertoft, 62-3, 109, 116, 235, 305
Sidney, Sir Philip, 318
Silkwomen's Guild, 84
Sittingbourne, 237
Sluys, 240, 263
Smith, Clement, 222, 231
Smith, Parson Philip, Staple Chaplain, 45, 78
Smith, Dr. Richard, 50-1
Smith, Sister, 93
Smith, Thomas, merchant of the Staple, 132-3, 213, 219, 230, 236, 253
Smith, Mrs., 150
Smith, Sir Thomas, 312, 314
Solme, 189
Solme, Edmund, 262, 279, 283, 288
Somerset, 92
Somerset, Duke of (*see* Edward Seymour)
Sonning, Robert, 76
Southampton, 228, 246, 316
South Sea Bubble, 274
Southwell, Sir Richard, 46
Southwell, Sir Robert, 46
Southwick, Henry, merchant of the Staple, 118, 128, 132, 155, 181, 210, 244, 246-8, 251, 254, 259-60, 271
Southwick Wood, 92
Spain, 32, 51, 141, 144, 237, 259, 272, 277, 282-4, 296, 298, 300, 304, 311
Spaniards, 39, 111, 272
Spanish, bankrupts, 294; cloak 65, 155; far-thingale, 158; treasure ships, 312; wine, 144, 276-7, 282-4; wool, 251, 257
Speke, Sir Thomas, 270
Spencer, Alice (*see* Alice, wife of Evangelist Johnson)
Spencer, John, 299
Spender, Laurence, 80
Spender, William, 141, 158, 241-2, 244
Spenser family, 25, 169
Spenser, Edmund, 318
Spicer, Aunt, 78, 80
Stafford, Lady, 236
Staple, 68, 176, 223, 250-1, 253, 257, 271, 307-8, 314, 317 (*see also* Wool Trade)
Staple, Chaplain (*see* Parson Philip Smith)

Staple, Chapel, 79
Staple, Charter, 307-8
Staple, Clerk (John Johnson), 317. Under Clerk (Edward Johnson), 317
Staple, Constable, 251-2
Staple, Inn, 251
Staple, Lieutenant, 56, 251
Staple, Mayor, 251
Staple, Merchants, 21, 250-5, 271, 307
Staple, Regulations, 223, 252
Staple, Shipping, 253
Steen, Jan, 114
Stevens, William, 21
Stevenzon, Jacop, 256, 258-9, 261, 263
Stockbridge, Richard, 300
Stokes, Adrian, 81
Stokes, Thomas, 225
Strangers' Post, 237
Strasbourg, 47
Street, William, 161
Strozzi, 249
Stubbes, Philip, 126, 161, 163
Suffolk, 214
Suffolk, Duke of, 35
Suffolk, Duchess of, 81
Suffolk, sons, 270
Suffolk Men's Play of the Battle between the Spirit, the Soul and the Flesh, 43
Suierpont, Arnold de, 283-4, 301
Summerson, Esther, 234
Surrey, 140
Surrey, Earl of, 33, 35, 49, 67
Sutton, 34
Sutton, John, 244
Sutton, Mrs., 244
Sweating sickness, 266-74, 283
Switzerland, 268
Symons, Peter, 258
Syon Cope, 149
Syon House, 37, 49

TAGUS, 31
Tailor, Thomas, 152
Tanfield family, 25
Tanfield, Francis, 216
Tasso, Ercole, 156
Tate, Mr., 115
Taylor, Ralph, 280-1
Teken, 88, 107-9
Tempest, Robert, 27, 112, 218, 271
Tendering, William, 173
Tewkesbury Abbey, 34
Thames, River, 89, 237, 261, 281, 283, 296, 305
Thelbie, John, 187
Thickthorns, 189
Thomas, 73, 186
Thompson, William, 247, 249
Throgmorton family, 25
Throgmorton, Mr., 294
Tickford, 26, 53, 80, 105, 137, 189, 204, 221
Tickford Church, 66
Tickford House, 63-6, 91, 104, 110, 121, 173, 189, 235
Tickford Long Close, 189
Tickford Priory, 26
Tintern Abbey, 34
Tintoretto, 32
Titian, 32
Tortyfuma, 297
Tournai ribbons, 298
de Tournon, Cardinal, 243
Towcester, 235
Townshend, Turnip, 131, 181-2
Trade, general, 21, 30-1, 40, 76, 202-5, 215-18 (*see also* Wine Trade and Wool Trade)
Treaties:
   Commercial Convention of 1522, 255; Inter-cursus Magnus, 239, 255-6; Peace of Ardres, 249, 261; Peace of Crespi, 246, 260; Spanish Alliance, 239; Treaty of Blois, 314

329

INDEX